SECULARISM AND COSMOPOLITANISM

EUROPEAN PERSPECTIVES

EUROPEAN PERSPECTIVES
A Series in Social Thought and Cultural Criticism
LAWRENCE D. KRITZMAN, EDITOR

European Perspectives presents outstanding books by leading European thinkers. With both classic and contemporary works, the series aims to shape the major intellectual controversies of our day and to facilitate the tasks of historical understanding.

For a complete list of books in the series, see pages 247–49.

ÉTIENNE BALIBAR

SECULARISM AND COSMOPOLITANISM

Critical Hypotheses on Religion and Politics

COLUMBIA UNIVERSITY PRESS   NEW YORK

COLUMBIA UNIVERSITY PRESS

Publishers Since 1893

New York   Chichester, West Sussex

cup.columbia.edu

"Saeculum" published in French as *Saeculum: Culture, Religion, Idéologie*, copyright © 2012 Éditions Galilée

"'God Will Not Remain Silent': Zionism, Messianism, and Nationalism" published in French in *Agenda de la Pensée Contemporaine*, No. 9, Hiver 2007. English translation published in *Human Architecture. Journal of the Sociology of Self-Knowledge*, VII, 2, Spring 2009, 123–34.
© Reprint by author and journal permissions. Balibar, Etienne (2009) "'God Will Not Remain Silent': Zionism, Messianism, and Nationalism," *Human Architecture: Journal of the Sociology of Self-Knowledge*: Vol. VII, Issue 2, pp. 123–34; issue title: *Historicizing Anti-Semitism*. Issue co-editors: Lewis R. Gordon, Ramón Grosfoguel, and Eric Mielants. Journal editor: Mohammad H. Tamdgidi. Available at http://www.okcir.com/16HAVII2Sp2009.html.

Library of Congress Cataloging-in-Publication Data

Names: Balibar, Etienne, 1942– author.

Title: Secularism and cosmopolitanism : critical hypotheses on religion
    and politics / Etienne Balibar.

Description: New York : Columbia University Press, 2018. | Includes
    bibliographical references and index.

Identifiers: LCCN 2017061567 (print) | LCCN 2018010919 (e-book) |
    ISBN 9780231547130 (e-book) | ISBN 9780231168601 (cloth : alk. paper)

Subjects: LCSH: Secularism. | Cosmopolitanism. | Religion and politics.

Classification: LCC BL2747.8 (e-book) | LCC BL2747.8 .B2954 2018 (print) |
    DDC 201/.72—dc23

LC record available at https://lccn.loc.gov/2017061567

JACKET IMAGE: LEE EUNJONG, GM #0416, MUSEUM PROJECT 2011
BOOK AND JACKET DESIGN: CHANG JAE LEE

CONTENTS

PREFACE

In this book, I have collected three groups of texts, to illustrate what I believe to be the importance of a new "critique of religion" in the contemporary world, to indicate some of its objects, highlight some of the reasons for its practical urgency, and contribute to its development.

The first part consists of the retranslation into English of my essay *Saeculum: Culture, Religion, Idéologie*, published as a book in France by Editions Galilée in 2012, itself an expanded and adapted version of the lecture on "Cosmopolitanism and Secularism" that I gave in November 2009 as the Anis Makdisi Memorial Lecture in Beirut. In this essay I argued, on two correlative planes, that current disputes concerning the uses and misuses of the concept of *religion* and the *religious* (clearly Eurocentric, but also deeply rooted in the legacy of rival Western monotheisms, which include Islam)[1] would greatly benefit from the theoretical distinction between "religious" and "cultural" dimensions of social practice that a renewed concept of "ideology" in the post-Marxist sense makes possible; and, second, that confrontations between "religious" traditions and "secular" discourses and institutions must now become reframed from a *cosmopolitan* point of view that fully takes into account the relativization of borders, the hybridization of cultures, and the migrations of populations which have restructured our post-colonial world. I proposed that these phenomena intensify and redefine the perception of "anthropological differences" which are permanently at stake in symbolic differends, particularly among religions and between religions and secular discourses. These issues are intrinsically philosophical (if we understand philosophy as a discipline that continuously exchanges questions and notions with anthropology and other social sciences), but they are also immediately political, with highly conflictual or violent dimensions that verge on a state of endemic war of all against all, leaving us no intellectual or moral security. Because I wanted to overcome past shortcomings, introducing what I hoped was a better sense of the complexity and ambivalence of our historical, juridical, and hermeneutic categories, while not avoiding taking sides in the controversies about the universal in which some major intellectuals of our time have been involved—which also matter to every citizen—I tried to define a strategy through the somewhat utopian notion of the *secularized secularism* (or *desacralized secularism*). Borrowing Fredric Jameson's famous category and using it in my own way, I proposed that it could serve as a "vanishing mediator" in the multifaceted conflict of rival universalities. However elusive it may appear, this notion remains the guiding thread of all the subsequent parts of the volume, not as a "solution" or a "fixed" concept, but as an instrument to criticize existing rules, construct genealogies, and make room for political imagination.

As a complement to this principal essay, I have collected two groups of independent essays or texts. In the first group, titled "Essays," I put together three articles, all written before *Saeculum* (in 2005 and 2006), one of which had already appeared in English, which can be said to highlight the continuity and pervasiveness of the "theologico-political complex" a symptomatic "grammatical" difficulty indeed), even if it leaves room for dissent, heresy, resistance, and rebellions. This is what makes critique necessary and possible. There is more in my introduction, but why say it in advance? I will take the liberty of redirecting now the reader who is willing to examine my reasons to the text itself.

I want to express generic gratitude to all the institutions, friends, and colleagues who sponsored, commissioned, and commented on the following essays and interventions, as well as the journals and publishers in French and English where some of them appeared, and last not least to the translators (or first translators) of my French into English, particularly Michael Goshgarian, who translated or revised the greatest part. They are all referred to by name in the volume.

Russilly (France), August 25, 2017

INTRODUCTION
CRITIQUE IN THE TWENTY-FIRST CENTURY:
POLITICAL ECONOMY STILL, RELIGION AGAIN

We gather once again to examine the question of "critique."[1] We do so not just after Kant, Marx, Nietzsche, and their respective descendants, but also after the innovations of the Frankfurt School (which only came to receive serious attention in France after some delay) and the critique of the foundations of psychology, to evoke Georges Politzer's title, which, albeit with a number of adjustments and reversals, runs through the whole French epistemological tradition, both during and after the "structuralist moment."[2] Needless to say, we don't embark on this examination from an abstract or timeless perspective, but caught up in the middle of a conjuncture that we are all trying to understand. What are its tendencies and conflictual stakes? What alternatives does it present? From the place where we find ourselves, we try to assess the characteristic features of this conjuncture—the signs of the times—in order to reformulate the meaning and fields of critique and perhaps also to refound it. As unrepentant "moderns," we believe that critique has not ceased to designate philosophy's most characteristic gesture, and we seek more than ever to understand how the current situation must change critique itself, conceived as an analysis of "what we are," as Foucault used to say—which in reality means an analysis of what we are becoming, or turning into—one that cannot prescribe its culmination in advance. Through an essential circularity, we need to recast critique in order to provide a diagnosis of the present, but we can only orient this recasting by following certain paths derived from the way we already presuppose, if not prejudge, a diagnosis of the present.

CRISIS AND CRITIQUE

As a supplementary determination to these general points, I shall borrow from the famous title of Reinhart Koselleck's 1959 book, *Critique and Crisis* (poorly translated in French as *Le Règne de la critique*). Beyond the book's contents (essential reading for any discussion of the origins of the Enlightenment program), Koselleck's title trades on an idea that, for one reason or another, we have never quite managed to escape: namely, that "critique" is essentially related to "crisis," or to the manifestation, through certain signs, of a time as a time of crisis. The crisis renders the contradictions visible, and in so doing brings to the fore the internal structure of the world (particularly the political world, the social world) that is to be the object of the critique. Or, inversely: crisis *summons* critique to produce the instruments, the elements of intelligibility, which would allow for an analysis and resolution. And as it happens, we are at this moment and in this place, besieged by signs of crisis and by interpretations of its nature, which start with ways of naming it. Maybe that should put us on our guard, because, in a certain way, the crisis-critique correlation works a little too well. But how to elude it?

There are two remarks I would like to make on this score. The first is that the couple crisis-critique has determined the program of the social sciences from the start of the nineteenth century up until today. More generally, it has determined the program of the "social philosophies" (to which Marxism belongs) that have sought to define the objectives and practical functions of these sciences, because critique is rooted, on the one hand, in the manifestation of phenomena of conflict, contradiction, alienation, anomie, or pathology, all of which form the reverse, or the repressed, of the regularity of social relations, and hence hold the hidden truth of that regularity; or, on the other hand, in the manifestation of phenomena of interruption (provisional or definitive) of their regulation, or of their *reproduction*, which convey that combination of contingence and necessity upon which "societies" and "social formations"—in a word, their historicity—rests. Hence the privilege enjoyed by the idea of revolution, even under the form of an unfinished or suppressed revolution.[3] One of the terminologies available to us to express this dialectic is the antithesis of *organic* phases and formations and *critical* phases and formations (meaning crisis formations). In the prevailing representation—elaborated by the Saint-Simonians at the start of the nineteenth century and rediscovered by Gramsci in the middle of the twentieth—these phases or formations succeed one another periodically, though they can also be understood as "instances" imbricated in one another, with fluctuating relations of dominance.[4] The underlying idea is that critique, as a mode of thought that proceeds from critical phenomena, must in the end *return* to those phenomena if it wants to elucidate or transform them.

Here, though, I must make another remark. That we are, here and now, in Europe and elsewhere, knee-deep in a "critical phase," or a phase in which the pathologies of social life, of the mode of economic development, of collective identities, are all coming to the fore, is a widely shared sentiment and an intensive object of study for sociologists, psychologists, political commentators, etc. More and more, however, these judgments are overdetermined by *eschatological* connotations.

This is especially the case with the insistence on the notion of "world," which is called forth by the reference to globalization as the site and origin of the crisis, but whose evocation is filtered through the multiple registers of the social world considered in the totality of its extension and determinations, as "world system" for some, as "civilization" for others (Immanuel Wallerstein, Jean-Luc Nancy).[5] What is in crisis is a "world on a world scale" (or on a planetary scale). Linking these two gives rise to an issue that impacts, to a whole new degree, the circularity in the formulation of our critical tasks and objectives. It is by no means a given that the antithesis—organic/critical, normal/pathological, regular/state of exception, constitution/dissolution—remains an applicable tool of investigation in the context of the "global crisis" or, to parody Marx, of the "developed totality" (*The German Ideology*). Or it could be that the antithesis of two stages and two phases—which, if we think about it, is constitutive of the very idea of *society* or *social relation*—is what has to become the very object of critical reflection, or, if you prefer, of its deconstruction: it is what deterritorializes critique by depriving it of the possibility of positioning itself either from the perspective of normality (so as to identify the exceptions and pathologies) or from the perspective of pathologies (so as to discuss the value of norms and the degree of organicity of social forms). If that is the case, then the legitimacy and orientation of critique no longer stems from a foundational antithesis, but rather, and only, from its exercise, from the way it criticizes itself, and that is perilous. . . .

And yet. And yet, it is my plan today to stick to that old schema, and to give it a formulation that may, I hope, echo the concerns of many of us gathered here. It seems to me that the source of the calls for a renewal, maybe even a displacement, of critique, is the fact that the crisis affects, and globally so, the possibility of politics as a collective activity, and hence as a privileged form of the articulation between institutions and modes of subjectivation that allow human communities to represent themselves as agents in their own history—a form of self-consciousness for which the West, at least, has developed and universalized a number of names, *citizenship* chief among them, both in the privileged case of the nation-state, and in the forms of protest that have always accompanied it. Citizenship, under siege and reduced to impotence, has been devalued or deprived of meaning—as have, indeed, other categories closely associated with it, such as conflict, representation, militant activity, participation in public affairs. A particularly acute manifestation of this, as we know, is the fact that democratic institutions have degenerated and been emptied of their content in that part of the world where they were erected as a dominant value, while remaining conspicuous by their absence in other parts of the world, where they are perceived, at best, as an artificial foreign graft and, at worst, as a masked form of domination and alienation.[6]

There are exceptions to this, of course, and thankfully so. But their viability and mutual compatibility have still to be demonstrated. One hypothesis we can formulate, adhering closely to a certain Marxist logic while turning it against some of its postulates about the philosophy of history, is that we are *only now* entering capitalist society (and, as always, we are only noticing this after the fact, when it is late, perhaps even too late)—or, if you prefer, we're only now entering "pure" capitalism, which does not have to deal constantly with heterogeneous social forces that it must either incorporate or repress, or with which it must strike some sort of compromise. Pure capitalism is free to deal only with the effects of its own logic of accumulation and with those things necessary for its own reproduction.[7]

Now, it could be, regardless of what Marx thought about this, that modern forms of politics, and in particular the forms of this "great politics" whose stakes are the antithesis and the varied combinations of the relation to the nation (hence to the state, to the law and legal subjects, to *laïcité*, education, war), as well as the relation to class and class differences (hence to social inequalities and social policies, to reforms and revolutions), are characteristic not of capitalism as such, but of the *transition* to capitalism. This would be a very long drawn-out transition, certainly, and we are only now realizing that it needed nearly four centuries to run its course—assuming, that is, that we situate the beginnings of this transition to capitalism in mercantilism, manufacture, the "discovery" of a world to colonize, the proletarianization of farmers, and the emergence of constitutional states that "monopolized" legitimate violence and the power to judge. As it happens, that is where Koselleck situates the origin of the articulation between critique and crisis. But what is its "end," exactly? What are the determinations of this end, and, more specifically, what is it that, with it, *starts to exist* and to *dominate*, in the Marxian sense of *"herrschend"* (*herrschende Klasse, herrschende Ideologie*)? These questions are as much epistemological as political, and they are among the most urgent tasks facing the efforts to renew critique, or give it a new foundation.[8]

ECONOMY AND THEOLOGY:
THE *CHASSÉ-CROISÉ* OF VIOLENCE

Let us venture a step further. I would say that what seems to characterize the world-scale dimensions (*la mondialité*) of the "crisis"—which is at once local and global, and is not foreign to the eschatological connotations it takes on in our discourses and conscience—is the superposition of two "phenomena" that seem at first sight heterogeneous, but that we can try to relate to one another in a quasi-analytical, or perhaps pseudo-analytical, schema. The first is the emergence of an economy of generalized violence that cuts across borders and combines endemic wars with other forms of exterminating violence—indeed, eliminating violence, since what is involved is not death in the strict sense, even if there are at this moment many deaths, under different modalities.[9] Exclusion, for example, or, perhaps even better, to use the category that Saskia Sassen recently deployed with impressive force and scope, the generalized *expulsion* of individuals and groups from their "place" in the world, in any world whatever.[10] No one doubts that violence is immemorial, that it assumes myriad forms and has myriad causes, or that it is an anthropological characteristic of the human being as such. But the violence that seems able to cut across any and every border, and indeed to use borders themselves as the instruments of its own generalization, is in a way a new phenomenon whose novelty rests on the fact that every person may in time be potentially confronted by it.[11] The second phenomenon I have in mind is the superposition or, better yet, the *chassé-croisé* of political economy and political theology, or the theologico-political. We are now approaching the question that we need to ask. To convey what seems to be a widely held view today (and I don't believe this view is exclusively French, even if it undoubtedly owes a fair share of its evidence to a certain "French" way of thinking of the autonomy of politics), I would propose the following formulation: we no longer have enough political economy (or politics in economics), but we have too much political theology (or too much theology in politics).

In what we commonly refer to as the "return of the religious," I include certain ways of asserting or imposing laïcité, as themselves deeply religious forms of reacting to what is perceived as a "re-theologization" of social conflicts or their modalities of self-consciousness. (But how to separate social conflicts from their self-consciousness, since the latter is precisely what renders them "conflictual" in the first place?) There is no need here to try to retrace and survey the entire field of fundamentalisms—Islamic, but also Hindu, Jewish, and Christian (Christian above all, in a significant number of countries in the West and the South)—in the face of which one would also have to describe the no less impressive range of practices of non- or antiviolence that find their inspiration, language, and the models of conduct they want to put in place and share with others, in religious traditions, which they have reinterpreted to a greater or lesser degree. Hence Jacques Derrida's question (thinking primarily about the Middle East):

> Wars and military "interventions," led by the Judeo-Christian West in the name of the best causes . . . are they not also, from a certain side, wars of religion? To determine a war of religion *as such*, one would have to be certain that one can delimit the religious. One would have to be sure that one can distinguish all the predicates of the religious.[12]

For my part, I would say that the phenomenological criterion at work in current analyses is that the religious emerges where the economy ceases to be thought and practiced as a *political* institution, in keeping with its old denomination as political economy, a perspective which was gradually abandoned as the power of states seemed more and more out of step with the autonomization of markets, and of financial markets in particular. In other words, the *chassé-croisé* is always already present within each of the two phenomena, neither of which is independent from the other.

Hence the two questions that preoccupy our contemporaries, not separately, but in tandem: How to rethink the theologico-political? And how to evaluate the degree of distance possible between the economy and its modes of political regulation? The term "governance," thematized for the first time by the World Bank in the 1990s and now in general use, pinpoints the ambivalence of the second process, because it can designate, depending on the author, either a real withdrawal of politics—whose function is to support and manage social adaptations to the self-regulation of markets—or, conversely, the emergence of, or simply the demand for, a new political practice, reserved for new actors whose transnational legitimacy no longer depends on their authorization by a state.[13] As for the first question, about the meaning of the theologico-political complex, it continues to turn within the circle that was assigned to it by the two inventors of the formula, who are separated by nearly three centuries, at each extreme of modernity: Spinoza and Carl Schmitt.[14] That it is to say, it is taken to indicate either that the "theological" or the "theocratic" is a specific political regime (or more precisely, a *tendency* toward the sacralization of power, and likewise of any counterpower, at work in every other political regime), or that secular models of political authority (notably those founded on the *law* as a more or less complete subordination of the exception to the norm) derive their meaning and symbolic power from religious models. If this circle has started turning anew, is it not because the reference of the political (and of political action) to the state—whether as its necessary framework or as the system of power that it tries to overflow, or from which it wants to free itself (and, by the same token, to which it risks being eternally dependent)—is a reality that is less and less consistent, or, at any rate, less autonomous?

To Derrida's question regarding the "predicates of the religious," we cannot but add at least two more questions, about the predicates of the political and the economic. The economy of generalized violence manifests both the phenomenon of the withdrawal of politics into economics (that is to say, the disappearance of the political for the benefit of the economic, and the absorption of the political by a "pure" economic logic even when the latter can be described in its own way as a new politics that functions on the mode of denegation) and that of the vacillation of the theologico-political between a politicization of the theological and a theologization of politics. Nevertheless, the economy of generalized violence can be described as a double crisis: of the historical affiliations and memberships of individuals (which means also a hierarchization of these memberships for the benefit of a sovereign political order), and of the established modalities, gradually institutionalized, of social *conflictuality*—or, if we prefer, of the "struggles" among "parties."[15]

In this conflictuality, the class struggle represented, for two centuries, both in Europe and elsewhere, a limit form, or a form of radicalization that situates itself on the "shores" of politics (to evoke Jacques Rancière) or, more precisely, on the shifting border that separates and articulates *civilized* modalities of the "social war" (also called "civil war" by antiphrasis). And it does so while opening up the possibilities for transcommunitarian and, in particular, transnational, memberships that could be called nomadic in relation to instituted and territorialized political communities.

You can already see the position I am heading toward. On the one hand, we must take seriously the hypothesis that the "return of the religious"—under the form of a growing affirmation of collective identities of the religious sort (for all manner of mutually antithetical ends), to the detriment of identities assigned or recognized by the state, in competition with them, or seizing them from within—is a consequence of the decline of "collective subjectivations" that were elicited by earlier forms of political conflictuality or civil conflict. (Rancière suggested this in a recent interview).[16] On the other hand, this hypothesis can be no more than a starting point, a provisional formulation, since we are not in a position to tell whether the religious that "returns" is actually the same as the one that had—only more or less, in reality—"departed," like a return of the repressed. That is to say, we don't know, deep down, what the "religious" is, or indeed whether there is such a thing at all, and under what perspective it can be unified, or even compared. Likewise, we don't know how economic governance, which subordinates states to the imperatives of the market, a process that is tempting to explain in terms of an entrance into pure capitalism, is articulated with the affirmations of religious identity in order to engender the new field in which societies are confronted with inconvertible violence.[17]

A DETOUR THROUGH MARX

At this point, I shall take a detour through Marx, or at least through certain moments of his thought, because a lot is being said today about how Marx contributed to obscuring the importance of the theologico-political problem, and more generally the problem of the religious factor in history, because he trained his attention exclusively on the social causes and economic contradictions of capitalism, arguing that, "in the last resort," these are the determining factors of the historical processes whose manifestations we find in our present.[18] This is both true and false. In this instance, though, the modality is more significant than the overall thesis, or rather it helps to determine its meaning.

We can, once again, start from the famous formulations that open (and close) "A Contribution to the Critique of Hegel's *Philosophy of Right*: Introduction," which appeared in 1844 in the *Deutsch-Französische Jahrbücher*:

the *critique of religion* is essentially completed; and the critique of religion is the prerequisite of every critique. . . . The foundation of irreligious criticism is this: *man makes religion*; religion does not make man. . . . But *man* is not an abstract being squatting outside the world. Man is *the world of man* (*der Mensch, das ist die Welt des Menschen*)—the State, Society. . . . Thus, the critique of religion is the *critique* in *embryo of the vale of tears* of which religion is the *halo*. . . . Thus, the critique of heaven is transformed into the critique of the earth, the *critique of religion* into the *critique of law* [*Recht*], and the *critique of theology* into the *critique of politics*.[19]

I don't believe Marx ever revisited this formulation, and even if it is important to mark the difference separating the critique of right and politics from the critique of political economy—regardless of whether we call it a "break"—the idea that the critique of religion has been *completed* remains a presupposition of his entire critical enterprise. Indeed, we can even say that it becomes more than that when the critique of the "vale of tears" became "earthly" or, at least, more tightly bound to the study of the conditions of production and reproduction of the material conditions of existence in human societies.

What is immediately striking, upon rereading this text, is the extent to which it appears indissociable from Marx's insistence on the anthropological question. "Materialist" anthropology against "spiritualist" anthropology. First, it's the social human being who makes religion, rather than having been made by it; anthropology itself, in other words, *determines* the modalities of the constitution of the religious imagination and the functions it can fulfill in history, whether this be to consolidate modes of domination or to "protest" against them. Second, an anthropology of the relation or "link" (*rapport*), and not an anthropology of the essence or "genre."[20] I think we can see in a text like this (and in others from the same period that complete it, particularly the "Theses on Feuerbach"), the foundation of a Marxian *philosophical anthropology*.[21] "It is the human being who makes religion" is, by definition, a humanist thesis; we might even say—in the context of a *critical* enterprise—that it is the humanist thesis par excellence. But the fact of calling it into question, particularly by adopting a materialist approach to the question of what precisely "the human world" means, does not ipso facto eliminate the anthropological question. Quite the contrary: it is a way of reformulating and giving a different orientation to that question.

We can see this clearly if we just focus our attention on how the two reductions that Marx needs to operate in order to interpret "the human world" are connected. There is, on the one hand, the reduction of being or of the human essence to a "set of social relations." I am myself tempted to call this an *expansive* reduction, paradoxical as the expression may seem, because it shines a light on a generalized intersubjectivity or transindividuality, of which the construction of religious communities is a part, as are the construction of imaginary communities and "civil societies." There is, on the other hand, the reduction of the set of social relations to the form of labor or the status of a labor product that is in the final analysis derived from productive or reproductive activity itself, both "manual" and "intellectual" (*The German Ideology*). Nor can we forget or overlook the fact that what human beings "make," they can likewise "transform" (*verändern*) or "remake" differently. In sum, we cannot forget that the reality human beings make is a transformable (*veränderbar*) reality.[22] That is why Marx will say later that mankind "inevitably only sets itself such tasks as it is able to solve."[23] Here, once again, we notice a bifurcation, though not between (humanist) anthropology and (materialist) ontology, but within anthropology itself, even though the latter implies an ontology.

What conclusions, then, are we to draw from this observation, which is in some ways a critique of Marx, or a redoubled application to Marx himself of the critical instrument? We need to proceed slowly here, or rather, with a certain sense of discernment. On the one hand, we can say that Marx shares the thesis that the movement of history in the modern period is that of a gradual secularization, though there is something original in his formulation of it. For Marx, the principle of the transformation of societies is the restoration or the becoming visible of the material causality that, from their "origins," would have engendered all the modalities under which societies "make" or "produce" their own social relations, as well as the *phenomenal form* (*Erscheinungsform*) under which these must appear to their subjects or bearers. This, incidentally, goes hand in hand with a fundamental evolutionism, one that is not original to Marx in the nineteenth century, though he did elaborate an original variant of it, more contradictory than other versions, but ultimately more unstable as well. On the other hand, the radicality of his thesis—that the source of religious alienation is to be found solely in the anthropological function of labor and in the relations of production that give it its historical expression—is the very thing that opens the way for the analysis of the economy as an "anti-religion"; or, if you like, for the analysis of the economic representations of the "world" constructed by the economy in the capitalist epoch. But in *Capital* Marx will show that the economy *does not exist* without the "representations" or "appearances" that render its own "economic laws" operational. In speaking about antireligion, I intentionally use the prefix, "anti," in its double logical sense: antireligion is what opposes itself to religion so as to destroy it, to "profane" it, as Marx says in *The Communist Manifesto*, and it is also what *faces* religion and reproduces—as if in a mirror, mimetically— its imaginary functioning, particularly the effects of belief and subjection. Thus, a reflection on Marx and a rereading of his work does not render impossible and unthinkable those critical gestures aimed at reintroducing the theologico-political question as a fundamentally political question in the wake of the question about political economy, as a question lodged in its heart and always intertwined with it. On the contrary, such reflection and such rereading are one of the conditions of possibility of this reintroduction.

What we must retain from Marx is that there is something of the theological (for example, in money) in societies "secularized" by the always increasingly totalitarian grip of the economy, and even of the religious, under the forms of the rituals of daily life that are guided by the fetishism of exchange value, and by the hallucinatory perception of the "bodies" of merchandise as the "incarnation" or embodiment of their value, even if these rituals take place outside the traditional space of "religion" in the historical sense of the term, that is, an institutional space that enjoys legal and political sanction. If we do not take antireligion into account, in the sense above, then perhaps the entire question of the metamorphoses of the religious in the capitalist epoch (including here the "returns of the religious" in the moment of its crisis) will remain inaccessible to critical analysis. That said, we must also, tirelessly, raise the question of the blinding consequences that his opening postulate operates across his work: "the critique of religion is complete," particularly in the form of a persistent denegation of the fact that, in the anthropological thesis that reduces the essence of the human being to the idea of the *producer* (which contains the connotation of *creator*), there is an antireligious signification that can always be turned into a religious one.

The Regime of the Constitution of Bodies

There is no need to insist too much here on the way in which, at the end of the same text from 1844 ("A Contribution to the Critique of Hegel's *Philosophy of Right*: Introduction"), the messianic figure of the proletariat appears as the redeemer of humanity: the producer radically dispossessed of his or her own creation, a figure that becomes even more emphatic in the later "expropriation of the expropriators," and in the way this messianism was later "routinized" by the secular religions of historical or so-called actually existing socialism. That's too well known to detain us.[24] It seems more interesting to try to identify a *sensitive point* where a new critique of political economy—one that extends and deepens while also rectifying Marx's—can be articulated with a critique of religion, and this in the double sense of understanding its signification, and resisting religion's pretensions to an exclusive universality. I am tempted to use for that the expression "point of heresy," in the etymological sense of choice or theoretical bifurcation, even if, in this instance, the aim is not to describe a divergence starting from a common "epistemological" ground (as in Foucault's *Archaeology of Knowledge*), but rather to arrive at a virtual convergence, one that cannot, for all that, issue in any real reunification.[25] It seems to me that we can identify this point of heresy in the way in which a critique of political economy and of political theory (or of the religious) must treat the status and function of bodies, and consequently describe the anthropological differences that are inseparable from the way human beings use their bodies. *L' uso dei corpi*, Agamben would say. They are also inseparable from the way "human societies" humanize themselves (and do so by dehumanizing themselves) by prescribing to the individuals that compose them a certain use of differences linked to the body—particularly the difference between the manual and intellectual aspects of labor, and sexual difference. This, of course, opens the way for different forms of "embodied" resistance and emancipation.[26]

I would like to advance two hypotheses that strive to distance themselves somewhat from the discourses currently in the air about "biopolitics," while nevertheless intersecting with them on several points.

The first concerns the idea that the point around which collective cultural practices and a symbolic architecture of the religious type are articulated is a prescription that concerns the body, and in particular the manifestation of the difference of sexualized bodies (be they two or more).[27] As we know, cultural practices can be very diverse and mutually contradictory, not just because they develop over long periods of time in very different contexts and civilizations, but because they combine different forms of "invention" and "respect" for the tradition, with contradictory tendencies about how to adapt to, or resist, modernization and commodification. In religious discourse (particularly that of revealed, monotheistic religions), rituals and beliefs are tightly superposed and intertwined. And so too, as Derrida suggests in his rearticulation of the idea of "the two sources of religion," are the hope of salvation, of deliverance from evil, of immunity, and the reference to the name (*au nom*), to the law that forges the communal link (ideal or institutional) among believers and the faithful. This name can be equivocal; it can be "instrumentalized" by forces, ideologies, and powers, though it must first be *inscribed* in a form of sacredness or prohibition. That is what makes the difference between the religious, strictly speaking, and the simply cultural, what determines that which, in religion, is always *in excess* in relation to the cultural, but eventually returns to mark and guide it. Let's say, then, that the difference between religious discourses and their point of mutual untranslatability resides, in particular, maybe even specifically, not in the difference between dogmas, or in their narratives of origin (even if these are always strictly linked to the institution of anthropological differences), but in the different regimes, incompatible among themselves, that prescribe and prohibit the uses of bodies, or institute the visibility of bodies and their accessibility.[28] So that these *concrete universals*, or these *practical universalities*, which is what religious discourses are, particularly the discourses of "revealed" religions, are not in contradiction or in conflict with one another when they announce general truths, salvific beliefs, and prescriptions for a universalizable morality as the object of a predication—on this point, ecumenism or "interreligious dialogue" is always at least virtually possible. But they do contradict each other and fight over the extent to which the sexualized body must be seen as the very site where signs of purity, election, obedience, sacrifice, asceticism, and alliance are to be made manifest.

That is no doubt why all the studies of the religious character of humanity are comparative. But this comparison lacks an external point of view, since there is no human perspective sufficiently "distant" from the body to see from outside it the *difference of differences* inscribed on the body.[29] Hence the violence of the conflicts that have flared up, here and elsewhere, around the question of the Islamic veil and the regime of *manifest invisibility* it imposes on sexual difference. Far be it from me to deny that the Islamic veil has something to do with the reproduction of a hierarchical relation between the sexes, one that can nevertheless be modulated or negotiated (or, as Butler puts it, "resignified") in different ways. But in the phobic reactions it provokes in a French-like space of laïcité—and especially when these reactions are institutionalized and prescribed as rules for the functioning of public institutions—we see quite clearly that what emerges is a religious conflict—albeit one heavily mediated and instrumentalized by secular power relations. It's a conflict of religious universalisms concentrated around the singularity of the bodily regime that lies at the core of each of these universalisms. The question remains open, incidentally, whether this is an *old* conflict, for example between the two dominant versions of institutionalized Western monotheism (I'm not sure that it is), or a *new*, or at least relatively new, conflict: one that entails, in equal measures, a work of interpretation and the repetition of theological archetypes. This is as such a religious way of reacting to the violence of other social conflicts, especially since they are not regulated by a classical form of the state, with its "organic" or "hegemonic" social system, or taken in charge by revolutionary hopes and movements. I leave this question open.

The second hypothesis is intended to converge with the first without joining it, or to form with it a disjunctive theoretical machine (as Deleuze might have said) that allows us to "read" certain aspects of the generalized violence that characterizes the current crisis. This time I align myself with a reprise of the critique of political economy. The critique Marx leveled at classical economic theorists produced a contradictory effect. It brought to the light of day an irreducible conflict lodged at the heart of the definition of capital, insofar as the latter imposes on "living labor" the law or measure (and the violence) of accumulated "dead labor." In doing so, however, Marx's critique also helped to obscure from view some ideological postulates of these same classical economic theories, notably the ones linked to the definition of the "substance of value" as labor (or abstract or generic labor), and those that tend to subordinate the crises of capitalism (notably its financial crises) to a finality, to a preestablished harmony ("the invisible hand") founded on a distribution, by society, of the labor forces available to it (and so, in the final analysis, of *productive bodies*) in function of the needs it must satisfy to perpetuate itself. All of that could be summed up in the idea that the political economy of labor, which is also a political economy of laborers (and of their organized political "movement"), stands opposite and against the political economy of capital, as its internal reversal and as the manifestation of its hidden principle.[30]

There is nothing simple about this. All the best commentators on Marx have shown, albeit through different paths, that Marx never appropriates a concept from classical economics without transforming it. This is particularly true of labor, or social labor, which in Marx becomes inseparable from *surplus labor*, the producer of *surplus value*: what matters then, and this is the very bedrock of the critique, is not so much the ability to invoke labor ideally, in its abstract "measure," in order to account for the commensurability of commodities on the market, but the fact that it must be simplified, timed, prolonged, and intensified so as to make it possible for it to be *added to itself* by creating a differential of accumulation. Marx's postulate, upon which rests the entire argumentation of his "critique," or upon which an analysis of objective categories and a phenomenology of lived experience are combined and complete each other, is that the articulation of surplus labor with surplus value (with the antagonism it engenders) must be thinkable at once on the level of the society as a whole (of the *Gesamtkapital* "organically" composed of a certain relation between dead and living labor) and at the level of the smallest unit of exploitation, i.e., each instant of a laborer's life, inasmuch as that is the life of an exploited producer, or an alienated productive life. But in this vast critical task, which brings to the fore the antagonism and exploitation at the heart of the "contradictions" of the economy, Marx nevertheless adopts, *uncritically*, certain fundamental ideas of political economy that allow him to represent to himself both society and the economy as balanced "machines" and "processes," self-regulating and self-productive, even if at the price of certain inequalities, crises, or class struggles, all of which will persist at least as long as capitalism has not reached its "historical limit." And the most fundamental of these ideas is precisely the idea of *reproduction*, as a moment separate from production but necessary to its perpetuity, without which there is neither society nor the accumulation of capital. Naturally, this is the place to recall that the notion of "reproduction" immediately produced schisms within Marxism—the most famous being the one that pit Lenin's interpretation against Rosa Luxemburg's—and these are still with us today. Moreover, the notion involves, whether consciously or not, a play on words, given its double—economic and biological—meaning.[31]

To say this does not take away the admiration we might have for the way that, in volume two of *Capital*, Marx constructs "reproduction schemas" that lend themselves to various readings. But it does lead us to try to lay bare the latent presuppositions that inform the crucial distinction between "productive labor" and "unproductive labor," among which fall a variety of "services," notably social and educational services, as well as the service of women, which render the consumption of laborers possible. I have come to think that, behind this aporia, there are not only sexist prejudices, or the inability to see exploitation in certain places and moments where it is nevertheless even more violent, as a whole body of feminist literature has shown, but also a *political* condition that is linked to my hypothesis regarding the transition toward a "pure" capitalism (or the entry into a regime of "absolute capital") and the transformations that transition imposes on the conditions of resistance, that is, on the very possibility of the class struggle. Because this resistance—from the Industrial Revolution and, most of all, from the first social legislations to those of the welfare state and of what Robert Castel and others call the wage-earning society—was also made possible by the fact that the life of producers was split into *two moments* by means of a major anthropological rupture or difference between the moment of labor and that of reproduction, each of which entailed different forms of socialization.[32] But this is no longer the case, at least tendentially, in "pure" capitalism, where reproduction—by means of the transformation of consumption, of health, of leisure, and, tendentially, of education into fields that capital invests in (fields called, precisely, "human capital")—is completely incorporated into production itself.[33] What that also means, again tendentially, is that sexual difference no longer has a "functional" need from the point of view of capital (which is of course not to say that it has disappeared, even as a difference in social status, because it has other functions and historical foundations). We should even ask if "intellectual difference"—between educated and uneducated workers—retains the same functions and content, since I suspect that there is an extraordinary mystification in what we call the "intellectualization of work."[34] The great and essentially floating division, which achieved a sort of projection in the instance that Marx called the "reserve industrial army," is the division between the precariously employed and the precariously unemployed. And we know that this difference, overdetermined by other factors of inequality with global reach, is potentially deadly.[35] It is a new regime of the production, the distribution, and the uses of bodies in capitalism, and it affects, without distinction, the "manual" and "mental" faculties, both of which have been profoundly dispersed and recomposed by information technology and a "post-Taylorist" organization of labor.[36]

As you can see, my efforts have not resulted in a theory, or even in a critical problematic, in the style of a theory of reification, of one-dimensional man, or of territorialization-deterritorialization, or even of a post-Foucauldian "biopolitics"—though I have tried to appropriate some of their questions. What I have tried to do is designate a "site," which is itself abstract, in order to analyze the overlapping effects of religious determinations and the economic determinations of the atypical, indeed exceptional, crisis we find ourselves in, a crisis characterized by its global reach and the deadly intensification of acts of violence (which, it goes without saying, also have all sorts of other causes). This site would be the "body," which is immediately split anew by a tension between two aspects at once inseparable and distinct, and whose unity is the enigma of anthropological discourse: the "symbolic (or signifying) body," and the "productive (or utilitarian) body," toward which converge, without being confused, a new post-Marxian critique of political economy and a critique of religion that does not yet presume itself to be "completed."

PART I
SAECULUM

1

CIRCUMSTANCES AND OBJECTIVES

S everal years ago, the American University of Beirut invited me to submit a few hypotheses on the relation-ship between cosmopolitanism and secularism—that is, the worldwide and the worldly in today's world—for discussion and, if need be, refutation.[1] What occasion could have been more appropriate—or more intimidating? The interest and stakes of this relationship are obvious. It sparks impassioned debate throughout the Mediterranean region we live in—and produces more doubts and misunderstandings than certainties or notions commanding common assent. How to approach the subject so as to steer clear of both pious wishes and standing divisions? The best way to proceed, no doubt, would be to lay one's cards on the table, however inadequate they might be. As I took pains to explain to my hosts from the outset, I am the product of an epistemological tradition based on the principle that one really learns only from one's mistakes. It remained, however, to put this principle into practice, and I was counting on my hosts to help me do so. All of us had also learned from Edward Said that differences of culture and origin need not stand in the way of mutual comprehension, if we take them into account and subject the prejudices they may mask to systematic criticism.

This section of the book is an expanded version of my November 12, 2009 lecture titled "Cosmopolitanism and Secularism: Controversial Legacies and Prospective Interrogations."[2] I revised the text of the original lecture for publication as a book in French, fleshing it out with a few more quotations, elaborations, and references. I also wrote an envoi for the French edition. The resulting essay, which by no means lays claim to the status of doctrine or theory, will, I hope, help to reopen and sustain the transnational, transcultural debate that many of us have been calling for, by investing it with a philosophical dimension that is occasionally neglected in order to suppress the distance (and the distinction) between history and politics. On that condition, the critical ambition inherent in the universalism that we have inherited from the Enlightenment may avoid transformation into its opposite: a purely ideological tradition given locally institutionalized form in the interests of a now untenable hegemony.[3]

2

SECULARISM AND COSMOPOLITANISM: AN APORIA?

In my title the conjunction of the terms "secularism and cosmopolitanism" seems to announce a complementarity to be discovered or constructed through an effort at definition and proposition. I make no secret of the fact that these two notions are, for me, associated with basically positive values: they make up part of what characterizes democratic politics. Yet, as contemporary debates unfold in what has become a transnational framework, it is no longer possible not to see that their combination conceals profound contradictions. I am now persuaded that, in the current situation (the final result of a long history), each term calls the validity of the other into question or, at any rate, undermines its stability and deconstructs its apparently solidly established meaning.[1] As a result, it has become much harder to consider them complementary aspects of a single civic or democratic project. That is why I do not here intend simply to wed cosmopolitanism and secularism in a single problematic—which it would be quite natural to associate with the Enlightenment tradition or the project of modernity, even if it remains "unfinished" (Habermas), an association that would lead some of our contemporaries to proclaim their abiding value, and others, on the contrary, to denounce, with varying intentions, the indelible trace of a hegemonic discourse in them, supposed to be the discourse of a Eurocentric ideology's conquest of the world. Instead, I propose to discuss the presuppositions underlying them, and, thus, to complicate our representation of them.

Whence the questions, anything but natural, that I propose to explore here. The following question, for example: supposing that, under the conditions of contemporary politics, no cosmopolitical project is tenable without secularization (in other words, supposing that the idea of a "religious cosmopolitanism" is untenable per se), why is it that holding up a secular or secularized perspective for the construction of the cosmopolis only adds (at least initially) new problems and contradictions to those already entailed by the idea of moving from citizenship at a national level to transnational citizenship? In other words, why does the idea of a public sphere that is "secularized" or freed from the grip of religion (an idea that seemed straightforward enough even if it did not command unanimous consent) at the level of the polis or nation, become confusing, impracticable, or even self-destructive when we shift our concept of politics to the level of the world or humanity, that is, to a space a priori free of limits and exclusions? How must we proceed so that the obstacles before such a representation of things do not simply accentuate its hopelessly utopian or potentially destructive character, but, rather, foster discussion of intellectual tasks and rules of governance that put our societies in a cosmopolitical perspective?

Inversely, however, let us suppose that—in some parts of the world or even, perhaps, all of them, albeit differently in each case—it is no longer really possible to implement a secular or secularized conception of politics, to institutionalize secular modalities for regulating social conflict, improving public services (education, health care, urban development, and so on), and broadening access to means of communication without building a "cosmopolitical" dimension into the very definition of the political. In that case, no truly secularized democratic politics that is socially and culturally progressive is tenable short of cosmopolitanism. This comes down to admitting that a secularism (or *laïcité*) that defines itself along communitarian lines, guided essentially by imperatives of national unity, national identity, or national security, will soon find itself entangled in contradiction and, eventually, become self-destructive. Why, then, do all these manifest realities not pave the way for institutional solutions, but, rather, seem to multiply ideological obstacles and obscure the very possibility of such solutions?

Let there be no mistake—not only do I not think that we can detach secularism and cosmopolitanism from each other as political concepts, but the heated debates they provoke have convinced me more than ever of the need to study each as a function of, and in terms of, the other.[2] By now, however, it is (or ought to be) very clear that a conjunction of this sort introduces a terrible uncertainty into each of the determinations that we are in the habit of placing under these two rubrics. Indeed, the debate is so vehement that we may well wonder whether they will still be recognizable after undergoing the trials they face today.

At this point, I am tempted to borrow the title of a recent book by the American historian Joan Wallach Scott on women's citizenship in the French Constitution (before returning to some of Scott's analyses of French laïcité): *Only Paradoxes to Offer*.[3] I believe that, here too, we touch on what I have elsewhere tried to analyze as the antinomic character of the development of citizenship as a historic institution: citizenship is intrinsically related to the processes of democratizing politics, yet is irreducible to "pure" democracy, for which liberty is the condition of equality, and vice versa. Citizenship can only represent the unstable, irreducibly conflictual balance between its own emancipatory and conservative—one might even say insurgent and constitutional—tendencies. That is also why the very existence of citizenship hinges, every time it finds itself caught up in a major historical transformation, on its capacity to be filled with new contents. Inevitably, the institution of citizenship as a whole is called into question, and presents itself to us in paradoxical form, because we find it hard to imagine (and thus to invent) the new in old language. That is, of course, a radically foreshortened way of stating the matter, but one that may make it easier to understand my motive for describing cosmopolitanism and secularism as two aspects of a project to democratize democracy that we can neither arbitrarily separate nor combine without, in both cases, also calling them into question. In other words, we here come up against internal limits on the democratic project that we can by no means be sure of overcoming in the foreseeable future. That makes it all the more important to discuss their nature.[4]

3

DOUBLE BINDS: POLITICS OF THE VEIL

Enough generalities—everything at issue here is a matter of concrete situations and depends on circumstances. I would therefore like to turn to an example in which the clash between cosmopolitanism and secularism is plain to see, so that we are left with no choice but to propose distinctions. I take my example from recent French history, but I do not believe that it is of merely local import: more precisely, I think that the echo it has found beyond our frontiers (often at the price of considerable oversimplification) helps bring out its significance, for this echo is not due to sheer hostility even when it takes the form of a radical critique of French conceptions.

My intention, needless to say, is to return briefly to the controversies occasioned by the French state's decision (now followed by several others in Europe) to make it illegal for girls to wear the "Islamic veil," or hijab, in public schools, in the name of a principle of laïcité understood as a constitutional principle grounding a collective political identity. In practice, the prohibition forces girls who have decided to wear the veil—for various reasons, personal or not[1]—to make the hard choice either to remove an article of clothing to which they attach value and

9

personal identity, or to find themselves excluded from the public school system (and thus lose their chances of professional success and social recognition). Let us note in passing that the widespread legal, political, and moral criticisms of this legislation have sounded all over the world (from conservatives and liberals, from academics, human rights activists, and spokespeople for religious communities, from the Indian subcontinent through North America and the Middle East). These criticisms are themselves part of the cosmopolitical framework and have major repercussions, in their turn, on the French debate.

We need first to review, however briefly, the question of the equivalence between laïcité and secularism.[2] Both should be put in a much more general historical paradigm. Manifestly, the English and French terms are not interchangeable; but neither can it be said that they do not overlap at all. If we take the series *secular-secularism-secularization* as our point of reference, what is foregrounded by the notion of laïcité, which has, in France, been institutionalized (and even enshrined in the constitution) is not the idea that all religious denominations have equal rights in the public realm, but, rather, the separation of church (more generally, religions) and state and, by extension, that of religious practices or beliefs on the one hand and, on the other, social functions placed under state authority, notably education. Laïcité, one of its most intransigent contemporary partisans tells us,

> has to do with the principle of unifying people in the state. It is premised on a basic legal distinction between individuals' private lives as such and their public dimension as citizens. . . . It will readily be seen that dividing the individual up this way is not always easy, and, above all, that to do so is acknowledged as legitimate only in a certain conception of law concerned with the individual's autonomy, a concern *laïcité* shares.[3]

As everyone knows, however, this public control over the school system accommodates, within the framework of what sociologist Jean Baubérot calls the "pact of laïcité"—a veritable *historical compromise* coextensive with the history of modern republicanism—for a broad denominational sector said to be "private." This "private" school system is more or less master of its curriculum. The situation is not quite the same in the other major field in which problems of secularization arise, the field of medicine. Here, the exception is much more straightforwardly defined in terms of people's class situation, even if inequalities have not reached the same levels as in the United States. Conflicts of authority have nevertheless begun to appear; they revolve, once again, around control over women's bodies.[4]

Elsewhere I have suggested that this orientation (which, of course, finds its explanation in both social developments and the centuries-old history of the relations between republicanism and Catholicism, in which various "minorities" have also been involved) should be traced back to a Hobbesian conception of the "social contract," which authorizes the state to represent a society regarded as a unified *whole*, rather than the Lockean conception of tolerance invoked by liberalism. This primacy of the state (or public power) over civil society, with its constitutive pluralism, certainly reflects a general tendency among modern nation-states, but it does not represent the only possible form in which secularism can be realized, nor even the one that became historically dominant between the sixteenth and twentieth centuries. Laïcité "à la française" (which, as is usually indicated by their adoption of the term itself, has been taken as a model by other countries not necessarily Catholic in culture), displays an absolutism that is not representative of the way "theologico-political" questions are posed in the Western tradition overall. This absolutism can nonetheless help bring out the contradictions underlying any consideration of secularism and secularization.[5]

That is why, although the commentaries—hostile or not—elicited throughout the world by the policy France has adopted are sometimes cause for dissatisfaction or perplexity for someone observing its aims and vicissitudes from inside the country, I take them very seriously and consider them illuminating or, at any rate, revealing. I do not, however, wish to be guided entirely by those commentaries.

I sharply criticized the French law in its day and am still in favor of repealing it, despite the relatively peaceful conditions in which it was ultimately implemented.[6] For I do not see how a constraint applied exclusively to individuals of the female sex who are portrayed as *victims* of religious oppression can have the slightest emancipatory or educational effect, cast as it is in the form of a rigid alternative: unveiling oneself in the presence of others or quitting public school and being confined to a private realm defined, by the same stroke, as religious and closed. Such a constraint reinforces the unequal treatment of the sexes that it claims to combat, denying the female subjects themselves any chance to explain their motivations or the meaning they attach to their behavior, and, as well, all possibility of self-determination or dialogue: for the law is the law. It turns the famous formula in Rousseau's *Social Contract* against its intentions: "whoever refuses to obey the general will be compelled to do so by the whole body. This means nothing less than that he will be forced to be free"; in the name of freedom and equality, it clearly treats these girls as *subjects*, while at no point treating them as the *citizens* that the "secular" (*laïque*) school postulates and claims to educate. It must, consequently, have other motives. Among them—apart from that of making a public show of the school system's jeopardized administrative authority, exercised in this instance at the expense of Muslim girls' freedom of conscience and movement—we cannot exclude, given the tenor of the debates and the circumstances surrounding them, the intention of pandering to certain racist,

Islamophobic elements of French society (thereby legitimating them). It would thus seem that we find ourselves in exactly the same postcolonial situation that Gayatri Spivak has described and interpreted with the famous phrase, "[European] white men saving [indigenous] brown women from [the oppression of indigenous] brown men."[7]

But are things really this simple? At the heart of the same situation, we surely find the opposite scenario as well. Its importance and means of action must be assessed as precisely as possible (their source is not law, but tradition, which can always be invented as need dictates), but it would be stupid to overlook it: "[indigenous] brown men making sure that [indigenous] brown women are not saved by [European] white men." This was illustrated in almost caricatural fashion in 2004 when, to protest the law prohibiting the veil, certain Islamic associations organized demonstrations in which girls marched through the streets wearing veils mockingly colored red, white, and blue, like the French flag; the girls, some of whom were quite young, were vigilantly escorted by adult males (clerics and Islamic militants) who saw to it that there was no discussion with journalists or passersby. Subjects are never ideally free; they are always the stakes of a conflict whose terms they are more or less capable of identifying and redefining.

It is time to return to the theses defended in Joan Scott's *Politics of the Veil*, a detailed analysis of the meaning and origins of the French law against the veil.[8] Basically, Scott demonstrates a continuity between the representations of "indigenous women" (especially Muslim Algerian women) that structured the colonialists' orientalist imaginary and the stereotypes that today's nationalist French discourse applies to relations between the sexes in immigrant (especially Arab) families. That continuity seems to me hard to dispute. However, bending the stick as far as possible in the direction of the postcolonial paradigm, Scott is led by her analysis to adopt the idea of a frontal opposition between feminine modesty, treated as a characteristic feature of traditional culture in the Muslim world, and the violence of the symbolic exploitation to which Western modernity subjects woman's body and image, especially in commercial advertising. Thus, we find her ranging, under one and the same concept, the tendencies of capitalist mass consumption (including the commercial sex industry, which *instrumentalizes* male domination and female submission in this sense) and the tendencies of French republicanism, which is based, notably, on *neutralization* (or even denial) of anthropological differences, whether they are, indeed, sexual, religious, or cultural. This is what Scott calls "abstract universalism." It seems to me, however, that this is to short-circuit the analyses we need, precisely, in order to account for the contradictions of universalism. This holds especially for the respective influences of commodity equivalence and equality before the law, both formally characterized by the fact that they "do not distinguish between individuals," although they manifestly do not bear on the same type of "subjects" or require the same type of consent from them. Scott's characterization of this "abstract universalism" is, in its turn, extremely abstract and ahistorical. Doubtless it is the very notion of abstraction which is equivocal. That cannot *not* have an impact on what we understand, correspondingly, by "difference" (particularly when the suggestion is that differences, for their part, are always "concrete," or tend to be).

In a crucial passage of her book, titled "The Clash of Gender Systems," Scott opposes Islam and French republicanism as a "psychology of recognition and a psychology of denial" of the difference between the sexes. Basing what she says, in particular, on a comparison between the controversies (incomparably shorter and less vehement) touched off when adolescent girls wore thong or "string" underwear to class,[9] Scott concludes that

There is, then, a persistent contradiction in French political theory between political equality and sexual difference. Politicians and republican theorists have dealt with this contradiction by covering it over, by insisting that equality is possible while elevating the differences between the sexes to a distinctive cultural character trait. . . . As if to prove that women cannot be abstracted from their sex (men, of course, can be), there is great emphasis on the visibility and openness of seductive play between women and men, and especially on the public display (and sexual desirability for men) of women's bodies. The demonstrable proof of women's difference has to be out there for all to see, at once a confirmation of the need for different treatment of them *and* a denial of the problem that sex poses for republican political theory. We might then say that, paradoxically, the objectification of women's sexuality serves to veil a constitutive contradiction of French republicanism . . . women are objectified in both systems, although in different ways. My point is that sex and sexuality are differently represented, differently managed in these two systems. Paradoxically, for Islam it is the veil that makes explicit—available for all to see—the rules of public gendered interaction, which are in no way contradictory and which declare sexual exchanges out of bounds in public space. It is this explicit acknowledgment of the problem of sexuality that, for French observers, makes the veil ostentatious or conspicuous in the sexual sense of those words. Not only is too much being said about sex, but all of its difficulties are being revealed. Women may be formally equal, but the difference of their sex somehow belies that equality. The pious pronouncements of French politicians about the equality of men and women are at odds with their deep uneasiness about actually sharing power with the opposite sex. These are difficulties that theorists and apologists for French republicanism want to deny.[10]

One can unhesitatingly grant Scott's point that the private-public regime for regulating the difference between the sexes, oscillating between exhibition and neutralization, reflects a "deep uneasiness." However, unless the aim is to suggest that "recognition" is a category encompassing contradictory practices, one is stupefied to find Scott describing as a "recognition of difference," without further specification, both the regime of the repression of sexuality in the domestic sphere, where man acts as the "guardian" of women's virtue, and the exclusion of "uncovered women" from public life:

> Islamic jurists deal with sexual difference in a way that avoids the contradiction of French republicanism by acknowledging directly that sex and sexuality pose problems (for society, for politics) that must be addressed and managed . . . Modest dress, represented by the headscarf or veil for women and loose clothing for men, is a way of recognizing the potentially volatile and disruptive effects of sexual relations between women and men, driven by impulses . . . that are a source . . . of dangers and conflicts. Modest dress declares that sexual relations are off-limits in public places. Some Muslim feminists say this actually liberates them, but whether it does or not, or whether, indeed, every woman who wears a headscarf understands its symbolism in this way, the veil signals the acceptance of sexuality and even its celebration, but only under proper circumstances—that is, in private, within the family. This is a psychology not of denial but of recognition.[11]

Do we not find here, induced by a fair critique of the hypocrisy that reigns over French egalitarianism (which in actual practice masks deeply ingrained forms of discrimination, both "public" and "private," that have not been fundamentally altered by the campaigns for parity between the sexes), an extraordinary blindness to the way a social order that is both patriarchal and monotheistic invests sexuality and the difference between the sexes with a symbolic function that is a frightfully effective means of reproducing its own power structures? Rather than alternately invoking the irreconcilable viewpoints of resistance to cultural imperialism and liberation from oppressive traditional cultures, I think we would do better to describe the reality of concrete double-bind situations. The fact is that, during the successive episodes of the controversy over authorizing or forbidding girls to wear the veil in lycées, and again during the more recent debate about authorizing or forbidding women to wear the burka in public (even if, in these two cases, the legal, theological, and social realities are not at all the same), female subjects found themselves caught between the battle lines and strategies of two groups that can both be described as phallocratic (this does not mean that they are made up solely of men) and that have made the regulation of women's bodies the battlefield and stakes of their will to power or a defense of their hegemony. (This is true even if, let me repeat, their forces are unequal or, rather, are not exercised in the same places with the same means of coercion.) One of these groups speaks the language of religious tradition (in more or less orthodox fashion); the other speaks that of secular (*laïc*) education and women's liberation (in more or less doctrinaire fashion). What holds sway on both sides of the line is power—that is, inequality, if not constraint—and, possibly, resistance.

I do not, of course, expect that such a view will command universal assent, especially when presented in such starkly unqualified terms. But it seems to me to be so powerfully suggested by the history of recent confrontations that we cannot shirk the obligation to examine its implications. However, before going to the heart of my discussion, which concerns the competing uses of the categories "religion" and "culture," I must make two transitional remarks. The first bears on the space in which the debates and conflicts just mentioned have crystallized: this space has become cosmopolitical, an expression each of whose two terms must be emphasized in turn. The second bears on the contemporary uses of the category "multiculturalism."

4.

COSMOPOLITICS AND CONFLICTS
BETWEEN UNIVERSALITIES

Basic disagreement over how to interpret the relationship between cultures, religions, and public institutions are well and truly *cosmo*political, in that they crystallize, in a specific national microcosm that is open and unstable, elements drawn from the whole world and its millennial history. Under contemporary conditions, the harder we try to close a "national" problem in on itself, the more we denature and destabilize it. That is plainly the logic of the unrest that has been erupting in what might be called the "global suburbs," where the upshot of migrations, diasporas, colonization and decolonization is that encounters between different cultural heritages and religions have become everyday realities, as have, consequently, the conflicts between them—all this against a backdrop of massive inequalities in social status and institutional recognition. The whole social formation is concerned by these clashes, their localization in the "suburbs" notwithstanding.

The postcolonial aspect is crucial here, to be sure, but it is also equivocal. The clash of domestic and diasporic cultures is prolonging the history of the colony beyond its official death (all the more insidiously in that that history has been repressed or travestied in institutional and collective memory). Yet the clash of cultures is not an exact reproduction of the colony, contrary to what militant discourses intent on undoing the repression of colonial history sometimes affirm. Rather, it translates and transposes it, and sometimes even constitutes a reversal of its effects. (Naturally, since relations of oppression and domination are at stake, this cannot happen in the absence of determinate struggles.) More than ever, therefore, we must acknowledge that the social environment in which we try to give our interests or beliefs political form is the product of a violent past whose traces continue to spawn new conflicts. There would be no globalized society without the process of "globalization of the globe" (*mondialisation du monde*) that began several centuries ago; its driving forces were, not just the anonymous capitalist processes of accumulation and commodification, but histories of empire, colonization, and decolonization or neocolonization—and, therefore, histories of domination and servitude. We must, however, also study the specific makeup of the social, cultural, and religious mélange precipitated by this history, whose development today cuts across the old frontiers of nations and empires.[1]

This much would suffice to explain why what seems to us to be *cosmo*political is also cosmo*political* in the full sense of the word: not just the object of legal descriptions and state interventions, but also the dynamic stakes of social and ideological conflicts that do not have a single, unequivocal meaning. But the example from which I set out shows us more than that. It calls our attention to the fact that, in a determinate historical and social situation, when discourses labeled "religious" encounter a counterdiscourse (for instance, that of institutional laïcité or state secularism), the counterdiscourse itself exhibits a symmetrical tendency toward sacralization; finds itself, that is, overdetermined by one or another typical trait of "the religious." This tendency is doubtless especially pronounced if our counterdiscourse is normative not only in the sense that it legitimizes values and endows them with a regulatory function (in France, one often speaks in this connection of the *Idea* of laïcité, in a sense that is more Kantian than Platonic), but also in that it associates the institution with positive legal *norms*, which prescribe or outlaw modes of behavior and thought in the cultural, educational, and social spheres (even—indeed, above all—if these modes of thought lay claim to scientificity, or proceed from what Georges Canguilhem calls "scientific ideologies").[2]

Should we conclude that the politics of secularization (particularly the politics of the secularization of education, public life, and public space) should itself be categorized as *religious conflict*? Quite the contrary: there is no such thing as a purely religious conflict in today's world; every confrontation between religious representations and communities, or between them and their secular antitheses, is always political. It is, moreover, always overdetermined by very material interests. It might be said that this has always been so, but there is also something new in the contemporary modalities of this theologico-political complex; it has to do with the fact that the relativization of national borders and the sovereignties that such borders distinguish, together with the growing importance of migrations, makes it increasingly artificial to assign the religious to the realm of the *particular* (or of "particularisms"), while the secular (in the guise of "public reason") comes by definition to occupy the place of the *universal*. This does not, however, lead to relativizing everything. The issue, rather, is *conflicts between competing universalities*.[3]

More precisely, the crisis of the theological universalisms (particularly the monotheistic universalisms of the West, which from this point of view necessarily include Islam) began with the dawn of modernity and has been raging ever since, without foreseeable end, whereas our time has seen the irreversible onset of the crisis of *political* or "civic" *universalisms*—premised on the principle, not of the existence of a revelation potentially addressed to all human beings "without distinction of origin," but of their equality before the law and, more profoundly, in Hannah Arendt's now-famous phrase, their "right to have rights" in the framework of a community of citizens. This explains, by the same stroke, why it is becoming ever harder to apply the legal distinction between mutually exclusive public and private realms to the difference between the community of citizens and the community defined by religious allegiance, in the absence of a supplementary political constraint. "Public" discourse and "public" institutions whose legitimacy essentially derives from a *national* (and, therefore, nationalist, even in the nation's republican form) historical formation are not more universal or universalistic per se than the discourse of a transnational religion. Their higher degree of universality cannot be proclaimed a priori: it must be proven at the level of experience, particularly on the terrain of the emancipatory possibilities that such discourses and institutions offer citizens. Whenever a religious or theological difference becomes a source of conflict (and it is incumbent on us to determine, case by case, the conditions that crystallize the conflict or make it an antagonistic one), that conflict is potentially *cosmopolitical*. That is why the closely related notions of *cosmopolitanism* (inherited from the ancient and classical philosophical traditions) and *cosmopolitics* (intensified by the effects of globalization) can no longer be articulated in linear fashion, as one might articulate an idea with its translation into realities and acts. Contemporary cosmopolitics is a particularly ambiguous form of politics; it consists exclusively of conflicts between universalities without ready-made solutions. It does not prefigure the realization of a philosophical "cosmopolitanism," but neither does it purely and simply do away with the possibility of taking it as a point of reference.[4] It would be more accurate to say that cosmopolitics clears the field for competition between *alternative* cosmopolitanisms.

In the same way, as I shall try to show in a moment, it is the theater for competition between alternative secularisms.

This brings me to a second, equally hypothetical proposition. We may unhesitatingly include "multiculturalism" among the varieties of cosmopolitanism that inspire political projects in the contemporary period. Must we not, however, now describe its political and philosophical power *in the past tense*? This is not to downplay its historical significance (still less to rally to a nationalistic discourse that has always ignored or denigrated it). Rather, it is to suggest that its fecundity now depends on an internal criticism of its own limits and ambiguities.[5] In every respect, multiculturalism today stands at a crossroads.

Everyone knows, of course, that the term has been used to cover a vast array of positions that contradict each other even in the way they utilized the idea of culture. Only because a multiculturalism such as Charles Taylor's or even Will Kymlicka's is designated by the same term as Homi Bhabha's or Stuart Hall's can they be ranged under the same concept. For multiculturalism of the first kind (which belongs to a tradition that ultimately goes back to European Romanticism and has drawn sustenance from an anthropological culturalism eager to rehabilitate "traditional societies" and protect them against the disintegrating effects and violence of colonization), cultures are mutually external *totalities* peculiar to historical communities to which one belongs by heritage or descent (and, sometimes, assimilation). It is a question of facilitating coexistence by means of a constitutional pluralism such that, for each individual, his or her membership in a particular community enjoys legal protection and the same recognition granted all the others; this community affiliation is, in the last instance, the vector of education and the condition for personal dignity. For the second kind of multiculturalism (which sprang up, notably, on the basis of the trans-Atlantic experience of post-slave societies, and was also prefigured, in the French intellectual realm, by an anthropology of "contacts between civilizations" such as Bastide's or Leiris's), the ultimate historical horizon is a never-ending process of cultural hybridization and interaction between communities; this leads to the idea that what makes subjects capable of individualization and historical metamorphosis is their aptitude for *translation* and thus for a disidentification that is at least virtual and can go so far as to become "double consciousness."[6] It is well known that modern postcolonial nations have given widely differing receptions to these two conceptions of multiculturalism over the years. In France, the dominant discourse has always rejected multiculturalism in all its variants; that discourse has today been joined by others in the framework of a Europe in which, there is reason to fear, it may become the one and only unifying idea. In any case, it seems clear that the contemporary phenomenon described as a "return of the religious" or "the sacred" cannot but turn the debate topsy-turvy, plunging the idea of multiculturalism as the realization of the cosmopolitical ideal into crisis.[7]

Here I do not primarily have in mind the effects of nationalist or xenophobic discourses—despite the seriousness of the problem they pose—that never tire of championing the idea, in defiance of all the historical evidence, that cultural homogenization within certain borders defined by sovereignty or alliance is the general condition for the survival of political communities in general, independently of any democratic politics. Rather, I am thinking of the thesis, which it is hard to contest, that projects to establish a "multicultural constitution" for democratic society considerably underestimate the acuity of religious conflicts (or conflicts based on religion) and, above all, misunderstand their true nature. For my part, I would interpret this phenomenon by setting out, precisely, from the idea that such conflict does not involve rival *particularisms* (if it did, the solution would consist in separating the clashing particularisms under the aegis of a superior, transcendent universalism, or in progressively integrating them in some syncretic culture); on the contrary, it brings *incompatible universalities* into collision. Thus, I am quite happy to grant that it is insufficient and ineffective to try to locate on a cultural terrain antagonisms whose essential determinants are partly religious, and then approach them in terms of multiculturalism. But this by no means traps us in the alternative of a generalized "war of religion"[8] or an ecumenical "interfaith dialogue" to which only voices officially defining themselves as those of religious communities would be admitted, so that political determination is subsumed under their narcissistic self-definition (or the reductive labels attached to such religious communities, as is often the case for "Islam," but also for the "Christian peoples," when both are perceived as unified entities). I prefer to look for a problematic that does not lock us into the language of either culturalism, theologism, cultural anthropology, or the classic alternative of tolerance versus intolerance, but, rather, analyzes, as such, a differend about citizenship whose stakes are political, although, to a certain (essential and doubtless irreducible) extent, its sources and self-consciousness are of the order of the religious or of criticism of the religious. In other words, I think that we must reopen, without offering any ready-made solutions, the thorny question as to what religious identities and beliefs do in the public realm, and what politics (whether it is a matter of institutions or movements) does with them. This is not the first time, incidentally, that such a question has been posed from the standpoint of a democratic politics. It was posed in Europe in particular, in a not-too-distant past, when the movements of resistance to fascism and later, in Eastern Europe, to Soviet-style state communism had simultaneously to rally "those who believed in heaven and those who didn't."[9] But the conditions resulting from the process of globalization now underway indisputably invest the question with a new urgency and a new uncertainty, inasmuch as they undermine the *national* form in which the solution has been prescribed until today.

At this point, another objection arises. To talk about the permanence or the return of the religious, about a "religious" or "theological" determination encompassing both creeds and secular critiques of them, is to make use of an imprecise if not deceptive category, one that rules out in advance, as certain philosophers and anthropologists tell us today, any comprehension of the cosmopolitical stakes, because it itself always already contains the principle informing a dogmatic deformation. In France, both Jacques Derrida and Régis Debray have outlined such a critique. Their formulations of it are the more important in that they are prudent, essentially tending to double their intervention in the contemporary "clashes of civilizations" with a deconstructive skepticism toward the basic ideas such clashes mobilize. In the United States, this critique has been developed, notably, by Talal Asad, whose formulations, as erudite as they are radical, have become very influential throughout the English-speaking world, especially after 2001, with the controversies touched off by the invasion of Afghanistan, one of the official justifications for which made constant reference to the "liberation" of

Muslim women from Taliban oppression and, more generally, Islamic fundamentalism.[1]

Derrida, setting out from a critical reading of Emile Benveniste's etymologies, points out that the word "religion," whose meaning still depends on its Roman and Christian sources, is, properly speaking, *untranslatable* into other languages and cultures. Use of this term accordingly imposes a "Romano-Christian" code on everything it is used to designate, even when non-Christian confessions (Judaism or Islam) have recourse to it to demand equal rights and recognition in a "religious" domain whose contours are in fact determined by a knowing or judging agency that claims to except itself from that domain by virtue of its secular nature (although, historically, it springs from it):

> [W]e will put to the test the quasi-transcendental privilege we believe ourselves obliged to grant the distinction between, *on the one hand*, the experience of belief (trust, trustworthiness, confidence, faith, the credit accorded the *good faith of the utterly other* in the experience of witnessing) and, *on the other*, the experience of sacredness, even of holiness, of the unscathed that is safe and sound . . . These comprise two distinct sources or foci. "Religion" figures their *ellipse* because it both comprehends the two foci but also sometimes shrouds their irreducible duality in silence, in a manner precisely that is secret and *reticent*. In any case, the history of the word "religion" should in principle forbid every non-Christian from using the name "religion," in order to recognize in it what "we" would designate, identify and isolate there. . . . Benveniste also recalls that there is no "common" Indo-European term for what we call "religion." The Indo-Europeans did not conceive "as a separate institution" what Benveniste, for his part, calls "the omnipresent reality that is religion." . . . There has not always been, therefore, nor is there always and everywhere, nor will there always and

everywhere ("with humans" or elsewhere) be *something*, a thing that is *one and identifiable*, identical with itself, which, whether religious or irreligious, all agree to call "religion." And yet, one tells oneself, *one must still respond*.[2]

That may be why the opposite happens in actual practice. Derrida calls it the "mondialatinization" of *religio* (it might also be called a Romanization of the world).

Yet this does not prevent Derrida from depicting the violence of the conflict raging around the city of Jerusalem and the national appropriation of its holy places, not merely as a phenomenon of a colonial type (the late development of European hegemony in the Mediterranean region due to dramatic historical circumstances: the persecution of the European Jews and, ultimately, their extermination), but also a "sovereign" intensification—and therefore a self-destructive or, to use the term he proposes for this type of violence, an "autoimmune" intensification—of representations elaborated by the three "Abrahamic" monotheisms over the sites and contents of the religious revelation that unites as it divides them.[3]

In a brilliant essay, Régis Debray takes a different tack. Debray denounces the modern (and, precisely, "secular") confusion between *religion* and *belief in God*, a confusion that obscures the greater generality of the relationship between religion and *membership* in a community or social body that assigns itself a collective identity (by fashioning or constructing it) transcending the sum of its members' individualities. Debray accordingly proposes to short-circuit the Christian legacy in order to return to a Roman definition of *religio* and, ultimately, replace it with *communion*, which, he says, is the modern term that better captures the intended meaning:

We do not pretend to believe in some policing of language that would, with one stroke of the wand, do away with a usage two thousand years old. The word "religion" appears to be here to stay; but let us note, for honor's sake, that there is a candidate fulfilling these various requirements: "communion." The narrowly liturgical meaning that Christianity has assigned the latter term—the reception of the sacrament of the Eucharist—fails to exhaust its resources. . . . Even if the Latin etymology of the word is not union (*cum* et *unio*), but a burden or mission to be shared (*cum* and *munus*), the word meets the purpose of breaking down the barriers between the domains of "belief" and "unbelief," which are all too piously segregated. "Communion" is charged with more meanings than "religion." It does not dissociate denomination ("the Anglican, Orthodox, Hindu communions") and empathy ("I feel a sense of communion with your ideas and sentiments"). It is simultaneously a socially recognized "denomination" and a gut feeling, a relation translated into emotion. Above all, however, the word joins the horizontal: "to be a member of"—and the vertical: "to adhere to." That, precisely, is the equation informing every assemblage that is destined to endure. . . . In order to become "brothers," people have to be "brothers *in* . . ."—in some overarching entity, noble abstraction, or sublime personage that precedes and exceeds us.[4]

This proposition, however, presupposes the primacy (which, Derrida would doubtless say, would have to be deconstructed) of the *communitarian* dimension (or effect of social *integration*, even if it continues to be ontologically marked by *incompletion*) over the individualistic (heretic, mystical, ascetic, or "virtuoso," in Weber's sense) dimension. It suggests, at any rate, that the latter is always an anomaly or excess with respect to the former. Ultimately, it conduces to an astonishingly skeptical version of the idea of laïcité:

We have concocted antidotes for overcoming the tragedies of credulity and lowering the mandatory rate of symbolic deductions. The first antidote is intellectual: science. . . . The second is political, and has been around for a century or two: *laïcité*. This defensive and extremely precious accomplishment safeguards, in the state, a kernel of indifference to symbols and the imaginary, by neutralizing, as fully as possible, their devastating effects on freedom of conscience and the coexistence of differences. . . . But let us not be duped: although law has an adequate knowledge of things, including things social and economic, and although the disjunction between citizenship and confession, law and creed, is nonnegotiable, it would be imprudent to expect them to be able to divest our minireligious, pluricultural societies of the inevitable little touch of madness deposited in their monuments, constitutions, and schoolbooks. What the blinding Weberian formula about "the disenchantment of the world" masks is, ultimately, the fact that every disenchantment of a symbolically invested realm, such as politics and its utopias today, precipitates the enchantment of another—in the case to hand, culture and its identities.[5]

The consequence of this may well be (and is it not what Debray himself would like to see come about?—I am not sure) a purely political *decision* in favor of one or another type of "communion" (or its institutional primacy), whether it is the communion oriented toward religious confession or that oriented toward citizenship.

The American anthropologist Talal Asad has suggested an altogether different formulation in a series of essays on the genealogy of the opposition between the religious and the secular; they are becoming steadily more influential today, especially in debates on Western societies' attitude toward Islam.[6] Asad's main idea is that "religion" is a purely Eurocentric category that Christianity forged in order to impose the Church's domination on practices and creeds that had to be either overcome or assimilated, but, always, assigned their subordinate place in one and the same field, although they themselves had nothing "religious" about them per se (for example, asceticism, charity, contrition, or prayer). Every classification and every interpretation of individual and collective non-Western experience based on the proselytizing, self-referential category of "religion" is accordingly certain to denature such experience, even when claiming to recognize and validate it. But "secular" discourse (in whose terms we formulate the program for the history of religions and, in our schools, our classes on "religious phenomena") has by no means abolished the theological antitheses intrinsic to the Christian tradition, which it both criticizes and preserves; rather, it has contented itself with displacing and amplifying them, superimposing the opposition between the secular and the religious on that between the orthodox and the heretical, or religion and superstition.[7] In so doing, it has constructed a *code*, dominant in certain societies in which it has been both institutionally (legally) established and intellectually elaborated; this code rules out alternate ways of constructing historical experience.

I think that this line of argument is ultimately aporetic, but I also think it should be taken very seriously, because it reminds us of the crucial fact that there can be no *recognition* without *representation*, and no representation without a *code for representation*. A code is dominant or dominated, but never neutral. It organizes what Jacques Rancière calls the "distribution of the sensible" between the representable and the unrepresentable; in other words, it totalizes the world in accordance with a rule of quasi-transcendental inclusion that also, inevitably, entails exclusion. Yet no code for representing differences is established from *outside the conflict* or the power relations constituting it, from some purely theoretical position: every code is itself party to the conflict and constitutes one way of managing it. This situation cannot but influence the way the problem of the relationship between democracy and representation is posed.

Edward Said and, in his wake, others who have taken up or rectified his analyses, have extended to the realm of "culture" as a whole, with its normative, performative, and figurative dimensions, the antithesis, classic in political sociology (beginning, at the latest, with the Marx of *The Eighteenth Brumaire*), between dominant and dominated positions in the field of representation (in other words, the difference between *being represented* by imposed powers or theoretical discourses and the act of *representing oneself*, that is, in fact, of *presenting oneself* in the form of a political demand for emancipation).[8] But the debate on Orientalism is not only not over, it is also shifting to the terrain of the relations between religion and culture—as we saw when the Catholic Church, in the person of its supreme doctrinal authority in Rome or intellectuals close to him, endorsed the idea that European identity (or, more generally, Western civilization) has "Christian roots" and that this establishes a supposedly unique relationship between faith and reason.[9] It would be easy to multiply examples; for, of course, certain critiques of imperialist domination in the extra-European world, or on the part of intellectuals attempting to theorize its emancipation from the mind-sets established by colonization (including "modernity," "rationalism," and "historicism"), are quick to adopt the same idea in order to apply it in inverted fashion against what they designate with the blanket term "the West."

However, if we take seriously, as I suggested above, the idea that there exists a multiplicity of cosmopolitanisms, and if we bring it into relation with the internal critique or deconstruction of the secularism historically institutionalized in the framework of the nation-state, as one of the instruments of its sovereignty and cohesion, we are led to a different way of posing the problem of coding and codification, which is also that of the *regime of translation* through which *collective subjects represent themselves for one another* (generally speaking, through the mediation of discourses with which certain "organic intellectuals" and institutions of "power knowledge" provide them). Clearly, we cannot simply dismiss the injunction, issued by Asad and others, to question the religious code and, with it, the secular code bequeathed us by the history of Christianity, together with its juridical and theological elaborations and internal conflicts, all of which turn, precisely, on the category of religion. Does it follow that that injunction is itself free of all contradiction, and is by itself sufficient to free us from the dominant code that prescribes and limits the possibilities for the translation and representation of differences? I am not at all sure, for the logical reason, to begin with, that we will not be able to dispense with the category of the religious without mobilizing other anthropological categories, such as that of culture or tradition, defined as "agency is a complex term whose senses emerge within semantic and institutional networks that make possible particular ways of relating to people, things, and oneself."[10] If, however, we pursue the deconstructive project to its term, the category of culture, like the category of society, law, politics, nation, or even the state, must necessarily appear just as Eurocentric or Western in our eyes as the categories of religion and secularism (or laïcité). For the category of culture results, no less than they do, from the functioning of the major ideological state apparatuses that have been put in place by the West and serve as transmission belts for its hegemony: among them is academic research and scholarship, with the various historical and anthropological disciplines that make it up. The problem, therefore, is perhaps less to eliminate one or the other of these disciplines than to rectify them all, as well as the borders between them, by confronting them with what they have historically grasped in a strange relationship of recognition and miscognition.[11]

6.
CULTURE, RELIGION, OR IDEOLOGY

Have we simply been turning round and round in the same circle, spawning nothing but a sterile skepticism? I think that that can be avoided, but only if we come up with a new conceptual dispositive that is not based on a forced choice between a problematic of culture and a problematic of religion, or the reduction of one of those terms to the other. What I propose instead, as an experimental hypothesis, is to put the *very duality of this pair of concepts* to critical use in such a way as to identify certain differences which, although they are, to be sure, subtle, are nevertheless essential for any analysis of conflicts involving religious and cultural stakes or ideals.

I shall make no secret of the fact that this also represents an effort on my part to rehabilitate a category that has become rather unfashionable today: *ideology*. Why this odd attempt, even if the term "ideology" is here taken as the name of a formal, heuristic tool the application of which varies with the object itself?[1] The aim is emphatically not to *reduce* any and all discourse to an "ideological function," which would also be a way of disqualifying it, but, rather, to *complicate* the semantic demarcation of culture from religion, and thus to *displace* it.

My aim is not simply to clarify the debates about the political (and politicizing) effects of religion and culture, but, at bottom, to explore the ways a theory of ideology (or what was once called, in Althusserian circles, the "ideological instance" of social practice) might gain from this utilization of it, which effectively makes it a mediating category articulating the cultural and religious dimensions of social life, but, by the same stroke, without ceasing to generate contradictions inside each. Formally, then, I shall attempt to describe not just a logical relationship, but also a dynamic of transformations and activities. I set out from two ideas: the idea that processes of cultural generalization, routinization, and hybridization are capable of modifying and even, in the long run, breaking down religious models of existence, subjectivity, and community life; and the complementary idea that religious symbols associated with rites, conversions, and creeds (which can be of the order of revelation, myth, or dogma) have the power to crystallize and intensify cultural differences. Thus, such symbols can limit the malleability of cultures, homogenize them and isolate them, but also, in certain cases, *radicalize* their internal tensions and transform those tensions into political conflicts. We might further hypothesize that what a Wittgensteinian philosopher or anthropologist might call "forms of life"—cultural habits and the corresponding imaginary representations—circulate only with the human groups that are their bearers, whereas one can transmit the more "abstract" systems of religious symbols (that they are "more abstract" does not mean that they correspond to less intense subjective experiences) over much greater distances, a process that is today facilitated by the new technologies for the communication of messages and the multiplication of images. (Such technologies are one focus of Régis Debray's analyses). Thus, one converts, individually or collectively, to a creed, acknowledges the authority of a law or the truth of a dogma, chooses a road to salvation, serves a god or even a name, and becomes the adept of a ritual, whereas one can only adapt a culture or, more or less easily, adapt to its forms of life, because they do not invest the body and affect the unconscious the same way. This implies that there is a universality to the religious modes of ideology or, perhaps more exactly, a dialectic of belonging to a community and of confronting the universality of the world (or the truth) that is not to be found in ideology's cultural modes, which are essentially particularistic or differentialist—except, precisely, to the extent that they are articulated with a set of religious symbols.[2] However, a culture, in its turn, could not be individualized and experienced as a form of collective belonging that is always already given for each subject if it were not embodied in *nongeneralizable* norms, codes, or signs of mutual recognition (such as the famous "shibboleth" in the Bible story).[3] The age of globalization is therefore, par excellence, the age of a destabilization and politicization of the relations between culture and religion, because the frontiers of what can be pooled, shared, generalized, and communicated have lost their institutional or traditional identifications.

But I have another reason for thinking that we might gain from resuscitating, in as undogmatic a form as possible, the category of the ideological: the fact that, however general the concept of ideology may be, *it always implies a constitutive relationship with its own outside*, and, consequently, inscribes lack or inadequacy in its very constitution. It is contradictory to talk about ideology if one thinks that ideology is everything, contains everything, or covers everything. Thus, the suggestion here is that culture and religion, or, if one prefers, the cultural and religious aspects of ideology do not in themselves contain either all the causes that produce the combination of religion and culture within ideology itself or all the effects that that combination engenders in specific conjunctures. The equation that we must keep in mind cannot take the form *culture + religion = ideology*, but must rather be written *culture + religion ± X = ideology*.

Ideology, as a combination of culture and religion in variable "proportions," always exhibits a structural *deficit*. But, further, the *excess* represented by each term of the ideological "combination," and, a fortiori, the ideological instance as such considered with respect to its component elements (religion is something more and other than culture, but culture is also something more and other than religion), remains the index of a *lack* or an *absence*, inherent in their "sum," which, *taken together*, they make visible.

What, more exactly, is this X that marks the element of externality internal to ideological processes, this X that we must attempt to discover in the realm of both causes and effects? A Marxist would say that it is "the economy" ("production," capitalism, class relations); a Foucauldian would say that it is "power" (or "power relations"); a Weberian would say that it is "domination" (legitimate or illegitimate); a Bourdieusian would say that it is "practice"; a Lacanian would say that it is "the real," and so on. Of course, all these categories are different, differently constructed and justified in the light of different historical and social analyses, although, from our present standpoint, they stand as so many attempts to zero in on the same lack or absent cause. We must bear in mind this irreducible externality (and, at the same time, its ambiguousness) when we set out to analyze political situations regarded either as subject to dynamics basically rooted in culture (or, as one says today, in "identity") or else dominated by irresistible religious forces (unless we are to fall back on a bastard synthesis of religion and culture, such as the "clash of civilizations"). Not only can religion and culture not be spontaneously added together, but their combined effects are always overdetermined by socioeconomic processes and relations of domination or power that are in fact *neither religious nor cultural*. It is in this supplementary place carved out by their opposition that we must situate the absent cause, the effects, irrupting on another scene, without which religion and culture would themselves have no historical effects. It follows that if we were to content ourselves with a simple articulation of the cultural and the religious, we would never really escape the alternative between the two possible *reductions*, that of religion to culture or the other way around. Both reductions, let me add, have produced theoretical enterprises of great scope and sustained grand narratives about the way our societies develop. One could do worse than to try to draw lessons and even borrow tools from them.

For a strong version of the reduction of the religious to the cultural, one can still profitably turn to the work of Clifford Geertz. Geertz's guiding principle is to include religion in the set of cultural systems that symbolically confer an "aura of factuality" on the worldviews and modes of life that usually motivate people's actions (what Geertz calls "the general order of existence"). From this standpoint, obviously, culture constitutes the universal category, and religion is just one particular aspect of it, not only because religion, as "symbolic system," is simply one element of culture among others, but also—more crucially in the current conjuncture—because it is at the level of variations between cultures that we can, by endowing human societies and communities with a collective (quasi) personality or with *individuality*, conduct meaningful *comparative study* of their differences. Here it is not religions or religious systems, but lived cultures that come into contact, influence each other, and attract or repel each other by way of their individual or collective bearers. In this sense, culture is concrete and "comprehensive," while religion is abstract and "sectoral."[4]

Of course, we can ask whether the emergence, in the globalized age, of a deterritorialized "commodity culture" confirms or invalidates an analysis of this type, insofar as it calls into question even the tendential convergence between individualizable cultures and societies. Is it now opening our eyes to a possibility of universalization contained in the cultural itself?

Or should we, on the contrary (taking our inspiration from Marx's analysis of the "fetishism of commodities"), identify this culture of uniformity and equivalence (notably the culture based on mass *consumption*) as one of the most contradictory forms of the "return of the religious," one subject to stubborn denegation by both theologians and secular thinkers? We might also ask whether, in cultural complexes like the one that Scott, as we have seen, pinpoints as an embodiment of the "psychology of denial," the dominant norms proceed from old Christian family morality, a more or less completely secularized school system, consumerism and its standardized hedonism, or mixes of all three in different proportions, depending on the subjects and their social, generational, and professional situations.

We find a counterposed, equally edifying example of reduction of the cultural to the religious in Max Weber's program for a comparative sociology of religions. Weber, as everyone knows, not only argues that different "religious ethics" correspond to different historical economic formations and the social roles that spring from them (such as expenditure, saving, and accumulation); he also forcefully suggests that *religious individuality* depends, in the final analysis, on mutually irreducible *moral axiomatics* of "life" (or "meaning") that form so many attempts to represent and manage relations between the worldly and the otherworldly, the pure and the impure, evil (or sin) and salvation, action and contemplation, self-interest and charity, and so on. Here, then, it is religion or, better, *religious concern* which is universalized, while cultures are regarded as historical moments in the adaptation of religious axioms to circumstances. Weber's comparatism—structured by oppositions which, albeit highly abstract, are nevertheless capable of infinite variation, such as that between asceticism and mysticism, or salvation (*Heil*) and redemption (*Erlösung*), interiority and reciprocity—coincides only very rarely with the traditional taxonomy of religious confessions established by the history or science of religion, and more rarely still with the demarcations between ethnocultural groups or civilizations. Weber proposes, rather, to interpret their schisms ("heresies") and developmental tendencies by analogy: for him, they are torn between the force of charismatic events on the one hand and, on the other, evolution toward traditional or legal forms of reduction to the level of everyday life.[5]

Here I am tempted to pursue a quasi-Hegelian line of argument in order to transform the term-for-term opposition between these two classic viewpoints into a kind of dialectic: each is true in its own way or, rather, such truth as each contains resides in its *negative* relation to the other. The methodological consequence would seem to be that we are not very sure what, exactly, the categories of culture and religion include, taken separately and for themselves; yet even if neither term of the dichotomy is perfectly clear in and of itself, even if, in practice, the one and the other seem to designate "the same" activities and processes, we have formally to mark a *difference*, a shifting polarity of the religious and the cultural, in order to identify the becoming-cultural of the religious as well as the becoming-religious of the cultural. There we have the imperfect critical instrument with which we can try to pry open and problematize rigid notions such as community, or the membership of individuals considered as subjects in communities, while also making those notions flexible enough to accommodate the viewpoints of reciprocal action, changes in direction, or the aleatory evolution of institutions in which individuals' compatible or, under specific historical conditions, incompatible social or asocial destinies are crystallized. In this sense, the distinction between the religious and cultural aspects of the ideological process comes to resemble an intellectual weapon against indiscriminate utilization of the category of community and, a fortiori, of *communitarian identity*, which continues to vex and to skew debates about particularism and universalism.

The "community" as such (whether local, national, or transnational) is, it seems to me, neither religious nor cultural. It is not *given*, but autonomizes itself, relatively, and isolates itself, fictitiously, in a way that is more or less stable and imposes constraints, to different degrees, on other communities, in a process that is essentially political (or even, today, cosmopolitical). To that end, it combines religious and cultural moments that include more or less X as a function of "material" or "real" determinations of a different kind. These determinations are to be sought in class relations and power relations, but also—indeed, perhaps first and foremost—in their lack or limitation. This is to say that we have to look, in the real, for both "overdeterminations" and "underdetermination," as Althusser would say.[6]

7

RELIGIOUS REVOLUTIONS AND ANTHROPOLOGICAL DIFFERENCES

I would now like to introduce a final hypothesis (which I will doubtless be able to do little more than state): the determinations of culture and religion bear, not on distinct materialities, but on one and the same "object." That object, however, is so *malleable* that it lends itself to heterogeneous and even incompatible constructions or representations. The concept for it accordingly derives from a *disjunction* (a system of differences) rather than a *conjunction* (a synthesis based on a single criterion). Since it is clearly a question of general (or philosophical) anthropology here, we might be tempted to say simply that what is at issue is the human and its characteristic variability. Taking a step beyond this tautology (one step at best), I prefer to say that what is involved is *anthropological difference* and the way it is *constructed*, which never ceases to vary historically (this also means that "man" is never the same throughout history—except perhaps as biological species, at the level of genetic determinations, and even that is an open question). Several years ago, in the context of a discussion of the bourgeois ideology of citizenship, I tentatively proposed the category of anthropological difference in opposition to that of "ontological difference" to designate differences that are intractable (but, for the same reason, crucial) in that we can neither avoid them (or deny their existence) nor specify them in stable, univocal, incontestable fashion. Among them are sexual difference—as it structures the attribution of "masculine" and "feminine" roles on the basis of a more or less heavily marked conjunction or disjunction of reproduction and pleasure, affect and utility, love and genealogical institutionalization—but also the differences between the normal and pathological, mental ("intellectual") and physical ("manual"), and so on. The locus or the exact delineation of these differences as modes of classifying human beings and individual behavior thus remains, by definition, problematic, both socially and psychically, and even physiologically. We will never have a stable, indisputable answer to "essential," "existential" questions such as: What is specifically masculine and feminine (or appropriate to men and to women)? What is abnormal or "monstrous" from the standpoint of norms of thought or behavior? What puts the human in the animal realm or, on the contrary, distinguishes it from it? I presume that it is a question here of both an anchorage wholly immanent to the human condition and a radical indeterminacy (a "principle of insufficiency" in Georges Bataille's terms, or a "principle of incompletion" in Debray's) that rules out any common notion of the human, given once and for all and accessible to merely observing reason.[1]

Since such differences constitute, contradictorily, objects of fixation and displacement, normalization and perturbation, it is plainly tempting to postulate, if only as a working hypothesis, that culture does the work of normalization, or, in Weber's terms, of routinization, or, in Freud's and Norbert Elias's, of the civilizing of manners, whereas religion brings about the upheavals or sublimations, in revolutionary or mystic modes (which are not, of course, mutually exclusive).[2] The historical institutionalization of the human, whatever the material conditions of its "production" and "reproduction," can be thought only at the price of this tension.

One may object that this division of labor has something very mechanistic about it. That is true, and I have accordingly proposed it only as an allegory indicative of the fact that the opposed functions called into being by the uncertainty of anthropological difference do not fall under the same systems or the same actions in ideology. *Pace* the indications provided by anthropologists and historians intent on *reconciling* the religious and the cultural or *reducing* one to the other, I am taking the risk of pushing the idea of their polarity toward the dialectical figure of an antagonism: I put norms and customs, the "inventions of tradition," and the processes of "acculturation" at one pole of the opposition, and "conversions," "reformations" (or "counterreformations"), and "religious revolutions" at the other. The point is, obviously, to draw attention to the effectiveness of symbolic systems that are both *thought* and *institutionalized*, not only in the organization and sacralization of cultural structures of power and hegemony, but also in the investment of anthropological differences (such as the difference between the sexes), which accentuates and radicalizes the distribution of roles and practices that it is culture's basic function to render uniform and inscribe in the obviousness of the everyday.[3] What, however, does "radicalize" mean? It can mean, depending on the circumstances, intensifying, sacralizing, absolutizing, idealizing, and sublimating, or, on the contrary, deconstructing, indetermining, or opening lines of escape by introducing, via religious adoration or mysticism, an element of "additional significance" with respect to the everyday.[4] That is why this way of reconstructing the tensions within the ideological ultimately leads to limit-questions such as that of religious revolutions or *revolutionary transformations of religious tradition* (often called "reformations" [*réformes*] in the West, on the Lutheran or Calvinist model, or classified on the basis of an opposition between reformism and fundamentalism). It also leads to the question of the political effects they can bring in their wake.

More or less recent and still topical examples abound. The "secular religions" (or "political religions") that Nazism and especially Communism (whose messianic dimension runs much deeper) are supposed to have been may or may not qualify, but liberation theology clearly does.[5] "Islamic feminism" might well be counted as another example, if, in defining it, we privilege the symbolic and, equally, political objective of challenging structures of familial domination which, from the earliest stages of the Koranic revelation on (before or after the Prophet's death), must have been closely associated with monotheistic principles so as to inscribe the regulation of sexuality at the very point of articulation of the cosmic and social orders, between "revelation" and "community."[6] It may be that Islamic feminists, reenacting, in their fashion, a gesture made by other reformers, intend to isolate an element of "purely religious" revelation from everything that falls in the domain of culture or the traditional mores dominated by the patriarchate. It is more likely, however, that they will have to engage in interpretation of the revelation itself, which cannot be divorced from its founding history and, consequently, from that which symbolically institutes the tradition in Islam. At the intersection of tradition and revelation, the crucial stakes will be, obviously, *Islamic law*, derived from the revelation and the rules of conduct exemplified by the Prophet (*shari'a*), as well as the ways of understanding it (*fikh*).[7]

This last example—which would call for a long discussion—clearly shows that the domains of "the cultural" and "the religious" are never absolutely separate, not even when the logics informing them clash at a given moment in history and produce, as a result, a cascade of political consequences. The same lesson may be drawn from Saba Mahmood's work on the "mosque movement," with its radically different orientation. This movement, which Mahmood defines as a form of "piety" (in line with one possible meaning of the word *da'wa*, which may also be translated as "conversion"), has urban Egyptian women meeting under the guidance of a holy woman (*dā'iya*) in order to develop, together, the performance of traditional rites (particularly those involving prayer and modesty) and infuse their everyday existence with their spirit—in opposition to tendencies to laxity fostered by the modernization and Westernization of culture.[8] In the case of both Islamic feminism and the "mosque movement," it can readily be seen that only individual and collective *subjects*, constituted in and through this very experience, effect the overlap between the cultural and the religious in the conditions of a particular conjuncture. This is what lends the history of ideological formations its unpredictable and, simultaneously, never-ending character. Ideology, Althusser said, interpellates individuals as subjects; but subjects, Judith Butler points out, "counter-interpellate" ideology.

It is therefore just as crucially important to observe the emergence and development of *new*, more or less syncretic religions. They will confer a different meaning on the very notion of the religious by *reversing*, in some sort, the trend that—from the West's standpoint—shifted "polytheism" toward "monotheism" (albeit with all sorts of internal contradictions in the interpretation of the latter notion), thereby providing the history of religion in the Romantic period with a prototype for the subsequent shift from the theological age to the age of secularization. In what concrete context will these new religions emerge, if not, precisely, in the field of the mass "culture" fostered by capitalist globalization and the extreme tensions it is breeding—and thus also, as the need arises, *against* mass culture? I am thinking in particular of the "deep" ecological consciousness that manifestly has messianic and apocalyptic dimensions (with its quest for a *katekhon* or force capable of "warding off catastrophe"), but that may or perhaps even must also take the form of a revival of the "religions of nature" once known as pantheism or polytheism. They will quite possibly associate a personification of the Earth (Gaia, Pachamama), a "concern for life," a feeling of emotional community binding "human" and "nonhuman animals" together, as well as the imaginary panoply surrounding manmade life and the proliferation of constructs that are part human, part machine, while also prescribing new modes of life respectful of the environment and the corresponding dietary and health regimes.[9] I am not, of course, postulating that the environmental concerns spawned by the growing urgency of the global ecological problem can be expressed and disseminated in the culture of contemporary societies only by way of a religious (or neo-religious) revolution. But a revolution of that kind does seem to me to be well within the realm of possibility. It would be all the more likely if an essentially secular *civic universalism* were to remain the prisoner of productivism and its own "cult of progress."

Setting out from the hypothesis of *new religions*, we might further hypothesize a *new secularism*. But if the first hypothesis remains, to some extent, a matter of conjecture (even if it is based on numerous "signs of the times"), the second bears all the marks of a political and philosophical imperative, and it is urgent that we get to work on the ways and means of realizing it. In concluding, let me try briefly to say why.

8

SECULARISM SECULARIZED:
THE VANISHING MEDIATOR

The first and most pressing reason that makes imperative a new secularism brings us back to the preceding idea that the play of culture and religion in the ideological complex exists only as the function of an exterior (or, as the Lacanians would put it, a "real"): capitalist globalization itself, insofar as it is taking forms that are devastating or even catastrophic for the natural and cultural environments and, consequently, for humanity—even if it is also beginning to create planetary solidarities of a new type. From this standpoint, the question of a secularism for the global age does not really differ from that of the development of universalism or the very meaning of the category of universality in the current conjuncture. What language do we have with which to convince ourselves that there exist risks and interests "common to all humankind"? Or again: what are the *ideological alternatives* to which that proposition gives rise? Even if, following the suggestion of certain eminent contemporary postcolonial critics, such as Paul Gilroy and Gayatri Spivak, we use the term "planetarity" rather than "cosmopolitanism" to designate the set of constraints and imperatives that, in one way or another, must, after being formulated

in accessible terms, take their place in the political consciousness of all the planet's inhabitants, we will still not have eliminated all ambiguity.[1]

There is nothing in itself absurd in the claim that the idea
of a community of interests spanning all human individuals
and groups (or, more generally, all *living beings*) has to carry
the day if we are to limit the effects of unrestrained competition and capitalist individualism, avoid the self-destruction of
humankind, and move toward a civilization of the postmodern
age in which all kinds of communities, dependent on the same
environment for their survival, can coexist. But it is quite obvious that this idea must itself be universalized if it is to leave
the status of a moral horizon or utilitarian calculation behind,
and advance to the rank of a political construction. (This further implies, in all probability, that government and modes of
representation will have to be *reconstructed* on bases other than
those invented by the industrial nation-states in the period in
which they undertook to "divide up the world among themselves"). Or, to put the same thing in still other, Gramscian
terms, the idea of such a planetary community of interests will
have to become "common sense," translatable into a multitude
of discourses and languages spoken by a multitude of groups
and social conditions.[2] One hardly need be a Marxist-Leninist
to guess that such planetary universalization will come about
only at the price of very violent conflicts in which the immediate interests of the dominant and dominated, old and new, will
clash for a very long time, without an a priori prospect of reconciliation or even of reciprocal recognition. Science will not
suffice. Nor will law. Nor will humanism. Invoking "commons"
or "commonalities" names the problem, but does not yet determine a solution. I postulate, for my part, that the capacity to face
up to these conflicts and take part in them in a civilized way with
a view to changing the world will not depend on the establishment of a new religion, even if we should not exclude religious

components from the idea of planetarity, especially in view of the apocalyptic dimensions of the ecological risk and the fears it generates.[3] It will depend, rather, on whether we manage to discover a new "civic" articulation (*articulation citoyenne*) combining socialism, internationalism, multiculturalism, and, so to speak, a secularism raised to the second power—a "secularization of secularism" itself, that is to say, a *critical and self-critical* form of what has been historically thought and institutionalized under that rubric.[4]

In an articulation of that sort, nationally and internationally recognized legal systems, hence "secularized" states and "cosmopolitical" agencies, cannot but play an important role. For there is no citizenship, not even democratic citizenship, without institutions and institutionalization, and these are impossible without law. (This does not mean that there is an invariant legal form, especially not when the territorial framework of the law changes—but that is not my subject here.) But it may fairly be doubted whether states and international agencies will be, in the final instance, the decisive actors of such an articulation. For states and legal systems are, precisely, prisoners of national and, therefore, cultural particularism; they tend to reproduce forms of communitarian hegemony or, at best, to establish their limits. Above all, they are inseparable (however loudly they proclaim their devotion to laïcité) from theologico-political constructions, or present themselves as, in Hegel's terms, determinate negations and "sublations" of the theological institutionalization of sovereignty and the law.[5] That is why there is no reason to be particularly surprised that the idea of secularism—whether as the strict separation of the religious and the political along the same dividing line that separates private and public (this is what the French Republic officially means by *laïcité*), or as equal protection for all religious affiliations by a state and law that would maintain a rigorous "neutrality" toward all of them—has not been slow to lapse back into forms of a sacralization of power, not just as an absolutization of its authority, but also as an *immunization* of its discourse, which is thus placed beyond the reach of contestation and the conflict of interpretations. A state that holds a monopoly (within defined borders) on interpretation and enforcement of the law is always on the way to de-secularization even as it generalizes the field of secularization. That is the abiding lesson of Hobbes's *Leviathan* and Hobbes's own political theory: the substitution of the "mortal God" (incarnated, as a general rule, in the form of a national body) for the "immortal God" (assuming, let me add, that the mortal and immortal are separable attributes of the divine). The interstate negotiations from which international law derives occasionally *limits* the identity-based complex built up around the state and membership in the nation, but it cannot *do away* with it.

Thus, if the collaboration and cooperation of institutions such as states and international organizations, as well as advances in humanitarian and environmental international law, may well be required to regulate the problem of identity-based passions, communitarian hatreds or, more simply, the barriers to communication threatening to spoil, from the outset, the chances for the development of a new planetarity in the global age, it would seem that the solution to that problem cannot, in the final analysis, proceed from law itself. If so, it remains for us to grasp what *can* mobilize and articulate processes of cultural communication and the civilizing (in the sense of *civility*) of religious antagonisms. I have suggested elsewhere that the condition for defending and developing multiculturalism (jeopardized everywhere today by deadly combinations of postcolonial racism, a resurgence of nationalism, and defensive reactions brought on by globalization itself, to the extent that it "profanes" cultural identities and undoes social solidarities) is as radical a dissociation as possible between the traditionally contiguous (albeit not identical) figures of the *stranger* (*étranger*) and the *enemy.*[6]

The condition for multiculturalism is therefore also a politics of intercultural translation valorizing and fostering the phenomena of alliance and hybridization, of multiple affiliations, that form the material basis for encounters and exchanges between distant cultural universes, even if such phenomena have many obstacles to surmount and often come at the price, for the individual, of a melancholy bred by the experience of exile or, more simply, the existential problems inherent in life in a diaspora.[7] I have emphatically not changed my mind on this point. But I have to admit, on the basis of the preceding formulations, that none of all that precedes is sufficient. The *pacification of religious conflicts*, or, still better, their *conversion* or *sublimation* into ideals capable of relativizing communitarian affiliations, cannot function in the mode of multiculturalism because such pacification is not only based on processes of change, transition, and translation, however demanding they may be, but has also to do with what Weber calls "the war of the gods," that is, the incompatibility of axiomatics and ethical choices that such affiliations force individuals to make when the stake is the unbearable indeterminacy of anthropological differences themselves. What reigns between religious axiomatics is not necessarily war (for, as I recalled earlier, the causes of "wars of religion" are in fact never simply ideological), but what I have called a *conflict of universalities*; thanks to which difference is reduced to, or represented in accordance with, a certain code, a certain symbolic law. Here it is the regime of translation or "translatability" itself that must change. When it is possible to translate one religious universe into another, the reason is precisely that it is not purely religious. The "religious" as such always marks *the point of the untranslatable*.[8] As has been shown, however, by a major strand in contemporary philosophical thought, from Walter Benjamin to Jacques Derrida, the untranslatable is not just a barrier in this case, an external limit on the possibility of the encounter; it is, rather, the problem that must be confronted in common.

That is why I am inclined to think that if conflict, insofar as it is religious, cannot be resolved by purely legal or statist means (but can only be repressed or institutionally displaced in the form of a conflict between religion, relegated to the private sphere or particularity, and a secularism that sometimes tends to reestablish a "civic religion"), and if it also cannot be reduced to a system of cultural differences, then we have to agree to treat it as a *differend*.[9] That is, we have first of all to *state it* as such: to state it not as a juxtaposition of arbitrary constructs, but as a (forced) choice, for the subjects involved, between irreconcilable representations and prescriptions of the subdivisions of the human, of what separates the human from the inhuman, or of what separates the various modalities of the human from one another. It thereby allows us to bring these representations and prescriptions into relation. If there exists a symbolic element or a type of discourse that can here play the role of a mediation (or mediator), it cannot present itself as simply one more choice of the same kind; in other words, it cannot simply take its place in the system of religions, not even as a "new religion"—except, perhaps, as a sort of *generalized heresy*. Whence the idea, which has already appeared episodically in the history of ideas (in Spinoza, for example), that what obliquely makes the encounter of different religions possible, or allows them jointly to cultivate a "free conversation" in the public realm, is the introduction or intervention there of a *supplementary* element that is, as such, *a-religious* (although not necessarily *anti-religious*). Without this paradoxical element, which might be called atopical, internal/external, and be said to form something like an *edge* of the ideological universe, we would have no way of measuring the distance between the axiomatics of the difference, and no way of bringing their interpretations to converge on certain ethical or social rules, since there would be no discursive space in which these differences could be *presented* (*présenté*) as such, in comparative fashion, and thus "introduced (*présenté*) to each other" outside the framework of a codified domination or an imaginary reconciliation. It is this additional element, charged both with bringing religions together and recognizing the irreducibility of their conflict, that I am once again tempted to call, after Fredric Jameson, the "vanishing mediator" of communication between incompatible religious discourses. It must, accordingly, exhibit sharply paradoxical features, and we cannot be sure that they will not remain irreducibly contradictory.[10]

This vanishing mediator must always already have existed, even if it was not identified or was identified under assumed names, so that misidentification of it, its invisibility, is in some sort the rule. It is neither the discourse of universal morality nor that of the ethics of discussion, neither the discourse of scientific knowledge nor that of the rights of man; nor is it the discourse of tolerance, cosmopolitanism, or planetarity, although it has certain practical objectives in common with all of them.[11] Nor can it be identified with atheism, agnosticism, or skepticism, although it doubtless includes, as they do, a dimension of *negation*. It is easy to see, however, that each of these terms suggests negation in opposition to *just one religious form* or attitude. "Atheism," for example, is meaningful only in the case of religions organized around the representation of one or more gods; there are, however, religions without gods. As for "skepticism," which I have occasionally privileged, in the lineage of Montaigne and Bayle, it is meaningful only when the essence of religion is creed or dogma; the religious can, however, reside primarily in ritual.[12] For historical reasons, we can, for a particular place, call the vanishing mediator "secularism," on condition that our use of this term goes hand in hand with a critique of the institutions and reigning conceptions of secularization—heavily determined, culturally and politically, by the theological heritage and ecclesiastical institutions that secularization combated. Such secularism resembles a skepticism to the second power.

The vanishing mediator between politico-religious *differends* is effective only if it resonates within religious discourses, if it reveals cracks in their creeds, impossibilities in their prescriptions, or inconsistencies in their ethics. It has to divest them of their singularity and undermine their certainty that they hold the monopoly on truth and justice, without, however, thwarting their search for truth and justice ("salvation") on their own paths. Here we may, perhaps, once again invoke the category of *heresy* or try to imagine the vanishing mediator as the unlikely heresy common to all religious discourses, while leaving open the question of its relation to the heretical movements that have historically affected each particular religion. Not all heresies, of course, have been tolerant; far from it. Spinoza, for his part, preferred the term *wisdom* (manifestly inspired by a Greek and Latin tradition of "worldly wisdom" or "profane wisdom," *Weltweisheit*); yet the way he conceived wisdom was itself profoundly heretical, combining Lucretius' teaching with the Ecclesiast's.[13]

Be it added that this element is certainly a *public* discourse—in any case, *the function it performs is not "private"*—or always raises the private to the level of the political. However, as we have seen, precisely by functioning in such a way as to make the religious *differend* public, the vanishing mediator that we are identifying with (self-) critical secularism is necessarily at antipodes from the state institutions whose task is to regulate behavior in a legally enforceable way, while conferring an unquestionable obviousness on the distinction between public and private (which, in the order of discourse, is often redoubled by that between the expressed and repressed). More generally, it cannot be *normative*; it does not express an *imperative* in the Kantian sense—the less so in that, in our culture, the normative or imperative bears the indelible traces of certain religious constructions of the human, inscribed both in the inwardness of the soul and ethical consciousness, and in the externality of rules of prescription and prohibition (especially where sexuality is concerned). Yet it is also not purely *cognitive* or "theoretical," however important knowledge and an understanding of natural and social phenomena are for all secular thought. It might be called, rather, *declarative* or *performative*, in the sense, to begin with, that it effects its own free statement of truth (something the Greeks called *parrhèsia*, as Foucault reminds us) in the face of discourses of power based on myth, revelation, or the force of habit, but also in the face of the authority of science and law. Let us therefore forthrightly admit the fact: it is quite possible that this vanishing mediator is nothing more than a philosophical fiction. It is up to all of us to endow it with existence—or to invent it.

Before handing them over to the publisher, I have returned to the preceding pages to assess their imperfections. Without at all prejudicing what could be detected by readers whose critiques I await with impatience, I would like quickly to examine two possible objections.

The first has to do with the fact that the question of law (*du droit*) is treated in an incomplete manner and is too implicit even if, ultimately, it appears upon rereading, that issues of legality occupy a central place. Accordingly, the question is as central as it is problematic. I signaled that the constitutional value accorded in France (and in other countries, which often used it as a model) to the principle of laïcité is considered to be one of the outcomes of republican sovereignty. In a given situation, reversing its liberal interpretation and legislating matters of customs (*moeurs*) and opinion in a repressive way, it has a contradictory effect of accentuating the sacralization of the law and of weakening its democratic legitimacy. On the other hand, I submitted the negative thesis that problems of contemporary cosmopolitics taken in the alternative of a renewal of citizenship and an extension of governance without democracy, insomuch as they concern the formation, recognition, and transformation of cultural and religious communities, with very strong social tensions in the background, are not to be solved through law, whether national or international. This should not lead us to conclude that the legal instance is secondary or inoperative. If this instance appears, on occasion, to make up part of the problem, then it very well needs to take part in the solution, at the price of a transformation of its conception and practice; that is to say a reintegration of the legal into the political of which it always was, in fact, the instrument.

At least two reasons explain why the legal dimension is unavoidable (*incontournable*). First, the conception of secularism that makes up an integral part of the hegemony of the nation form in the institution of citizenship by the state (and especially with its laïque form in the French sense) implies a strict demarcation of *private* and *public* spaces, which ideally correspond to two types of activities, two personalities, two systems of speech. Just as, in the past, theology separated mortal man from his immortal soul, this laïcité institutes an anthropology of the split human nature (*homo duplex*). The expression of religious convictions, the accomplishment of gestures and rituals that signify belonging to the community or that simply perpetuate "cultural" memory are relegated to the private sphere, if not confined in secret, whereas public activities (whether contractual, educational, medical, social, or political) are supposed to be possible independent of any subjugation, of any cultural or religious affiliation, or more broadly, of any ideology. Since in reality this is not the case, one sees bastard forms appear that largely dominate the quotidian life of state citizens: an implicit civil religion sanctioning and reinforcing the norms of the dominant culture, more or less resisting its historical transformations, and the hypocritical use of the rule of "neutrality" in order to realize what in fact is a selection among religious confessions, or cultural practices to be tolerated, encouraged, valorized, or repressed. It goes without saying that the status of Islam, of Islamic symbols and discourse, of people who identify with it or who are conventionally linked to it in the European space, immediately illustrate this phenomenon. But Islam—like Judaism before—introduces an element of supplemental conflictuality. Because it is a religious discourse where the dimension of *law* (*loi*)—and of obedience to the legal rule—is prevalent and forms the basis of a community's point of honor at least as powerful as in republican legalism itself, its encounter with the "general will" is virtually explosive.[1] We find ourselves here in an acute form of what I have called the conflict of universalities (also conflictual in themselves), which apparently can be resolved only through force and violence, open or dissimulated.

But I touch here upon a second reason that makes the legal form a point that is as sensitive as it is problematic: from here on in, the conflict of universalities expands on a transnational scale, carried out willy-nilly (or tested within themselves) by subjects who already are no longer (and will be less and less) simply defined as the citizens of a nation. But the distinction of public and private spaces—not even considering the disruptions caused by new communication techniques—is irrelevant in a transnational space. It is directly tied to the territorialization of authority that circumscribes individuals and their activities in an institutional framework where power apparatuses work to have the nation represented by the state and frame it as the superior community, encompassing all communities. It is very difficult, although this task has already figured for a long time on the horizon of political philosophy and of democratic politics itself, to say in what a public transnational sphere consists; and it is completely meaningless to try to define private spaces on a world scale, unless we want to suggest that the only institution that subsists in a de-territorialized framework is the family, and to consider globalization as a type of generalized privatization of social life, that a simple economic governance would surmount and regulate. Obviously, the activities (that one could call civics) of networks or of organizations that take for a point of departure problems tied to the circulation of men across borders, and whose horizon is the emergence "from the bottom up" of a cosmopolitical citizenship, squarely deny this alternative. They seem to prefigure the overhaul of the very idea of right if not law. But this comes with a price: a dissolution of the public/private opposition as a means of *separation* (or even *cloistering*) between the subject's activities, at least for what concerns "ideological" matters. For someone who does not believe in the preestablished harmony of collective identities, or the possibility of regulating *without an institution* the differences and differends in cultural or religious matters, the question is then completely open: what type of legitimacy or symbolic authority will be at the same time superior to the state (*plus que l'État*) by its universalism and inferior to it by its constitutive pluralism?[2] By introducing in this essay the oblique hypothesis of a vanishing mediator, necessarily collective and disorganized (hence profoundly utopic), which one could also characterize as a *secularism secularized* (de-stated, de-Christianized, demasculinized . . .), I know very well that in no way have I resolved this problem. I am content with naming that which, arising from today's contradictions, seems to me to be the "negative theologico-political" dimension of its desirable evolution.

The second imperfection that strikes me, in retrospect, in the exposé that one has just finished reading, concerns the very articulation of universalism with the problem of *anthropological differences*. The fact that I have already tackled this theme in another context is not of great help here, because it is the case, in a sense, in a totally experimental way, of calling into question a concept at the same time that I try to make of it a new application. The reference to anthropological differences as a "thing in itself" (*chose en soi*), which is at the same time impossible to eliminate and inaccessible in a *direct* way, entirely immanent to historical experience and fundamentally insufficient or unstable, from which one could try to proceed to comparisons and analyze conflicts in the field of culture and of religion, does not pretend to reduce a knowledge of this field to a single principle, from which all of its expressions/demonstrations (manifestations) would derive. It only proposes a *point of view* on the differend. And it tries to be sufficiently general in order to neither be concerned with a single religious tradition nor a single cultural area, but also sufficiently determined, in its very opening (expounding, in some way, dialectically, the specific efficacy of indetermination) in order to displace and rectify what remains, in one way or another, the presupposition of any anthropology: that the cultural, religious (but also economic, political) express the power of "the human" to which, in return, they confer an infinite variety of institutional forms. What pushed me in this direction, in the end, was the possibility of sketching two types of analyses and linking them together: first, that of the "play" (*le jeu*) of culture and of religion (that, in an explicitly Weberian way, I imagine less as an opposition of the particular and the universal or the concrete forms of life and abstract prescriptions, than an opposition of the quotidian and the extraordinary, or the exception, in the reciprocal constitution of subjects), and second, the analysis of conflictual universalities (i.e., religious universalities between themselves, and above all religious universality and civic or bourgeois universality, which presents itself as modern and modernizing compared with traditions, revelations, asceticisms, and mystics).[3] One could approach the articulation of these two types of oppositions even closer in saying that what is at stake in this whole discussion (of which actual political conflicts in the world about religion and secularism underline the urgency), is knowing to what extent "secular" bourgeois universalism truly breaks (*rompt*) with religious ways (Christian in particular, or more generally monotheist) of instituting culture, and on which points. But it is also a question of knowing whether it would be necessary to add a "market-based universality" (*universalité marchande*) that is not the civic-bourgeois universality, to the extent that its definite principle is not equality or the equal liberty of citizens, but the measurable equivalence and monetary cost of needs, properties, and services. This is ultimately the same as Asad's question, but generalized and without a preestablished response.

But what pushed me in this direction, was also, obviously, the fact of the controversies that I started with and more generally all of those that, in the Mediterranean space, exacerbate the confrontation between supporters and opponents of secularism, between theoreticians of the clash of civilizations and critics of Islamophobia, crystallizing around the question of *sexual difference* (thus also of sexualities), and of its differential treatment by different religious traditions (fundamentally monotheisms) and by different realizations of "the principle of laïcité" extended to society as a whole. But here, I have to admit, a new difficulty presents itself, because on the one hand, sexual difference (even if we extend it from gender to sexualities, the domain par excellence of charges of abnormality) does not alone sum up the totality of "anthropological difference," and on the other hand, it could be that a general idea of "anthropological difference" is confused and confusing; in other words, that it only confuses the violent issue of sexuality in a generic and vague ensemble. Why not simply have posed, in accordance with a tradition that was reinforced by psychoanalysis but that goes back at least to Feuerbach, that the "secret" of the religious and their conflictual rapport with cultures or with politics and programs of secularized education always reside in a mode of treatment, of definition, of repression, of the sublimation of sexual difference?

I will say from the outset that this thesis would be nothing but absurd. It would not only permit, following a road opened by

Freud and pushed farther ahead by his successors (like Lacan), of tying together the violence of a conflict among pulsions to the efficacity of a symbolism that is probably (as Karsenti suggests) the key to any transmission (of names, of values, of powers, of knowledge). It would also allow us to problematize the "discontent of civilization" as it is specifically expressed in the relation of diverse symbolic orders and practices that they favor in matters of sexual relations (and more abstractly, relations between "femininity" and "virility"), in passing from one civilization to another.[4] At the same time, it would allow us to investigate the double bind which always constraints feminist politics and practices: they are at once omnipresent in the world today (which explains a good part of the intensification of sexual violence) and coming up against a multiplicity of obstacles contradictory between them, because they are anchored in "symbolic orders" as diverse as patriarchy, the caste system, monotheism, "exclusive democracy" (as used by Geneviève Fraisse), commodification . . . whose power of subjection is in no way identical.[5]

Nevertheless, I see an obstacle to conferring on sexuality *as such* and the differentiations that it (sexuality) engenders a monopoly of the "ideological" articulation between the religious and its cultural other (made from a multiplicity of social practices): it would confer on the very idea of sexuality (or of sexual difference, or of the relation of masculine and feminine) a signification or an *aura* which is itself religious. A more complete phenomenology of the manifestations of the sacred and of faith (or of obedience), insomuch as they fathom the exceptional in the quotidian, would not necessarily suppress the specificity of the sexual reference nor would it minimize the political conflicts that crystallize precisely around its regulation or its legislation. But it would point out *other differences*, which concern the impossible sharing of the human among humans. All of them are implied in the becomings that I wanted to exhibit (the becoming-religious of the cultural, the becoming-cultural of the religious): differences and even incompatibilities that affect food, health, and illness (so death itself as a condition of life), work and study (so skill and intellectualism), childhood and adulthood, reason and madness (or crime). All of this can be ritualized, sacralized, and submitted to the law, subjected to an eschatology or a cosmology.

It is true, however, that a theme never independent of sex (or of *desire* as its structure) in a way crosses all anthropological differences and the question, continuously shifting, that they raise that is continually displaced by what they give rise to: it is the question of the *body* as vital power and above all as the instrument or envelope of a soul that envelopes it in turn, therefore as beauty and obscenity or abjection, as a *condition* that is always "vulnerable" (Judith Butler) or "enslaved" (Bertrand Ogilvie).[6] Accordingly—in complete continuity with the debate on the trouble that the Islamic veil produced in the secular institution—I would perhaps have to admit that what creates a problem in and for religion (but also because of religious imperatives) is *the signifying use of the body* by human subjects, always obviously in the context of a certain reciprocal "perception."[7] And from this point of view, Joan Scott, whom I reproached for her "militant" way of simplifying the system of constraints in which conflicts of significations operate, is nevertheless unquestionably hitting the point. But then I would have to make equally explicit the fact that the body, whose dispositions and reactions crystallize all of the encoded ideological differences, is never assignable to *a single* way, to *a single* "public" or "private" place that cultures, religions, law look to be delimited. For this reason, veiled or unveiled in accordance with diverse styles, it will not stop changing the values that its "owners" (*propriétaires*) attribute to it, and in this way of expropriating the subjects of identities of which they believe themselves to be the masters, when they appear side by side, then face to face "on the world stage."

Have we lost sight of the discussion of the rapport of cosmopolitanism and of secularism in the present "age" or present "world" (*saeculum*)? I don't believe so. I wrote that I would *complicate* this problem in order to bring out some simplifications: the ones rooted in the dogmatism of ideological discourse, the others in the persistence of representations tied to another "age," from which we are now exiting irreversibly. It is just what was produced, also when, in the end, I attempted to identify shortcomings or hesitations in the text that weaken my argument. But this complication also produces, in its way, a confirmation: questions of cosmopolitanism (or transnational citizenship) and of secularism (and its own critical refounding) are indissociable one from the other. Each one complicates the other, but each one underpins and informs the other, or makes up part of its matter.

This arises undoubtedly from the fact that, for a certain period of historical transition (without assignable end), which corresponds precisely to what common sense calls globalization, two types of universalities have ceased to be relatively isolated from one another by a system of administrative and psychological borders: in another place I have called them an extensive and an intensive one, for the first relates to the possibility of communication of all humans within the same institutional space, whereas the second relates to equality, the nondiscrimination and the nonhierarchization of individuals (and communities in which they live).[8] This is equally true, of course, in the economic field, as shown by the fact that economists cannot study national inequalities anymore independently of transnational inequalities, and reciprocally. There are always multiple borders, more or less deadly and insurmountable. But these borders no longer stop the problems that I called the differends of citizenship: they only sharpen the differends and make them unavoidable.

PART II
ESSAYS

10

NOTE ON THE ORIGIN AND USES
OF THE WORD "MONOTHEISM"

Contemporary work in theology, the history of religion, and even philosophy[1] often makes use of the term
"monotheism" without indicating its origins. This silence
masks a complex historical problem. I shall try to sketch its
main lines here.

Let me begin by noting that the word "monotheism" belongs
exclusively to the Greek and Latin tradition. Doubtless Islam
has always designated itself as the (true) religion of *the one*
God. But this profession of faith (*shahâda*) is made in Arabic,
in a different terminology (translated in terms of "monotheism" today by Westernized Muslim theologians: in particular,
tawhîd, literally "to make one"). And it takes one of two basic
forms: *affirmative statements* (*La ilahah illah Allah*, "There is
no god but God," which is also attributed to the divinity himself: "I am He Who always turns to the repentant sinner . . .
Your God is one God; there is no God but He, the merciful,"
Koran 2:160–63; "verily, I am God, there is no God but Me!"
Koran 20:14), or *refutations* and *prohibitions*: ("God forgives not
associating aught with Him," Koran 4:116). It does not take the
form of universal descriptive categorizations. Denise Masson

observes that "the Koran uses the verb *ashraka* (and the active plural participle *mushrikûn*), which means simply "to associate someone or something with," whenever it is a question of those who attribute "associates" to God or put false gods (*shurakâ'*, literally, "associates") alongside the one God and worship them in a way that ought to be reserved for Him. *Mushrikûn* is translated (in French) as "*polythéistes*" (polytheists). Jacques Berque renders the same term as "*les associants*" (those who associate).[2] What Islam refers to when it asserts its conflictual kinship with Judaism and Christianity is less monotheism than the fact of the revelation (the "Book") and, above all, a common genealogy going back to Abraham: "Say ye, 'We believe in God, and what has been revealed to us, and what has been revealed to Abraham, and Ishmael, and Isaac, and Jacob, and the Tribes, and what was brought to Moses and Jesus, and what was brought unto the Prophets from their Lord; we will not distinguish between any one of them, and unto Him are we resigned," Koran 2:136). The convergence with what will be called monotheism in Christianity appears most clearly, perhaps, in the way the *singularity* of Mohammed's relationship to God is defined: "His" messenger in the full sense of the word, Mohammed represents the culmination of the entire line of the prophets ("Seal of the Prophets"). Some *sûfi* have gone so far as to conceive of him as having been *always already* engendered by God at the moment of creation. Yet no mention is made of the word "monotheism."[3]

Modern Judaism, for its part, "translates" the concepts of monotheism and polytheism as, respectively, *emunah bekel ehad* (literally, "belief in a one God") and *avodat elilim* (literally, "service/worship of gods"). Neither expression, however, is to be found in the Torah or Talmud. The daily prayer known as the *Shema* begins by repeating a verse from Deuteronomy: "Hear [or "listen"], O Israel, the Lord is our God [*Yhwh*, pronounced Adonai], one [or "unique"] Lord [*Elohim*], and you must love the Lord your God with all your heart and soul and strength" (Deut. 6:4, New English Bible). When it is a question of Moses's revelation, Judaism emphasizes less God's oneness than the unnameable, unrepresentable nature of the God who "chose," through Moses, the people of Israel as *His people* (*'am*, translated in the Septuagint as *laos*, as opposed to *gôyim/ethnè*).[4] The essence of idolatry resides in the attempt to *represent and incarnate the transcendence* that is at the origins of the law. Contemporary interpreters who mobilize the category of monotheism do so to hark back to this founding interpellation of the alliance and the paradox it involves. Thus, Levinas says that "the Old Testament Hebrew terms that we are inclined to translate as God, *Deus*, or *Theos*, are proper names for the Talmud. The name of God would always seem to be a proper name in scripture. Hebrew would seem not to have a word for God! A fine consequence of monotheism, in which there exists neither a divine species nor a generic word to designate it."[5]

Even today, then, ascriptions of monotheism set out from a Christian semantics, only to be disputed, in their turn, on the basis of that semantics. Matters are, however, more complicated here than is commonly assumed. Whereas the pair polytheism/ monotheism has acquired (at least since Auguste Comte and Renan in France) the status of a common antithesis, the two words are not equally old, nor do the same conditions govern the use of each. Polytheism, by far the older of the two, has a relatively clear, well documented meaning (even if its application is open to discussion). Monotheism has an obscure history that seems to attest not only to its late emergence, but also to the fact that powerful obstacles stand in the way of its utilization.

The first term in this (pseudo-)pair is derived from the classical Greek word *polutheos*. The word, used by Aeschylus, mainly designates an altar or a temple dedicated to the worship of a number of associated gods (for example, Letho, Apollo, and Artemis, or, again, Demeter and Persephone-Kore). *Thesaurus Graecae Linguae* gives, as Latin equivalents of this word, "*multos deos statuens*" and "*qui multitudinem deorum ponit*," even citing a superlative, *ekklèsia polutheôtatè*, "an assembly abounding in gods." The meaning of the word changes radically, however, with the debates of the Hellenistic period in which the religions of the Mediterranean Basin confront each other. The Hellenized Jew Philo of Alexandria, Jesus's contemporary, who is often said to have inspired the evangelist John, contrasts the Mosaic revelation of an unnameable, unrepresentable creator and legislator God, identified with the transcendent One, with the Greek and Egyptian religions, which he characterizes negatively as "polytheisms" (*polutheia, polutheotès*). He associates these polytheisms, which, he says, "mask the truth under mythical fictions," with the dispersion of the originary unity of the *logos* in a multitude of languages. (The Logos is for Philo not God, but His "image" [*theou eikôn*] and His "first engendered" [*prôtogonos*] or "firstborn" [*prototokos*]).[6] The great Neoplatonists and "pagans," on the other hand, make this polytheism an expression of the multiplicity of essences that proceed from the One, or the Principle, and the means of participating in its divinity. "According to Proclus, a god is a henad or power of the One. Through the henads, the Ineffable allows the different series that express unity in accordance with the character that each one confers upon itself (being, life, thought, the mental apparatus) to participate in the Ineffable."[7] This justification of polytheism on the basis of an identification of the divine as such with the One is, however, accompanied by an opposite move often called a "demythologization," which is inseparable from the foundation of "theology as a science."[8] It effectively replaces a mythical or symbolic theogeny originating in Hesiod and cultivated by the Orphic tradition with a speculative "procession" engendered in the heart of the intelligible by successive "triads" before this procession descends from the intelligible to the sensuous to animate the world. Such "demythologization" regards the traditional gods as *names* expressing this refraction of the One in the heart of the Multiple. This conception was perpetuated in Christianity and Islam as a "negative theology" grounded in the idea that the multiple *divine names* are so many (necessarily inadequate) approximations of divine ineffableness, "everything and nothing of that which is," according to pseudo-Dionysius (*panta ta onta kai ouden tôn ontôn*).[9] Finally, the Church fathers, turning the charge of impiety (*asebeia*) routinely leveled at them back on their accusers,[10] identified polytheism with the "idolatry" denounced in St. Paul's epistles[11]—an identification still current among moderns—and, ultimately, with atheism. *Polutheia* is an *atheia*, for to worship several gods or the images of false gods is to ignore the one true god—is, in fact, to have no god (Origen: *tès atheou polutheotètos*, "atheistic polytheism"; Justin Martyr: "impious are those who worship several gods, or none" [*asebeis, hoi polutheian è atheian thrèskeuontes*], both cited in *Thesaurus Graecae Linguae*).

Why, given these conditions, do we not observe the symmetrical emergence of terms such as *monotheos* or *monotheia*? As Philippe Borgeaud points out, the word "monotheism" does not exist in Greek, in which other oppositions prevail.[12] It is always extremely hazardous and, in a sense, futile, to claim to explain an *absence* rather than a presence, the more so as one's theoretical interpretation is at the mercy of the least little counterexample to come along. But the fact remains that the contexts in which "polytheism" looms large do not breathe a word about "monotheism," even as they theologize without respite about the One, unity, and the monad. Compound words beginning with *mono* and *polu* abound in Greek, often forming symmetrical pairs such as *monarchia/poluarchia*, *monoeidès/polueidès*, and so on, even if "poly" seems to be more frequent and, in some sense, more natural for Greek than "mono." If Hellenized Judaism or Christianity did not invent or borrow the word (and therefore the notion) of monotheism from the outset, is it not because it ran up against an obstacle? That is my thesis. But what kind of obstacle? Here, once again, I run the risk of simplification or overinterpretation.

It would nevertheless seem that we can privilege one line of approach. Erik Peterson, in *Der Monotheismus als politisches Problem* (1935),[13] uses the term "monotheism" from one end to the other of his famous monograph in discussing texts that never make use of it themselves; yet he provides us with a very valuable hint. Since Philo—decidedly rather hard to get around!—and the debate about the royalty of the Jews' God, in which Philo, too, takes part (he calls Him "King of kings" and "Lord of lords," playing on the fact that the Bible substitutes the terms *Elohim/Theos* and *Adonaï/Kurios* for the unpronounceable IHWH, and mimicking the oriental way of referring to royalty), the question of "polytheism" has been inseparable from that of "polyarchy," in both senses of the word *archè*: to talk about a plurality of cosmic principles is also to talk about a plurality of cults, commandments, and forms of obedience. The clashes between rival religious traditions and, in their wake, between sects in early Christianity provide the backdrop for the grand debate on both divine monarchy (*göttliche Monarchie*), a debate that goes back to Aristotle, and the analogy between *the unicity of the revelation* and *the unity of the divine principle* as well as that of the "universal" Roman Empire. This analogy culminates in the apologetic interpretation of the unification of the ancient world (the *pax romana* or *pax augusta*) as the providential condition for the coming of the Messiah and an anticipation of the final redemption. "For Orosius as for Eusebius, the unity (*Einheit*) of the *Imperium Romanum* is bound up with the unity of God: *unus Deus, qui temporibus quibus innotescere voluit, hanc regni statuit unitatem, ab omnibus diligitur et timetur; eaedem leges, quae uni Deo subjecto [sic] sunt, ubique dominantur* (V, 2, 5).[14] Orosius goes still further, attributing the foundation of Rome to the Christians' monotheistic God. . . . Thus, Augustus found himself Christianized and Christ was transformed into a *civis romanus.* . . . The political significance of this construct is patent."[15] It is, however, the partisans of Arianism or Monarchianism (condemned as a heresy by the Council of Nicaea in 325) who carry this "unitary," political-theological relationship to an extreme, maintaining, against the doctrine of the Trinity, that God's uni(ci)ty rules out the Christ's divinity, except when the latter is intended as metaphor. For their part, the theologians upholding the Trinity (which was to become official Church dogma) carefully avoid calling themselves "monotheists," despite the technical borrowings they make from Neoplatonism for the purpose of thinking the hypostases or distinct persons in the one God "equals," yet, at the same time, named in a progressive order (the Father, the Son, and the Holy Ghost). Inspired by a spirit "of insurrection [*Aufstand*] against both the metaphysical and political order" (57), these theologians ultimately dissolved the analogy between the two monarchies, heavenly and worldly (except when they transcribed it at the anthropological level theorized by Saint Augustine as a mystical correspondence between the divine nature and the tripartite nature of the soul). When that happened, the possibility of *affirming* "monotheism" as such was barred. Rather, that is how the possibility appears to us *in retrospect (par récurrence)*, since we have no other way of describing it. This "negative event" (a non-event, perhaps) was part and parcel, according to Peterson,[16] of the *separation*—fully achieved, in theory—between the spiritual and temporal or between Church and state (*imperium*), regarded not just as institutions, but as *ideas.* This can, however, be interpreted the other way around: as the result of an *ideological reduplication* of "polities," "powers," or "bodies" that paved the way for the entire history of Christianity as an instituted religion, if it did not, indeed, dictate it.[17]

The word "polytheism," rediscovered and translated into French in the sixteenth century (Bodin), was current in the classical age.[18] "Monotheism" was invented in English as a Hellenism by Henry More, according to the Oxford English Dictionary (*An Explanation of the Grand Mystery of Godliness*, 1660), but it was a polemical term aimed at the Unitarians (the most famous of whom was to be Newton), renovators of Arianism, which they grafted onto the naturalism of the new physics. More turned the argument that Origen and Justin had directed at the "polytheists" back against the "monotheists": in fact, he said, they are atheists. In 1680, however, he was to write, in his commentary on Revelations: "They destroy the worship of the Son of God under an ignorant pretense of Monotheisme; whereas the more distinct knowledge of that one God does not make us less Monotheists than they" (cited in the Oxford English Dictionary). Not less "monotheists" than they? One would perhaps have to be able to say, rather, *more* "monotheists" than they. That will come, but later.

For the moment, this use of the word as a form of retaliation masks an extreme tension. This can clearly be seen in the other great representative of Cambridge Neoplatonism, Ralph Cudworth, whose immense influence on modern European culture is appreciated for what it is today. In a 1678 book, *The True Intellectual System of the Universe*, which reconstructs the entire history of the religious problem since the ancient Egyptians and takes it for granted that there exists a primal theology (theologia prisca) common to Moses and Hermes Trismegistus, Cudworth adopts the theory of a "hidden God" that the ancient pagans are supposed to have veiled under various names (polytheism is defined as a polyonymy), and enters a plea for the fundamental identity, terminology aside, between Platonic philosophy and Christian dogma. For Cudworth, in essence, polytheism is unpronounceable monotheism in its exoteric manifestation, or doxa. The main enemy is atheism, materialism in its diverse forms; Cudworth proposes a classification of them and writes their history. But not only is polytheism not an atheism; Cudworth goes on to demonstrate that it is derivative and artificial. He multiplies neologisms: in addition to "polytheism" and "atheism," we find "ditheism" and "tritheism"! The only term in the series that never appears is, precisely, "monotheism." The reason is plainly his desire to refute a then resurgent Arianism: if there were monotheists, they would also be monarchians. . . . We might say that the doctrine of the Trinity (Deus Unus Trinus, as the Scholastic Doctors put it) has to keep an equal distance from two different heresies: it cannot tolerate being treated either as a disguised polytheism or as a straightforward monotheism. The consequence is that the word "monotheism" is tabooed, although, behind the repeated references to the theological truth of the "One (Supreme) God," it seems to us to haunt every phrase that the erudite Master of Christ's College utters.[19] We are here at a short remove from what Pascal, at the same moment (*Pensées*, Brunschvicg 733 / Lafuma 862) calls Christianity's point of heresy. Indeed, we are exactly at that point.

It is edifying to pursue our inquiry into the eighteenth and nineteenth centuries, beginning with Hume's 1757 work, *The Natural History of Religion*, which, it is today agreed, brought about the fundamental epistemological reversal in this domain, paving the way for evolutionism by refuting the idea that idolatry resulted from the degeneration of the revelation of a unique God, and making polytheism humanity's "natural religion," thereby transforming the revelation into a fiction. Hume's book systematically opposes "polytheism" to "theism." The word "monotheists" does, however, make one appearance at the end of the text, where it is used to describe the ostensible intolerance of the Zoroastrian Persians in contrast with the tolerance of the Greeks, whom the theological tradition accused of superstition.[20] Involved here is, obviously, a denunciation of Judaism (and its Christian posterity) by proxy: the kinship between the Mazdeans' and the "Judeans'" image-less religions was commonly noted in antiquity.[21]

Edward Gibbon, in his monumental *History of the Decline and Fall of the Roman Empire*, the first volume of which appeared in 1776,[22] takes his inspiration from Hume, his anti-Judaic tinge included, in describing the birth of Christianity and its conflict with the empire's other religions (chapters 14–26); but he eschews all reference to "monotheism." The French works that, in the same period, also treat this theme (Voltaire's 1763 *Traité sur la tolérance* and his 1736–1767 *Examen important de Milord Bolingbroke ou le tombeau du fanatisme*, as well as the great article in the *Encyclopédie* on "polytheism" that is doubtless due to Diderot) likewise make no mention of the word. Barring error on my part, it is not even to be found in the early nineteenth century French theorists of religion: Constant, Chateaubriand, Bonald, Maistre, or Quinet (whose lectures at the Collège de France, published in 1845 under the title *Le Christianisme et la Révolution française*, include a chapter on "Mohammedanism" immediately inspired by the new political-religious responsibilities that, Quinet explains, had been imposed on France by its conquest of Algeria; here it is a question of "the idea of the pure unity of God" that was revealed three times in history to "the same race of men [who] announced it to the world").[23] Littré cites an occurrence of "monothéiste" in a text by a certain Levesque [*sic*] in *Mémoires de la Classe des Sciences Morales et Politiques de l'Institut de France* (vol. 3, 1799/1800).

It would clearly seem to be in Germany, during the revolutionary period, in the context of a confrontation between the doctrines of the *Aufklärung* and those of a nascent Romanticism (which, let us not forget, witnessed the constitution of *orientalism* as well) that the decisive semantic changes came about.

To the best of my knowledge, the earliest text (a private text that is not cited in the dictionaries, although every philosopher is familiar with it today) in which monotheism and polytheism figure as the two poles of a balanced theoretical antithesis is none other than *Das älteste Systemprogramm des deutschen Idealismus*, a 1796 or 1797 fragment written on both sides of a single sheet and successively attributed to Schelling, Hölderlin, and Hegel by the commentators who discovered it early in the twentieth century.[24] Before the announcement of a new "mythology of reason" (*Mythologie der Vernunft*), we find the following formula there: "Monotheism of reason and the heart, polytheism of the imagination and art—that is what we need" (*dies ist's, was wir bedürfen*). This creation, as striking as it is enigmatic, seems to be modeled on the structure of Kant's transcendental schematism: it "synthetically" associates the opposing elements of representation, simultaneously shifting them toward a problematic of symbolism.[25] It seems to me that it must be interpreted as both crystallization and transgression of a complex ideological debate that welds together contemporaneous problems of several different orders—speculative, educational, and political: those posed in Germany by the *Pantheismusstreit* (a controversy about Lessing's reading of Spinoza as author of a natural philosophy capable of resolving theological antagonisms); those that arose from the revolutionary French project to create a "cult of the Supreme Being," opposed to the neopaganism of the "Goddess Reason" or the attempts to create a pantheistic "universal religion";[26] those thrown up by the Kantian idea of a "religion within the limits of reason alone," or a "rational faith,"[27] the polemical effect of which was radicalized with the "atheism controversy" (touched off by Fichte's teaching in Jena); finally, those that found expression in the Romantic call, inspired by the ancient Greek cults, for a *Volksreligion* capable of reinvesting Christianity, after the Enlightenment critique, with a function of social mediation—a call rooted in the rediscovery of the role of myth in constituting peoples (Herder, the Schlegel brothers), but tipped in a direction at once national and democratic by the Rousseauesque influence on Hölderlin and his circle.

A few years later, in 1810, this time in the broad light of day, Georg-Friedrich Creuzer began to publish his *Symbolik und Mythologie der Alten Völker*, a work that founded the history of religion as an academic discipline and sparked a tremendous controversy.[28] Not only did Creuzer maintain, against Hume, that in the permanent conflict between the "two main forms of religion, monotheism and polytheism," the former was the original and the second the derivative or reactive form (chapter 5); he also believed that the unity of monotheism reflected that of a people antedating the "Babelian" division of languages—what one might call an "archi-people" (*Urvolk*).[29] Creuzer likewise adopted the idea (chapter 6), drawn from hermeticism and the Cambridge Neoplatonists, that there had existed an "esoteric" Eastern religion (abstract monotheism) prior to the Greeks' "exoteric," anthropomorphic polytheism. This process of externalization and metaphor is supposed to have repeated itself throughout history in the relationship of the religions to popular mysteries and mythologies. Issued in an adapted French translation by Guigniaut beginning in 1825, Creuzer' s work found readers not only among historians (Michelet) and writers (Flaubert), but among theologians and philologists (Renan) as well.[30] The Oxford English Dictionary cites an occurrence of the phrase "pure monotheism" dating from the same period (1812); it is used in a discussion of Judaism and its capacity to resist persecutions and forced conversions, which suggests a debate related to the emancipation of the European Jews and therefore to their reintegration into the West's religious pluralism. Throughout the following period, the expression "pure monotheism" would likewise serve to designate Islam, that "religion of the desert," as Renan put it.[31]

Setting out from this opening, which founded the categories of monotheism and polytheism anew, making good a lag more than fifteen centuries old, we can, it would seem, identify three competing approaches to theorizing and historicizing the problem of religion in terms of monotheism. Let me attach the names Schelling, Schleiermacher, and Comte to them. Hegel, conspicuously, kept his distance from this theorization. His antagonistic relation to Schelling and hostility to philosophical Romanticism (especially as far as the theme of the *Urvolk* was concerned) may be one of the reasons for this.[32]

Whether or not he contributed to the *Systemprogramm*, Schelling has obvious priority here. In his early texts, he made systematic use of the designation "monotheism." An example is provided by his 1804 work *Philosophy and Religion*, in which he develops the same opposition between "esoteric" and "exoteric" religion that Creuzer (inspired perhaps by Schelling's own early texts) would later develop in connection with the project of a transcendental theogony. Another example may be found in Schelling's 1815 dissertation, *The Deities of Samothrace*, which includes a critical allusion to "this monotheism that is neither that of the Old Testament nor that of the New, but might perhaps be described as Mohammedan [*etwa mohammedanisch ʒu nennende*] . . . [monotheism] is foreign to all of Antiquity, with its splendid human society that finds expression in these words of Heraclitus's, applauded by Plato: the one wise being does not wish to be called Only-One [*alleinige*], he wants to bear the name Zeus."[33] It is, however, in Schelling's second ("positive") philosophy that the concept of monotheism comes to play a truly central role. It constitutes the object of the first part of *Philosophy of Mythology*, elaborated and regularly taught from

1825 on in Munich and Berlin and published in the 1853 edition of Schelling's posthumous works, to which it also gives its title. *Philosophy of Mythology* circulated widely throughout Europe even during Schelling's lifetime, thanks in part to (subsequently published) French transcriptions made for their own use by auditors whose courses would be inspired by their teacher's).[34]

In Schelling's speculative historical conception of monotheism (formally encapsulated in the affirmation, "No other god but God"),[35] monotheism intervenes twice: the first time as simple "theism" or "relative monotheism," corresponding to the fact that there can be no representation of a plurality of gods without a simple notion of the divine traversing all of them (the notion that Abraham and the prophets of Israel would seem to have isolated for itself); the second time as the "absolute monotheism" in which the identity of subject and object is realized: the self-relationship of the one divine Being by way of His own creation (his "desire to exist"). This identity sums up the Christian mystery of the Trinity as an "organic" idea (in the sense of Kant's *Critique of Judgment*) of unity in multiplicity or interiority in exteriority. The transition from a simple to a developed, self-conscious monotheism constitutes the *history of revelation*.[36] In this transition, mythological polytheism plays the key role of middle term, effecting the liberation of consciousness in the midst of life at the same time as the idea of God enters the real world. Schelling's presentation of this transition sometimes reproduces and sometimes rectifies Creuzer's. In particular, it assigns a central place to the mysteries of Demeter and Dionysius (the latter a figure who is himself polymorphous, answering as he does to the three divine names "Zagreus," "Bacchus," and "Iacchus"), which pave the way for the acceptance of suffering or pathos and the sublimation of sexuality (hence of the feminine) in Christianity. Jesus is the mystical truth of Dionysius, an idea that Nietzsche would adopt only to stand it on its head by making Dionysius the Antichrist.[37] This idea accordingly enables us to understand the way in which the theological question of the revelation of the divine Absolute in human life implies that of (positive) historical religion, and vice versa. By the same stroke, the notion of pantheism (or "Spinozism")[38] is short circuited, that notion to which, to his dying day, Schelling never ceased trying to devise an alternative compatible with revelation, even as he took from it the idea of a *natura naturans*, reformulated in *Philosophy of Revelation* as continuing creation: the idea of "Being as Potentiality" (*Potenz*), the effectuation of which is always still to come (and not to be sought in a lost origin).[39] In the lectures assembled in *Introduction to the Philosophy of Mythology*, Schelling discusses, notably, Hume, Cudworth, and Creuzer. He endorses, with reservations, the idea of a parallelism between the question of polytheism and that of the plurality of nations, while proposing to detach it from the core truth of what he calls "the monotheistic hypothesis."[40]

Schleiermacher illustrates the second approach. In *Der christliche Glaube nach den Grundsätzen der evangelischen Kirche im Zusammenhange dargestellt* (first edition 1821–1822; second, augmented edition 1830–1831), which founds modern Lutheran hermeneutics, he investigates what he calls "figures of devotion" or piety (*Gestalten der Frömmigkeit*), which have historical significance to the extent that they ground communities of believers (*Gemeinschaften*) and, at the same time, have a value for consciousness, that is, for interiority, which it is the theologian's task to express discursively.[41] All these figures take their inception in immediate consciousness of fault or sin and the aspiration to personal salvation inherent in human nature. The history of these figures of devotion culminates in the "three great monotheistic communities: Jewish, Christian, and Muslim," which have in common the feeling that "every finite being depends on One Supreme and Infinite [being] (*die Abhängigkeit alles Endlichen von Einem Höchsten und Unendlichen*)."[42] The three communities constitute, in their turn, an oriented progression (which is, however, not linear, since Islam is treated as a regression to the original Jewish form) within the order of self-consciousness. This progression culminates in the one form among the three that appears, on comparison, to be the "purest" and most "perfect": the Christian form—more exactly, the Protestant form.

Polytheism (the German term is *Vielgötterei*) and fetishism (*Fetischismus*) are presented as variants of idolatry (*Götzendienst*) repressed by the progress of consciousness. This also makes it possible to banish the notion of pantheism: its slogan, *Hen kai pan*, borrowed by Jacobi and Gotthold Ephraim Lessing from Neoplatonism and Egyptian religion as imagined by the Europe of the Classical age (the inscription in Isis's temple in Sais),[43] corresponds to forms of piety that can just as well proceed from polytheism as from monotheism. As for the doctrine of the Trinity on which the institution of the Church is based (since the Church is the "third person" of the Trinity, the community of Spirit or Holy Ghost), far from contradicting monotheism, it becomes its culminating point at the term of a dialectic that recapitulates a whole series of antitheses that had already played a part, as we have seen, in the process that engendered the notion: for an abstract monotheism that seeks to grasp the essence of the divine as being (*Wesen*) or causality (*Ursächlichkeit*), in other words, that seeks to grasp it by setting out from universals, the absolute equality or homogeneity (*Gleichheit*) of the two poles of the divine mystery represented by the unity of the essence (*Einheit*) on the one hand and the triplicity of the persons (*Dreiheit*) on the other remains irremediably incomprehensible. It inevitably lapses back, says Schleiermacher, into either the One, that is, an "impersonal" monotheism or a kind of *göttliche Monarchie*, or the Three, that is, a "quasipolytheism" (*die Dreiheit tritt als eine wahre Dreie fast polytheistisch hervor*) that Schleiermacher calls, like Cudworth, a "tritheism." To surmount this obstacle, one has to give up the viewpoint of ontology and logic for an eschatological viewpoint, that of the participation of the faithful, in "consciousness" (here, *Bewusstsein*), to the work of redemption, and the advent of the kingdom of God, that is, in the person of Christ.[44] Christ, insofar as he is our Savior or the Man-God always already present in us, is the truth of monotheism.

The third approach, finally, is that adopted by Auguste Comte, heir to Enlightenment philosophy and unfaithful disciple of Saint-Simon's, from whom he borrowed the term "positive philosophy," but, as well, an assiduous reader of the Scottish empiricists who was privy to the debates of German idealism thanks to Cousin's writings and to information he was given by his correspondents (Gustave d'Eichtal). As is well known, Comte orders the notions of polytheism and monotheism in an ascending series that he canonized, in some sort: fetishism, polytheism, monotheism, progressive moments of humanity's theological state, itself inscribed by the law of the three states (whose informing principle is change in the method of human knowledge) in the starting point of another fundamental series: theology (the "fictive" state), metaphysics (the "abstract" state), positivity (the "scientific" state). Comte did not, however, invent the ternary schema (the series fetishism-polytheism-theism may be found in Benjamin Constant).[45] All those who used the term "fetishism" in the nineteenth and twentieth centuries (from Hegel to Comte, Marx, and Freud) owe it to a book published anonymously by Charles de Brosses in 1760, *Du culte des dieux fétiches ou Parallèle de l'ancienne religion de l'Égypte avec la religion actuelle de Nigritie*.[46] Finally, the very series to be found in Comte is already presented in the seventeenth and last session of Year One ("The religious development of humanity: fetishism, polytheism, Jewish and Christian monotheism") of the *Exposition of Saint-Simonian Doctrine*, a transcription of the courses given by the Saint-Simonian religion's founders in 1829,[47] whereas Comte would only begin teaching the *Course of Positive Philosophy* in 1830 and would not reach the "historical part of social philosophy" containing the theory of the theological state until 1840. These precedents and parallels in no way detract from the important fact that Comte redefined all these concepts, conferring unequaled philosophical significance and scope on the series, which he theorizes afresh. They do, however, make it possible to bring out certain strategic choices.

The Saint-Simonians wanted to ring in humanity's religious future. Saint-Simon was its prophet by virtue of his book *The New Christianity: Dialogues Between a Conservative and an Innovator* (published in the year of his death, 1825), which, however, does not mobilize these categories.[48] The new religion was to mark the end of a transition from one religious principle to another: from fear, the mainspring of fetishism (where man is dominated by the forces of nature), which continues to make itself felt in Jewish monotheism (based on the "fear and trembling" of God's creatures before their creator and their fear of the fate reserved for all who ignored His commandments), to love, which begins to make itself felt in polytheism, a religion of "grace," and becomes the fundamental religious principle in Christian monotheism, where it informs the personal relation between the believer and the person of Christ. Conversely, however, like Judaism in this respect, the new religion was to be a political religion, or, more exactly, a social religion capable of organizing, not just inward life, but the community ("association"). (Freud would develop similar ideas when, toward the end of his life, he hypothesized in the 1930 *Das Unbehagen in der Kultur* that only love, *eros*, could combat the death drive and the destructive drives and, by ensuring mutual attraction among individuals, hold society together.) Comte's positions were quite different, at least initially. For him, the fetishism that constituted humanity's "spontaneous" religion was not a state of fear, but a "biomorphism," a projection of life onto its environment (the forces of nature) that freed up a universal capacity for fiction. (That is why not just human beings, but even certain animals are fetishists in an elementary sense.)[49] As for monotheism, it is the religion less of love or fear—or, generally, of the passions—than of spiritual power (which is, to begin with, a power of organization) that has attained dogmatic unity (one God, one Truth, one Church) and, accordingly, a certain simplicity or rationality, beyond the dispersion inherent in polytheism (or its polyarchic character, if one likes). Monotheism, in the domain of education to which it belongs (as opposed to action, which is in the domain of temporal power), is for Comte the great modernizing power: "The eminently social genius of Catholicism resided above all in the fact that it gradually brought about the greatest possible penetration of politics by morality in forming a purely moral power distinct from, and independent of, political power properly so called . . . and this basic tendency, at once agent and result of the continuous progress of human sociability, has necessarily survived the inevitable degeneration of the system that must have been its first general organ, in such a way as to characterize more profoundly than any other principal difference, with steadily increasing energy and notwithstanding various secondary or transitory perturbations, the radical superiority of modern civilization over the civilization of Antiquity."[50]

Thus the monotheism par excellence is, in Comte's view, not Christianity as such, but Catholicism, founded not by Jesus of Nazareth, but by Paul of Tarsus (a circumstance that undergirded the whole subsequent tradition of "political Catholicism," of which Maurras is the best-known representative and Schmitt is not very far—but at the price of closing off the universalist dimension that Comte explicitly designates as a latent "insurrection" within the Greek and Roman order, that is to say, a force sapping polytheism from within).[51] Monotheism itself, however, is just one stage in humanity's intellectual history: it is a revolution that lays the groundwork for another. The fact that Comte lends his evolutionary scheme a strictly linear form compels him to make room for "anomalies" that he himself calls strange, such as the great antiquity of Judaism,[52] and for "anticipations," the main one being the "admirable empiricism" of Mohammed, who prefigures, from the East, the "decisive revolution" thanks to which the modern West will overcome the theological as such.[53] But this linear form allows Comte to herald the emergence of a spiritual government of a new kind, which retains from monotheism the capacity to unify ideas in systematic fashion, while transferring its function, once the "critical abstractions" of metaphysics have been traversed, from the imaginary register to that of institutional rationality, both scientific and industrial.

This program of social "regeneration" is not, however, Comte's last word on the subject. His second philosophy, presented in *Système de politique positive*, after his 1846 "conversion," as well as in the 1852 *Catéchisme positiviste*, carries out a spectacular rehabilitation of feeling and fiction. The religion of humanity that he now proceeds to define is a new form of sublated monotheism. This monotheism worships the "Great Being," that is, the human race as such, of which modernity alone has been able to give us a unified representation. But the religion of humanity also carries out a kind of return to fetishism, a "fusion of the fetishistic with positivity (*fusion de la fétichité dans la positivité*),"[54] for it maintains an emotional and not merely intellectual relationship with this "rational fiction." At this point, one final crisscrossed exchange with the Saint-Simonian *frères ennemis* makes its appearance: whereas Enfantin had articulated his religion with a gender inversion imposed on the divine names (with *God the Father* becoming *God the Mother*, the better to ensure the equality of the sexes), Comte's religion of humanity is constrained to make Woman the mediator (or "Christ," if one likes), since she is the bearer of the powers of feeling without which humanity would be unable to triumph over its own archaic institutions of warfare. In both cases, however, it appears that the project to extend the movement of monotheism, by definition progressive, is inseparable from a return of monotheism's repressed, or the way it had abstracted from "gender."

At the end of this itinerary—long and meandering, yet still tentative and unfinished—I shall sketch five general considerations.

Firstly, the three explanatory procedures that went their autonomous ways at the moment of the modern "invention" of monotheism—they might be called, respectively, the symbolic, hermeneutic, and sociological approaches—are still active in contemporary thought. This means both that they are present and that they remain distinct there. They may well have been complicated as a result of overlapping or the incorporation of new points of view, associated, notably, with the development of comparativism and the emergence and integration of their repressed: the idea of God characteristic of the "other monotheisms," and the reality of "monotheism's other" (paganism with its own specific "spirit" [*génie*])[55]—without forgetting the most "subversive" of all: the religion without god(s), atheism or Buddhism. The fact remains, however—such, at any rate, is my hypothesis—that the problems and alternatives associated with monotheism's origins continue to be determinant of every utilization of the term. Monotheism is still a fundamentally *equivocal* notion.

Secondly, the fact that this notion was long blocked or retarded with respect to its point of application brings consequences of all sorts in its wake, at the speculative level as well as at that of concrete references. Not only does the theologically sensitive point of the enunciation of "monotheism," in a context polarized by its relationship with Christianity, reside in the mystery of the Trinity, as everyone knows; the transformation of the name into a concept is everywhere dominated by the formulas of Neoplatonism, the sole philosophy to identify the two grammatical significations of the One (*Monos, Hen*) as unicity and as unity (in a "beyond the essence" that appears, depending on the author in question, as overexistence [*surexistence*] or the limit of inexistence [*inexistence*]), but also the sole philosophy to have thus proposed a rational theoretical solution to the problem of the convertibility of the One and the Multiple (something that by no means excludes a privileged relationship with mysticism, quite the contrary).[56] We find the Neoplatonist heritage again when, in the modern period, the conceptual and existential impossibilities (including those bearing on tolerance and intolerance) are inverted and transformed into attributes of the divinity or conditions of possibility of faith. The specter of anti-Trinitarian Arianism that has, for fifteen centuries, shadowed recourse to the category of the "One" in the theological domain, before yielding to the specter of pantheism, accordingly seems to have been conjured away for good. In fact, it may only have changed its appearance, or pointed its canons in the other direction: for, increasingly, the problem is not the humanity of God, but its "correlative," the divinity or divinization of Man, his promotion to the rank of the Unique, *homo alter deus*.

Thirdly, the content of this modernity is unintelligible without reference to political, or, if one prefers, theologico-political determinations. We cannot treat as secondary the fact that the question of monotheism was overdetermined at the origin, if only negatively, by a representation of God as "lord" (Our Lord), and by a debate about the transcendent and immanent forms of monarchy; or, again, the fact that it emerged from what appears, for this reason, to be its latent state in the context of a "revolution," at once political and religious, that shattered or demystified the monarchical model and, irresistibly, threw up the question of a "democratic" community that would be its own sovereign or transcendence in every domain falling under the purview of "spirit" (as German idealism puts it)—if one prefers, of culture. It by no means follows that the very question of principle (or of the principle of unity) has been abolished. Quite the contrary: it has been liberated as such. That is why, in a sense, the theorist of monotheism who, of the three we have singled out, comes closest to a certain aboriginal monarchianism is Auguste Comte. For that very reason, he is the one who best helps us understand how a certain "secularism" (laïcité) of yesterday and today is more than ever fundamentally monotheistic, in the sense defined by that secularism itself. But, more generally, how could we understand, without reference to this determination, that the "onto-theological" equivocalness of the One (a totalization of all that exists) and the Unique (alone vis-à-vis the others, or even excluding the possibility of their existence) ends up as a characteristic of the positive notion of "monotheism," the agent of its comparative exportation and the debates about the relationship between the "monotheistic" model and "universalism"? We have to pay special attention, in this connection, to the fact that the old theme of the unity and plurality of languages (glôssai, "fragments" of the logos), and therefore of nations and peoples or even churches, insistently returns to overdetermine the invention of monotheism as a historical category in the democratic age—at the price, of course, of being immediately pulled in contradictory directions.

For, fourthly, this structure of latence and conversion of the principle turns out to be inseparable from a temporal determination—better, from a determination of historicity. What we must think in order to characterize the modern emergence of the category of monotheism is not just the problematic of the reunification of the community; it is that of *the community "to come,"* the universality to come, and the equality that will be distributed on the condition and on the prescription of unity.

"Monotheism" represses a "polytheistic" past; it names this repression, while also seeking to appropriate all the positivity of the repressed (that is why it is basically a *Gegenreligion* or "counterreligion," to borrow Jan Assman's formulation, while giving a certain twist to it).[57] Thus, even when this notion is not evolutionist, it is ineluctably historicist. But the historicity that it registers permeates it and propels it toward an eschatological horizon, toward a beyond-rationality in which it must seek its definition, toward the effectuation of its own ontological potential, or, again, toward that which would overcome it, yet always find formal expression in line with the logic of monotheism itself. The modern discourse of "monotheism," which never ceases to postulate an original surpassment (*dépassement*), simultaneously seems always to be awaiting a meaning, realization, or mutation that would, at last, allow it to renounce nothing of what it has excluded. It is perhaps here, in particular, that we should begin to seek the reason for the obstacles that prevent it from serving as the object of a simple *auto-attribution* ("We, the monotheists"), until such time as it finds the path of what would have to be called an indirect attribution or a *auto-hetero-attribution* ("We, the true, the only monotheists"; "We, monotheists like you"; and, finally, "All of us, we the monotheists").

Fifthly and finally, the simple history of the origins and uses of this word reverberates, as Foucault might have put it, with the noise of all sorts of battle. The name that affirms the unicity of God or of the divine message itself only owes its existence and power to the fact that it conceals unending divisions. Some are "on the surface": that is, they manifest themselves in the discourse of monotheism itself, whose rhetorical effects they may, at the limit, appear to be. This holds for the never-resolved question as to what would make it possible to save monotheism from its perilous proximity to atheism or pantheism, without reducing it to anthropologism, to anthropomorphism, and thus to the polytheism of which it is the theoretical antithesis. Let us put this better: at the *point of heresy* that we may call, generically, X-theism, there once again meet and clash with the trace of polytheism not only monotheism itself (this comes down to saying that Christianity is its own heresy), but also ditheism (its gnostic, Manichean tendency), tritheism, atheism, and pantheism. Nothing of all that is external to monotheism, insofar as it is logos, discourse. But the nature of the question has already shifted when it comes to the relations between "the monotheistic hypothesis" and the differential of mythologization and demythologization characteristic of religious thought in general (unless we should put the matter the other way around, and argue that it is from the standpoint of a Christian or post-Christian history of monotheism that there exists something like "religious thought," the site of which is, par excellence, this differential and the symbolic labor that it forces spirit to perform). The nature of the question shifts once again when what returns beneath the category of the One is an alterity such as gender or sexuality, in the form of a difference that is not simply anthropological, but theological as well: *différance* in God Himself. Perhaps we can suggest, accordingly, that the concept of monotheism is from the outset the agent of an oblique thought of difference (and of conflict without resolution, without sublation) even more than, tautologically, a thought of unity or unification. As for the question of saying how, and with what stakes, it is obvious that the history of a word is not by itself enough to provide an answer. It can only suggest that we need to find an answer, for sentences once uttered can never be completely reduced to silence.

11.

"GOD WILL NOT REMAIN SILENT":
ZIONISM, MESSIANISM, AND NATIONALISM

A t a moment when the expropriation of the "occupied territories" by Israel has finally voided of its content the
hypothesis of two states in Palestine by destroying and frag-
menting the country in seemingly irreversible fashion, and
when the conflict as such has largely lost its autonomy within
the context of a regional war marked by the confrontation
between U.S. imperialism, its allies, and its diverse opponents
(Islamist or otherwise), what purpose can possibly be served
by new analyses of the constitution of Zionism?[1] There would
seem to be an abysmal gap between the complex historical and
theoretical references these analyses propose, the distance they
establish with respect to stereotypes, and the starkness of the
choices that a century of wars, violence, diplomatic maneuvers,
and false political solutions offers in the end to the parties to
the conflict: elimination or "transfer," in the short term, of the
Arab populations with the exception of a few zones of concentration and surveillance, or, in the longer term, of the Jewish
populations, at the price of a massive new emigration. Or, first
one and then the other.[2]

And yet such analyses are important in many ways; I am convinced that it is always worthwhile to take the time to conduct them and discuss them. First of all, they reveal the internal contradictions of an ideology and a policy which, under given conditions and a given balance of forces, has contributed like very few others to "making the history" of which we today are the subjects, wherever we may be in the world. We can of course use them as polemical arguments against given actors, but one can also see in them an indication of potentialities of division that crystallized in the past and could do so again if circumstances lend themselves to such an outcome, i.e., as a means contributing to avoiding the worst. The rise of critical thought in Israel—sometimes referred to as a whole as "post-Zionist"—within the small minority that truly opposes the settlements and seeks to act in concert with the Palestinian resistance, is indeed impressive. At the same time, such analyses open pathways for comparison between an "extreme" and even unique case, and a multiplicity of state formations that also represent associations—of very different sorts—between "messianic" and "national" components, in a synthesis that is more and more problematic today. On the one hand then, the idea is to bring out, against appearances, the indetermination lodged in the heart of a determined *situation*. On the other hand, the idea is to contribute to a comprehensive reflection on the forces and representations implicated in the changes on our cosmopolitical horizon. In both cases, we must recognize the capacity of the past to act in the present, by applying as much rigor as possible to understanding its powers.

This is the perspective in which I would like to discuss three recent works on Zionism—a notion which continues to dominate the "common sense" of perceptions of the Jewish question and its entanglement with the history and the functions of the state of Israel. Despite the difference of positions they take on key points, they all challenge the idea of a separation (*coupure*) between the religious and the political and they all bring out, in Israel's trajectory, a history that is not "sacred" but rather a history of the powers of the sacred in the secular world and its effects on those very actors who make use of it. All three books have the added interest of articulating in timely fashion an astonishing intellectual conjuncture that has seen successive convergences and oppositions between the critique of the idea of a "Jewish state" in Palestine, the defenders of an alternative, "cultural" Zionism, and the partisans of a cosmopolitanism rooted in the Jewish experience of exclusion, the most striking episode of which was the confrontation between Gershom Scholem and Hannah Arendt just after the latter published her "report" on the Eichmann trial.

The first book to which I refer does not come from Israel, even though its author has multiple relations with that country: Jacqueline Rose's *The Question of Zion*, which came out of a series of lectures delivered in 2003 at Princeton University.[3] In the first chapter ("The Apocalyptic Sting"), Rose examines the messianic foundations of political Zionism by drawing inspiration from the now classic though still controversial analyses by Gershom Scholem of the history of the Kabbalah and Jewish messianism.[4]

It was Scholem himself who, shortly after he moved to Palestine, brought about a rapprochement between Zionism and Sabbateanism, in which he saw the two "political" moments of the history of the Jewish people in the modern era. The "historical" character of redemption in Jewish messianism (as opposed to the Christian idea of salvation in another world), associated with the hope for an end to persecutions endured in exile and during the enslavement of Israel, engendered a revolutionary ideology that Scholem calls "utopian" and "apocalyptic." This ideology, the result of an "intense messianic expectation,"[5] represents the messianic age as the moment of a "final confrontation of Israel with the Gentiles," a conflagration with a cosmic significance whose cataclysms form the condition of the national renaissance. To this representation of the role of violence in history (which also became an element of Marxism), identified with the suffering of "giving birth," a particular tradition from the Kabbalah adds a specifically antinomic dimension: the messianic era is not only that of the reunification in divinity of parts of the world that have been "broken" since the creation; it is also—with a view to "hastening the end"—that of an inversion of the law or its realization through its transgression ("it is by violating the Torah that one accomplishes it"), a specific form of "the activism [which takes] utopia as a lever in the aim of establishing a messianic kingdom"—however undecided the figure of the messiah himself may be.[6]

Traditionalist and rationalist Judaism (Maimonides) has always vigorously resisted this revolutionary conception, which Scholem did not hesitate to see as a "circuit of mutual influences" of Judaism and millenarist Christianity.[7] But the episode of the rise, recognition and apostasy of the "false messiah" Sabbatai Zevi, the repercussions of which were immense in the seventeenth century in Jewish communities as well as in the Christian world, confirmed this idea in spectacular fashion. "Redemption through sin" here forms the "political" bond between the charismatic power of the messiah and the hopes of the people, leading to the auto-dissolution of its traditions and giving rise to a nihilistic conception of destruction as the path to redemption.[8] Scholem himself saw in this episode a first manifestation of Jewish nationalism and its projects of liberation— an anticipation of Theodor Herzl's Zionism. As a result, he never ceased to warn against the "messianic" identification of the return of exiled Jews to Palestine with redemption; he sought to "neutralize" the apocalyptic dimension of messianism without liquidating it altogether, by keeping the political moment, having to do with national, state, and territorial structures, separate from the spiritual moment, and by staking out a mystical interpretation of the redemption as reestablishment of the unity and harmony of the world.[9] He defines this separation in many writings, in particular during the years when he was associated with Martin Buber, Rabbi Judah Magnes (founder of the Hebrew University of Jerusalem), and other intellectuals living in Palestine and belonging to the Brit Shalom movement, which fought Zionism's rallying to the vision of conquest advocated by Jabotinsky and his "revisionism." The most remarkable of these is a letter to Franz Rosenzweig in 1926, in which he expresses his worry over the consequences for sacred language, but also for the collective consciousness and the future of Jews settled in Palestine, of the transformation of Hebrew into a national language: "God will not remain silent," he writes, meaning that despite the apparent secularization of language, the apocalyptic powers implied in invoking of sacred narratives will tend to realize themselves, whatever the obstacles and the human price.[10]

Jacqueline Rose uses Scholem's notion to interpret the historical trajectory of Zionism from the writing of Herzl's utopian novel *Altneuland* (1902) up to the foundation of the state of Israel as "Jewish state" in Palestine (1948) and the current situation of occupation and progressive destruction of Palestinian society. She sees in this history the realization of the antinomic element of messianism transformed into a program of political action, both destructive and self-destructive. The analogies between the manic-depressive personality of Sabbatai Zevi and that of Herzl serve as leverage for her argumentation, which has not failed to provoke controversy.[11] However, the essential contribution lies in the relationship she establishes between two questions: that of the national territory as a "land of redemption" ascribed to the people by revelation or by history, but contingent upon a never-ending process of appropriation, always "insufficient"; and that of the collective narcissism that tends to transform all "foreign bodies" into enemies and to turn a people of victims into a people of oppressors. Rose develops her thought with the help of psychoanalytical notions (using Freud, Bion, and Lacan) of collective identity and defense mechanisms against the reality it engenders. Everything revolves thus around the patterns of extreme violence and their imaginary *elaboration*. The myth of Palestine as a "land without people"—an act of denial that can affect either the physical presence of "nomads" (who are in fact peasants), or the legitimacy of the historical settlement of Arabs in the "land of the Bible," or the national identity of the Palestinians—must be forced to fit reality against the "evil powers" that resist it. At the same time, the historical reality of anti-Semitism and its traumatic culmination in genocide is turned into the conviction that the victims of Zionism are in fact its persecutors.[12] In this manner, any manifestation of hostility becomes a threat of annihilation (physical annihilation but also symbolic annihilation: degradation and collective "shame" expressing the powerlessness of the Jews, as the Shoah was presented for a long time in Israel), against which all means are justified and even sanctified ("every soldier in the Jewish militia is an actualization of the messiah").[13]

The heart of this analysis is thus a psycho-political reflection on the way in which anti-Semitism has come to constitute not only—as Herzl never tired of repeating—the objective ally of Zionism, by destroying illusions of assimilation and persuading Jews that persecution is the only destiny outside "their" nation-state, but also the projective structure (*schème*) of a melancholic conception of self in which the group sees itself (while also fearing to see itself) as absolute victim, object of the murderous hatred of an Other that is both omnipresent and radically evil. This conception of the collective identity avoids any calling into question of one's own politics and allows one, in advance, to attribute any criticism to hostility. It is obviously not the only possible conception, although in certain circumstances that "liberate" the antinomic element of the unconscious itself, it is perhaps irresistible. That is why Rose attributes essential importance, at the heart of her book, to the alternative advocated by the "spiritual" current of Zionism, founded by Ahad Ha'am (Asher Ginzberg),[14] in whom she sees not only a precocious source of inspiration for a critique—aiming at Herzl—of exclusive nationalism that makes the prior occupants of the promised land invisible, but also—in anticipation of *Freud's Civilization and its Discontents* and in continuation of a rabbinic tradition—the initiator of a "clinique" of melancholic identifications, which would liberate the collective consciousness from grief and the cruel injunctions of the ancestors.[15]

The relation to ancestors, treated with a completely different method, is also the subject of Idith Zertal's work *Israel's Holocaust and the Politics of Nationhood*, which seems to me to have received up to now insufficient or biased attention.[16] Zertal takes an interest as an historian in the constitution and the functions of collective memory, drawing on the works of Maurice Halbwachs and, among more recent scholars, Benedict Anderson and other historians of national culture. In her conclusion, she converges with the positions of Hannah Arendt, which she attempts to adapt to the current conditions of Israeli politics.

The main portion of the work is a detailed study of the way in which a whole set of commemorations and educational institutions constructed and incorporated the notion of a "crucial and exclusive link" between the memory of the Shoah and Israeli defense policy.[17] The perverse effect of this notion was to inscribe at the heart of collective consciousness an equivalence between the Arab world (and today, more and more, the Muslim world) and a new Nazism, as hammered home in the discourse of the political and military elite (with the partial exception of Rabin before he was assassinated) and largely adopted in public opinion.

It should be noted here, to preclude shrill protests, that Zertal does not contest (any more than does Rose) the idea that Israel has enemies, nor that these enemies wish for or fantasize about Israel's elimination.[18] Nor does she contest the fact that, as early as the period of the Yishuv and during World War II, certain Palestinian leaders imagined an alliance with Nazism against the "common enemy"[19] and that revisionism or negationism (Holocaust denial) are broadly encouraged today in the Arab and Islamic world. That is not the problem she addresses, however; what she does treat is the *endogenous* construction of a collective self-image[20] through the superimposing, via certain symbolic events, of two systems of representations—one of which reconstructs ancient or recent history while the other interprets politically the contemporary period—which constantly draw on each other in configuring reality in order to delegitimize and dehumanize the enemy. It would not be forcing the meaning of Zertal's argumentation to define as its motive, not an underestimation of the importance of the Shoah in Jewish consciousness and contemporary history, but rather a revolt against the instrumentalization and even the banalization of the Shoah,[21] which deprive it of its historical reality and dispossess its victims while promoting its imagined imminence in a completely different political conjuncture—thereby rendering the violence and crimes of the present invisible and inconceivable, given the effect of disproportion.

Her analysis reveals the articulation among several moments. The first concerns the fiction of a chain of heroic sacrifices for the nation beginning long before the proclamation of independence, the war of 1948 and the appropriation for *Eretz Israel* of the European model of the sacred bond between "land and blood," with the difference that the mission in Palestine is to create, displace, and defend the frontier against an *internal enemy*. The model invoked here is the resistance to the death of the settlers of Tel Hai in Upper Galilee against their Arab assailants in 1920.[22] With two other key examples—that of the exaltation of the insurrection in the Warsaw ghetto (1943) presented as a "Zionist combat for the honor of Israel"[23] and that of the tragedy of the *Exodus* as managed by the leaders of the Jewish Agency in order to influence the debates within the U.N. Commission in 1947—we move to a second and even more sensitive question, that of the selection in Israeli policy among testimonies and even among persons (i.e., survivors). This leads to a discussion of the way in which the state-led construction of memory represses what it considers "shameful" from the standpoint of the "new man" and constructs scapegoats among the victims themselves, while exonerating certain veritable collaborators.[24]

What emerges, in Zertal's striking expression, is a "memory without subjects" (121), a "mixture of appropriation and exclusion" (36), the ideological thrust of which is to construct a "civic religion" (82) and to "purify" Israel itself of the "Jewish shame" represented by the ignominious death of powerless victims (91, 115).

Without restoring to the survivors their right to expression, of which the state (but also, secondarily, the army and the settler organizations) took on the role of "certified heirs" (237), the officializing of the cult of the Shoah dead, of which the Eichmann trial in 1961 constituted a key moment, nonetheless represented a significant shift. The Shoah is no longer categorized as a sign of degeneracy and "passivity" of the ghetto Jew as opposed to the "new man" embodied by the Zionist pioneer; it is transfigured into a founding event of the national renaissance and the negative sign of Israel's chosenness, which guarantees a priori the holiness of its objectives and the means (in particular military means) used to the achieve them.[25] Its "unique" character is no longer discussed—as it still was at the time of the Biafra war—but proclaimed and sanctified. Once again then, and on a much greater scale, a situation is systematically read in the shadow of another, thus instituting a collective psychology of angst which exceeds all the particular circumstances that might nourish it (regional wars, suicide bomb attacks, the Palestinian demand for a "right to return"), and resulting in an Israeli self-consciousness as a "refugee nation," placed permanently under the sign of extermination. "In this universe where all meanings are inverted and all projections permitted," writes Zertal, "the conquered peoples become conquerors; persecutors are turned into the persecuted, criminals into victims, and this upside-down world is sanctioned thanks to the supreme hallmark of Auschwitz."[26]

Under these circumstances one can understand why Hannah Arendt, expressing herself "as a Jew" in her report and interpretation of the Eichmann trial, while refusing all group affiliation,[27] provoked a scandal that continues to this day. After having published in Hebrew, for the first time, Arendt's letter to Scholem—which he had promised to have published with hers—Zertal devotes a long chapter to this apology for free thinking (*Selbstdenken*, in Lessing's expression) against "the catastrophe of political messianism," and draws inspiration from it in her conclusion. In her view, and above and beyond the criticism of the great historian's failure to keep his word, this polemic is exemplary of the way in which the current that had believed in the utopia of Jewish-Arab understanding became divided between a cultural nationalism, powerless to dissociate itself from mythical extrapolations from history despite having studied its genealogy methodically, and a "world citizenship" for which the essential political problem to be resolved is how to achieve the historical conditions for coexistence between different demands for self-determination, mutually antagonistic and yet equally and unconditionally justified.

The Scholem-Arendt controversy also occupies a central place in the third work I examine here, Amnon Raz-Krakotzkin's *Exil et souveraineté. Judaïsme, sionisme et pensée bi-nationale.*[28]

However, against the background of their common friendship with Walter Benjamin (whose inspiration Arendt and Scholem had in some way incorporated into their thought), this controversy is reexamined from the standpoint of the "political theology" which undergirded the construction of the state of Israel and its colonial expansion to the (undetermined) limits of the Biblical *Eretz Israel*. Here, then, is a third perspective that cuts across and displaces the two previous ones.[29] It is impossible here to account fully for a work so worthy of discussion (which I hope will occur), stunning in its erudition and its theoretical ambitions. I will first indicate the meaning the author attaches to the notion to which he refers in his title, and then concentrate my remarks on three plurithematic (*transversaux*) points.

Raz-Krakotzkin takes care to distinguish what he calls "binational thought" from any particular institutional solution to the Israeli-Palestinian conflict in the form of one or two states. As outlined in the interwar period by Buber, Magnes, Scholem, and Arendt, and as it survives today in Israel among the minority that struggles for the rights of Palestinians, it consists first of all in an effective recognition of the presence of the Arabs, in the midst of which Jewish communities have always lived, as the first residents of the land of Palestine; secondly, it refers to the idea that "the rights of Jews and Arabs form a whole" such that one cannot make democracy progress without "treating simultaneously both facets,"[30] which requires reasoning no longer in terms of exclusive sovereignty but rather limited or shared sovereignty. Finally—and this is a knottier problem—it affirms that for the Jews themselves "Palestine is a country of exile," as it has become for the Palestinians, in such a way that there is no eschatological identification possible between the "return" of the Jews to Palestine and the construction of a state in the Middle East.[31] Binational thought thus constitutes both an "intellectual and moral reform" and a political methodology in today's situation, whose outcome cannot be predicted.

In this perspective, the first thesis of the book is that the distinction often acknowledged in Israel between a "secular" camp and a "religious" camp is meaningless. It was secular nationalism, and socialism in particular, predominant at the time of the state's founding and in charge of its policies for decades alone or in coalition, that carried out the "secularization" and the conservation of theologico-political schemas, sacralizing national symbols (the flag with the star of David reproducing a prayer shawl), making the Bible the absolute reference for the representation of borders, and making Israel a chosen land that could only be appropriated by the Jews. Raz-Krakotzkin sums up this "inverted secularization" with a witticism: "God does not exist, but he promised us this land." This theology, denied and yet omnipresent, associates in close combination the political aspect—the absolutization of the national state form—with an apocalyptic religious deviation[32] with respect to the idea of the human condition as exile, seen as the ethical and mystical foundation of Judaism, in correspondence with the prohibition on "hastening the end."[33] As a paradoxical consequence, we must look for the opponents of political messianism among the religious thinkers and parties who oppose the idea of the Israeli territory as a holy land, rather than among the self-proclaimed "secularists."[34]

The negation of exile, this time in a directly historical sense, is at the heart of Raz-Krakotzkin's critique of the "orientalism" (as defined by Said), which according to him pervades the self-images and the cultural policies of the state of Israel. The paradox is that a nation born of persecution of the Jews in Europe conceives of itself (starting with the writings of Herzl) as the vanguard of the Europeanization of the Middle East; and that, in turning against itself—not without extreme ambivalence—the system of "stigma" invented by orientalism, that nation comes to hunt down ferociously, in its history, cultural traditions and ethnic composition, everything that evokes "otherness" with respect to the models of community developed by European nations and colonial empires. This "delocalized" orientalism, "projected" out of its place of origin, holds naturally for the systematic negation of the rights and the very existence of the Palestinian Arabs and for the representation of Islam as a backward and fanatic religion. But it holds as well for the symbolic violence to which the "oriental" Jews are subjected and the erasure of Judeo-Arab culture, in both its popular and its learned guises, despite its ties to the great moment of renaissance of medieval Judaism in Yemen, Baghdad, and Cordoba.[35] What a paradox for a state building itself in the Middle East, and of which—leaving aside the 20 percent of Israeli Arabs—nearly half the Jewish majority population has origins in Yemen, Iraq, and North Africa! Greater still is the paradox concerning the way in which, in denying a specifically Jewish conception of historicity (as Benjamin attempted to retrieve it in combination with another messianism) in favor of a "grand narrative" of state modernization, the dominant discourse in Israel presents Jewish history of the past millennium, under conditions of diaspora, essentially as a long, negative parenthesis and an experience of alienation from the collective identity. The construction of the new man thus becomes not only an instrument for "eradication of the past," but also the process by which the stereotypes of European anti-Judaism are assimilated and ratified.

At the most advanced point of his critique, Raz-Krakotzkin, developing an intuition of Scholem against Scholem himself, argues in favor of the thesis that the "secularized political theology" guiding Israeli policy is not so much the effect of an internal deviation of Jewish messianism as it is the result of its own impregnation with specifically Christian schemas, from the appropriation of Protestant principles of literalist reading and exclusive authority of the Bible to the use of extermination as a theophanic founding moment, a sign of God in lay history, via the representation of the "end of exile" as an "entry into history" in the progressive and positive sense of the term.[36]

It is against such an inversion of perspectives, which is much more alienating than the "degeneration" to which it claims to put an end, that Raz-Krakotzkin invokes the Benjaminian idea of a history of redemption as a "history of the defeated" (or, in the language of Arendt, the "pariahs").[37] This history is by no means purely speculative since it opens in his view the possibility of exercising *political responsibility* for the consequences, for others and for oneself, of the Zionist conquest—a responsibility on which depend the chances, which in truth are very tenuous, of not paying collectively the heaviest price.[38]

To conclude, I would like to stress two problems that clearly call for further reflection. One point in common between the analyses of Rose, Zertal, and Raz-Krakotzkin, which the very divergence of their methods brings out even more strongly (and even violently) is the pervasive presence of anti-Semitism within contemporary Jewish identities, and the profundity of the deferred effects that its internalization never ceases to produce in the self-consciousness or *Selbstthematisierung* indissociable from the Israeli national construction. It will no doubt be admitted that no form of identification with Judaism and with Jewishness (*judéité*)—and we know that there are more than one—can emerge unscathed. The traumatism of the Shoah, transmitted from generation to generation, adds to it a dimension of inevitability which is difficult to resist. But the situation is qualitatively different for Israeli national consciousness because the relationship of the "self" to the "other" (the foreigner, the enemy) becomes the object of an institutional construction, a political "appropriation," and this construction takes place under conditions of colonization, and thus a "vital" denial of the condition of oppressors on the part of former victims (or rather their heirs, which is not the same thing). Everything thus occurs—as an effect of the "perverse debt," in

Zertal's expression—as if Sartre's formula ("it's anti-Semitism that makes the Jew") had found its deferred realization: it is anti-Semitism that constructs Jewishness (*judéité*) for Israelis, both in the definition of what they reject as foreign to them and of that with which they identify. The supremely ambivalent category of "victim" paradoxically joins together the two aspects.

The resulting practical consequence is twofold and of course does not concern only the Jews or the Israelis. First of all, it is important to explore in more depth, as Hilberg, Arendt, and Poliakov had all begun to do in different ways, *the nature of the historic ties between anti-Semitism and extermination*, since these ties are by no means logical or linear. Further, it is essential to place a merciless ideological struggle against current forms of anti-Semitism (in both the East and the West) on the agenda of any attempt to contribute to a solution of the Israeli-Palestinian conflict through the "neutralization"—insofar as possible—of nationalist messianism, because the latter draws nourishment from any circumstance in which the real provides opportunities to confirm its imaginary. This implies no necessity of giving in to the blackmail to which any critical examination of Israeli history and politics is exposed. The difficulty arises from the fact that anti-Semitism is of course used tactically by Israel but also forms, in a much deeper way, an unconscious basis of its identity, associated with the discourse of Zionism from its origins, which obstacles and refutations do not weaken but instead reinforce.

At another level, the analyses of our three authors pose anew a complex but crucial question: in what sense is the ideological formation referred to here as "nationalist messianism," or sacralization of the nation by the "angel of death," specifically Israeli? Could it not be that a part of the fascination exercised by Zionism, in the West or elsewhere, on the minds of people who have no particular sympathy for colonization, but who may on the other hand be attached to a "civic" or "republican" conception of the nation and its particular manner of combining universalism and communitarianism, egalitarianism and exclusion, comes from the fact that Israeli nationalism brings to an extreme point (and even to a breaking point) an ideological formation that is not—or not entirely—unique to it? At a time of general questioning of the combination of messianism and nationalism—which is more or less indissociable from the translation of an historical identity into state policy and attaches itself, according to the circumstances at hand, to the ideas of "civilizing mission," "elect nation," "land of resurrection" where the New Man is born, or "nation victim of history" (France, U.S., U.S.S.R., Poland, India, Iran, etc.)—the particular case of Israel appears as the stronghold of a certain image of sovereignty and as the place where it is (always and already) in the shadow of death.[39] The very Spinozian formula of Rabbi Haim Grodzinski quoted by Raz-Krakotzkin—"Israel is a state like any other"—takes on a different meaning.[40] It calls for a more complete investigation into everything that the couple formed by the land of the ancestors and sacrificial patriotism, exacerbated by Israeli nationalism, owes in fact to the European history of nationalisms (including Maurice Barrès!). It further calls, of course, for investigation into the fact that this history has never ceased to reactivate and exploit Biblical models—and here we encounter the "circuit of mutual influences" of which Scholem spoke. Finally, it demands of us that we pose the problem of the specificity and the singularity (the uniqueness, if one prefers) of Jewish history in Israel and outside Israel, not in terms of essences or identities but in terms of internal relations and othernesses, in the past as in the present. All states are "like the others" but no national history is "like another," since it reflects within it all the others.

12

WHAT FUTURE FOR *LAÏCITÉ*?

What do I want to achieve in this essay? To make it as clear as possible, let me begin with a commentary on its title.[1] First, the fact that I use the French word "laïcité" does not mean that I intend to discuss purely national issues in a parochial manner. On the contrary, I believe that French national issues do have a general relevance and import. But I also believe that this general character of the problems concerning relationships between religion and state, religion and society, religion and politics, religion and ethics, that we imagine to be associated with the notions of laïcité and secularism, can only be addressed and discussed in a proper manner from a *comparative* point of view, through the critical examination of singular histories and languages. This is what I have in mind when attempting a discourse which, spoken and then written in today's transnational or cosmopolitan English, will maintain the word "laïcité" in "national" French, as consistently as possible, drawing its main references, accordingly, from the French case.

There are many intellectual risks involved here, not least to surreptitiously produce a reiteration of a narrow Francocentric understanding of the problem—not to say a typically French illusion of universality—while pretending to be critical and self-critical. I am aware of this risk, and, in a sense, it is precisely why I insist on the specificity of my references: I expect objections and critiques, which will help me relativize my point of view, in the sense of a national historical location. This is, I submit, the only way to avoid the twin illusions of abstract universality and narcissistic exceptionalism.

I use such terms on purpose, because, as readers will notice, my reflection is haunted by the twin problems of universality and universalism on the one hand, exception and exceptionalism on the other hand. As for universality, this comes from the fact that "laïcité," spoken in French (a French that is framed and inhabited by the legacy of the complete set of Western, Euro-Mediterranean politico-theological notions, however) illustrates and touches the very heart of what we might call the *intrinsic paradox of universalism*, namely the fact that universal principles, values, and truth contents, while removing the limits of particularism (specific memberships and cultures, etc.), are always of necessity formulated and enunciated in a given time at a given place, and above all in a given idiom. [2] This does not destroy universality as such, but right away inscribes in its heart a contradiction or a tension, a dialectics of limitation and expansion, negation and affirmation, institution and transgression, which can never become stabilized and reach an end.[3] In particular, the institutions (political, in the broad sense) which claim to incarnate universality in history—including the one that in our post-Latin languages has been named *universitas* or "university"—are bound to be consumed by this tension, which is also one of the reasons why they become powerfully sanctified in legal practice and the collective imaginary. As for *exception* and *exceptionalism*, the difficulty comes from the fact, particularly illustrated in the French case, that we have to do here with a double determination (at least): a singular history of relationships and conflicts between politics and religion, more precisely between Church and State, which has completely dominated the imaginary of the "common" and the representations of "authority"; and a long and prominent role of European nations and nationhood in the Western appropriation of the world, with its inextricably mixed progressive and regressive effects, combining hyperbolic ambitions and never-ending resentments, which gives a *messianic or quasi-messianic character* to the nation and everything that becomes closely associated with it and "intrinsic" to its typical common culture. This is eminently the case for the idea of laïcité. What I want to suggest, in short, and before entering into more specific discussions, is that in the French "case" (as in others, each in its way), the propensity to claim exceptionalism, and also the desire of others to applaud or deride this propensity, to a large extent come from the fact that the paradoxes of universality and the *conflicts* between different claims of universality, have become an object of public discourse itself, almost an obsession. And laïcité, inside and outside France, is one of the *proper names* of this obsession. This makes its genealogy and a structural analysis of its social and political functions, and an understanding of its limits, transformations and crises, all the more necessary and perilous.

Ideally, a critical discussion of laïcité in the past, the present, and the future would involve a twofold cross-examination. It should involve a relativization of the terminology itself, being compared with other terms such as *secularization*, but also *enlightenment*, *tolerance*, *pluralism*, *civility* or *civilization*, etc., each expressing a point of view on the institution of the political with respect to the religious environment, highlighting one of its aspects and reflecting a specific history. The list of alternative terms is open; it is not even sufficiently indicative, because it would be necessary to turn to the different national and cultural idioms and install a *multilinguistic confrontation*, beyond the limits of Western "universalistic" languages themselves.

This is or will become increasingly part of the problem in the years to come.

The discussion should also involve a confrontation between typical forms of the crisis and transformations that the theologico-political complex is undergoing everywhere in the world today: Israel is attempting to build a "secular" (or modern) state based on the religious identity of its dominant community; the United States has its "manifest destiny" challenged from outside and from inside, but also sees a new wave of politicization of the faith (in particular Protestant Evangelical revivalism); Algeria suffers a lethal conflict between religious fundamentalism and military secularism, which perhaps expresses only part of the crisis of the so-called Arab-Islamic identity; Iran oscillates between moments of forced westernization and moments of "religious revolution" combining anti-imperialism and clericalism; the Indian subcontinent combines a violent conflict of monotheistic and polytheistic cultures with a specific crisis of "national secularism"; Europe as such witnesses a renewal of the idea of the "Christian roots" of its cultural identity because of the postcolonial confrontation with Islam but also the divergent ways of instituting the relationship between church and state in its different "nations" (which to a large extent became autonomous entities in the premodern era around the solution that was found for this issue, deemed the "Westphalian compromise," each becoming in a sense an "exception" to an absent rule).[4]

Clearly the study of laïcité in the French variety is only a very partial, one-sided point of view on the multifaceted theologico-political complex which, to the great surprise of many, becomes (again) a key issue of our present, globalized history. The paradox and the challenge that we address in conferences prompted by the anniversary of the establishment of laïcité in France, I believe, lies in the fact that we are fully aware of this narrow limitation, while trying to formulate a general set of questions, through the critical discussion of this case, and the deconstruction of its presentation as a "model."[5]

Let me now indicate the order in which I shall examine the problems of laïcité, and foretell some of my hypotheses. This is not a deduction, only a juxtaposition, highlighting different sides of the question. In the first part, I will address what I have just called the "theologico-political complex," and I will present the hypothesis that, in French modern history, i.e., after the revolutionary reconstruction of the nation-state, whose core is a certain legal and symbolic definition of the universalistic *citizen*, the representation of the *community* and the attachment of the individual to the community have been negatively determined by the *failed attempt* at building a "civic religion" on a Rousseauist model.[6] So the ghost of Rousseau, the greatest French philosopher between Descartes and Comte—although he was not "French" himself, or perhaps just for that reason—was permanently haunting the French political machine, especially through his way of constructing the relationship between the law and the principle of equality. And laïcité in a sense is a *real*, historical *substitute* for this imaginary construction, which means at the same time achieving some of its goals and reversing its logic. In the second part, I will move to a more sociological point of view, trying to give some indications (i.e., again, formulating hypotheses) concerning the *hegemonic function* of laïcité in modern French history. The category of "hegemony," as you can imagine, has a Marxist background here: more precisely, it derives from Gramsci—who paid a keen attention himself to the French post-revolutionary history, comparing it with other European cases: the Italian *Risorgimento*, the German *Kulturkampf*, etc.[7] Therefore it deals with a certain institutional form of the reproduction of class domination, which does not rest on absolute political rule, but rather on a certain equilibrium of forces, and it involves the development of cultural and ideological forms which we may also call a *discourse*. However, to this broad idea of laïcité as a "bourgeois," therefore also "liberal," hegemonic public discourse, which provides a certain "language of politics" for the bourgeois state, I will add some other dimensions, in order to be able to explain—or simply discuss—the current manifestations of the crisis of this hegemonic model, probably irreversible, which is more acute because it is so deeply entrenched in the articulation of the state and the civil society. Finally, I hope to return to the philosophical side of the problem of laïcité, albeit always from the same historical perspective. I will argue that laïcité has—or, I should say, it *has had*, but this past not only weighs upon the present, it also prescribes tasks, and it opens a question for the future—a very contradictory relation to what historians of ideas and culture, but also sociologists, after Weber, have described as the continuous movement of the "secularization" of politics and society in the West. To describe laïcité as a simple expression or a particular institutional realization of this movement is misleading; it misses the contradiction and the tension involved here.

What seems to me to characterize the trajectory of laïcité, not as a destiny that would have been predictable in advance, but as an aleatory result of practices, compromises, inventions, displacements, is the contradictory fact that it can be considered in a sense a regression with respect to secularization, expressing a resistance to the "neutralization" of the religious element, while on the other hand it pushes it far beyond mere neutralization (or privatization), to embody a certain critical or skeptical aperture of the relationship between faith and reason, or belief and knowledge. On the one side, therefore, you have what I will dare to describe as the "monotheistic" (rather than *sacred*, or *pious*) character of laïcité, something that is easily perceived from outside France (only the French themselves have difficulty admitting it . . .), but which is also difficult to precisely interpret. On the other side, you have what I consider to be the permanent legacy of the Enlightenment—or perhaps we should say rather, again in French: *les Lumières*—in the history of laïcité as a spiritual and philosophical framework. But we also have the very problematic adaptation of this legacy to completely new conditions and forms of belief and knowledge, which derive in particular from the new global hegemony of *communication* processes and media.

On the background of this triple discussion, I suggest that my title should become reversed: namely, we should not only reflect on the *future of laïcité*, but we should also reflect on the (contingent and hypothetic) *laïcité of the future*. And beyond that: not only on the laïcité of the future, but also on *the religious and the religions of the future*, with which laïcité maintains such an ambivalent relation of internal opposition, involving both distance and iteration.

Theologico-political Complex, Nation as "Community of Citizens," and the Impossibility of "Civic Religion"

This is my first point—Rousseau is constantly behind us, but also ahead of us, as he was behind the revolutionaries and ahead of them: continuously revived, read otherwise, and criticized each time a restoration or a renovation of the republican form of the state was on the agenda during the nineteenth and twentieth centuries. This was the case several times, as we know. But Rousseau ought not to be the only reference. Contemporary scholars have initiated an original use of the work of Kantorowicz to interpret the process of secularization or *laicisation* of politics in what might appear at first as a paradoxical manner: since the famous scheme of the sovereign's dual nature in medieval and classical Europe, apparently concerns just the opposite, a persistent anchorage of the political in the realm of the sacred.[8] The problem here would be: what happens to the "two bodies" when the sovereign is no longer a *real person*, or an individual, but an ideal and practical *community*, i.e., a polity or citizenry. It would seem that this community must become duplicated itself, in order to allow for a *transcendent foundation* of its unity. This was more or less, we may remember, Marx's vision of bourgeois politics, especially in its French version (but he considered it "typical"): it worked as a "projection" of the actual divisions of the civil society into the "heavens" of the national unity, without which there would be no "body politics" (Karl Marx, *On the Jewish Question*, 1844).[9] But in Rousseau we find a different conceptualization, which does not operate at the level of transcendence: on the contrary, it operates in the horizon of *immanence*, forming an internal, and practical, relationship of the community with (and within) itself, with its own members. This is what Rousseau in the *Social Contract* defined as a "double rapport" (a *twofold* or *double relation*), which from one point of view regards the legislative function of the citizen, his (rather than her . . .) forming an "indivisible" part of the Sovereign, or the Nation expressing its perfect unity in the General Will (but also creating this unity through the General Will, which acts as *causa sui*); whereas from the opposite point of view it concerns the differential belonging of the citizen— qua "subject"—to what Rousseau (only then) calls *l'Etat* (the "state"): in this sense we would rather say today *la société*, since it is on this side that individual citizens emerge with their particular interests which, whatever their nature, can become the basis for the formation of "parties," claiming to represent their particularity in the realm of politics.[10] The key idea is that *the Law is not transcendent*, it is immanent to the community of the citizens, and the citizens have a double relation to it: collectively but also ideally, *they make it*, thus transforming themselves into a unitary or indivisible ("mystic") body; individually— *singulatim*, as Foucault would write—they are subjected to it, and it regulates their activities from outside.[11] As we also know, there is a normative, even a coercive character of this representation, not to say a "terrorist" one—which is what the counter-revolutionary rhetoric has continuously sustained.[12]

Now there is no doubt that what allows Rousseau (and the whole democratic and republican tradition after him) to hold this idea of an *immanent process* of unification and construction of the Sovereign People as a community of its own citizens, is his very strong concept of *equality*, or *equal liberty*.[13] And, in fact, Rousseau's notion of equality is just as twofold, or double-sided, as his notion of the citizen/subject itself: it is *equality in the making of the law*, "constituent power," or equal participation in the legislative function (even if through representatives—and we know that this posed a serious problem of "losing" equality, the reason Rousseau tended to reject it in favor of "direct democracy"), and it is *equality in the obedience to the law*, equal treatment of individuals, groups, interests, social responsibilities, by the law to which they are subjected (with equally well-known difficulties, as soon as the social differences also involve relations of power, which is inevitable with property, but also with education, culture, etc.). We retrieve these two sides of the law and their common foundation on the equality of citizens in famous passages of the *Déclaration des droits de l'homme et du citoyen* from 1789.[14]

Now my argument is the following: in the broad sense, as a "block" or a "system" of constitutional measures—ranging from the separation of Church and State in 1905 to the complete secularization of administrations, particularly the administration of *Justice*, and the establishment of a public, and (at least ideally) unitary school system, which would closely associate the development of rational knowledge, the teaching of morality, and the impregnation of the individual with patriotic values and legal principles—laïcité in Modern French history is nothing but *the political ideal of a community of citizens that is not transcendent*, governed from the inside in an immanent manner *by the rule of equality*. The creation of such a community, as Rousseau perfectly understood, would have required the emergence, and therefore the invention, of a *civic religion*: not in the sense of a sacralization or deification of the State, or more abstract political entities, but in the sense of an absolute, unconditional primacy of the value of equality, the mutual recognition of citizens as equals, over their divergent interests and relations of power. And it is the practical *impossibility to create such a civic religion*, despite repeated attempts (of which the *morale laïque*, to which I will return, with the active support of the school system, was a privileged and strikingly contradictory example), that may allow us to understand the much more complicated pattern that *actual, historical* ("really existing") laïcité in fact has taken in France. Tocqueville's testimony (in *Democracy in America*, vol. 1, 1835) is crucial here, because it shows that the only form in which a "civic (or civil) religion" can exist as a "religion of equality," is precisely one *that cannot exist in France*, but only in a "new nation" like the United States of America, where the relationship between religion, State, and society, reflects a totally different history (more "individualistic," but also more "communitarian" . . .).[15]

On one side we will observe the return of the sacred within the secular or the political discourse—or to put it à la Kantorowicz, the imaginary projection of a transcendent community, mainly in the form of *the sacralization of the Nation* as a quasi-divine, trans-historical entity (sometimes more "racial" or exclusive, sometimes more "cultural" or inclusive, but in practice always both), for which the citizens ought to sacrifice their lives: *pro patria mori* as a substitute for the "indivisible" participation in the collective sovereignty—especially activated in times of war.[16] And on the other side, what has been described as the final result of the century-long struggles between Church and State, nationalism and socialism, counterrevolutionary clericalism and liberal political ideologies—some rooted in the emancipation of discriminated religious communities (like the Protestants and the Jews), some rooted in the republican and democratic turn of the dominant Catholicism itself, others in the discourse of the positivist or rationalist sections of the bourgeoisie—namely a *compromise* (although an unstable one) between the religious and antireligious forces of society *regulated by the state* (what historian and sociologist Jean Baubérot calls *le pacte laïque*).[17] This is a typical product of "organic liberalism," as it was theorized between Guizot and Durkheim, half way between a *state-controlled* regime of cults (a "concordat" in the Napoleonic sense, whose memory is still haunting government policies toward Islam in today's France), and a more or less inclusive *self-regulated* form of religious autonomy of the civil society, usually referred to in the English speaking world as "toleration" in the Lockean tradition.[18]

Allow me to add four remarks on this interpretation of the genealogy of laïcité in terms of a failed attempt at establishing a "civic religion" in the Rousseauist sense, which means that it will remain permanently haunted by its ideal model, and that it practically works on completely opposite bases: not exactly *civic*, but *national* and *social*, or civic only inasmuch as the *citoyen* is a national subject and a social agent.

The first remarks concern the notion of laïcité as a *constitutional principle*, whose importance has been repeatedly emphasized in recent debates.[19] As I already mentioned, it was only rather late, in the 1946 Constitution, that the principle was enunciated as such: "La France est une République indivisible, laïque, démocratique et sociale," (France is an indivisible, secular, democratic, and social Republic) a formulation clearly determined by the fact that the French were reestablishing a Republican order after the tragic episode of the Nazi occupation and the Vichy regime, which had all but undermined these principles. But we should also remember that the Third Republic, the one that in the short time span of fifteen years passed all the great *lois laïques*, beginning with the creation of the public school system and ending with the compromise with the Catholic Church on the "separation," *did not have a formal Constitution*.[20] Leaving aside other more accidental reasons, I think that the two facts are closely associated: The Third Republic (the Republic of "les Républicains"), did not inscribe laïcité in the narrow sense in its implicit Constitution, but it progressively placed it at the core of the *material Constitution*, i.e., the block of political principles that must become intangible (sacred if you like) because they define the political regime, and in the end the very form of the State. But in reality, this was the completion of a much longer process, arising from the moment in which the transcendental foundation of the political community had been destroyed and rebuilt on different bases, with all the contradictory consequences that this Revolution produced over time.

Hence my second remark. I agree that laïcité should not be identified with, or reduced to the separation of Church and State, even if or precisely because the symbolic event—the one that is continuously invoked these days—coincides with an act of *separation* which—we ought to remember—explicitly concerns the material basis, the status of properties, or clerical assets.[21] The secular character of the public administration and the legal apparatus itself existed long before: it has roots in the Roman tradition, and the autonomization of the Monarchic State power in the premodern and modern periods. On the other hand, laïcité is not a principle or a rule that only governs the relationship between two powers, or two apparatuses (the Church and the State); it is a principle that regulates the relationship of the State with the society, the *standing* of the State within the Society that it rules. In Foucauldian terms, we might say that it is a principle of "government." In the middle of the evolution, the crucial turning point concerned the new representation of the national community, defined in terms of republican citizenship. And if the notion of laïcité in the French case was so closely associated with that of *citoyen-neté*, this was perhaps, negatively, because up to then the government of society, particularly at the moral level, had been so completely performed in a religious code by the Catholic Church, which itself had a religious monopoly granted by the State (a "monopoly of legitimate belief," so to speak); but it was above all, positively, because in a secularized society, where the state has become the sole representative of the society as a whole, mechanisms of *self-regulation*, self-limitation of the moral or ideological power of the State over the individuals were needed. The State should not become *sacred* itself. The "nation" as an ideal, a sublime body of the society, was sacralized, but not the State. Laïcité paradoxically worked as an internal limitation of the sacred, with it and against it.

Hence my third remark: in debates over the meaning of French laïcité, a recurring dilemma concerns whether its equation with *neutralité* refers to a neutrality or *neutralization of State interventions* within the realm of values, morality, religion, consciousness, or *the neutralization of religious influences* and memberships or forces within the public sphere (from justice to healthcare or *Santé publique*, and also, in the French case, the school system, or the established part of it (often referred to as *l' Ecole* with capital *E*). This dilemma again played a great role in recent debates about the Islamic veil and the displaying of religious symbols within the educational and medical institutions. Both interpretations are relevant indeed, which is a good index of what, after other writers (such as Pierre Rosanvallon), I have called here "organic liberalism."[22] But also, clearly, there is an unstable equilibrium here, in which either the State imposes constraints on the "free" development of religious (or cultural) tendencies originating within the society, or religious and cultural movements try to modify the definition of the public sphere. As all the best historians of laïcité—Baubérot, Poulat, Lalouette, and others—have observed, laïcité does not make religion a *private affair* which would be confined in private or rather domestic spaces, even if this motto regularly returns in the controversies: but it prevents religion from explicitly taking part in the definition of "public values," and for that reason it defines it as an expression of "private," meaning *particular, non-generalizable* interests or convictions.[23] What seems to lie behind these complicated shifts and balances is not simply a *religious neutrality*, it is something much more decisive: a relative or partial *neutralization of politics* itself, in the Schmittian sense, i.e., a delimitation of the sphere where the political conflict cannot rise to the extreme, or take the form of *"two nations" existing within the "indivisible" Nation*. What is at stake is, thus, the drawing of a line of demarcation between legitimate political competition and illegitimate political antagonism. At a certain point in history, this menacing possibility, which would undermine the State's monopoly of regulating the society ("government"), was represented or represented itself as a religious divide (Catholics and Protestants), or a "civil war" between religion and antireligion.[24] This has led to imposing upon "religions" a definition which makes them in the principle "apolitical," for them not to become *antipolitical*. It is indeed, historically speaking, a complete abstraction, if not a denial of reality—which also explains why, when social or cultural or ideological conflicts again seem to become polarized along religious lines, the whole "constitution" is shaken. The legitimacy of power is threatened. But to be honest, there is also the possibility that a political discourse *pictures a social or political antagonism as a religious conflict*, in order to raise the specter of a constitutional crisis and instrumentalize it . . .

Finally, I would insist on the idea which will provide us with a transition to a second set of problems, namely the originary association of laïcité with a conception of citizenship based on *equality* as a legal and political principle, without which liberty itself could not exist, thus becoming a paradoxical characteristic of the citizen as such (transforming a relation into a predicate: the republican citizen is "the equal human," for whom equality is part of his/her nature).[25] This has also very contradictory effects. It makes *discriminations*, including "religious discriminations," radically *illegitimate* (the problem becomes more difficult with "cultural" discriminations, or perhaps many uses of the concept "culture" are precisely meant to cover this gray zone). But it also provides the Nation (the National State, the French Republic) with a powerful instrument of social hypocrisy: The Republic and its political representatives can always tell the citizens: it is true, you don't enjoy perfect *égalité* (far from it), but you have *laïcité*, which is its quintessential expression in the realm of individual autonomy. However, this discourse also works conversely, as a permanent incitement to claim equality: because laïcité, which has replaced to some extent the missing civic religion, teaches that equality is inalienable, that it should prevail over other values if the community is at all to survive, citizens who are explicitly or covertly discriminated against because of their religion (or the quasi racial use of their religious affiliation, e.g., Muslims) can invoke the protection of a (somewhat idealized) laïcité to fight for recognition.

BOURGEOIS HEGEMONY AND REPUBLICAN *LAÏCITÉ*: THE QUESTION OF *POTESTAS INDIRECTA*

I associated a second set of problems with the notion of *bourgeois hegemony*, in an enlarged Gramscian sense.[26] I will skip theoretical and methodological considerations on the relationship of such a notion with the discussion of power structures, and the discussion of forms or modes of *domination*—only simply to admit that power structures, as Foucault has shown, are always unstable: they meet with resistances, they build on the capacity to control resistances or even to co-opt or instrumentalize them, and they are always heterogeneous, combining discursive elements and bodily elements, power in the form of knowledge and power in the form of discipline.[27] Let us also admit, with Max Weber, that the ultimate measure of domination is the probability to have its injunctions obeyed, i.e., to obtain *consensus*, legitimacy.[28] If laïcité has played such a decisive role in the progressive construction of what we may call a bourgeois hegemonic regime in France, with its astonishing capacity to survive dramatic political crises by providing antagonistic parties with a common language and cultural code, this is probably because laïcité really forms a crucial part of a bourgeois hegemony rooted in power-knowledge, in disciplines, in procedures which anticipate and reproduce a consensus prevailing over social antagonisms, while not abolishing them entirely. But isn't it also for the very same reason that it proves so difficult to adapt to other circumstances in which neither the social problems nor the cultural horizons and codes have remained the same—especially because they are less and less defined or definable in purely national terms? After the hegemonic moment comes the *crisis of hegemony*, and the crisis displays aspects that mirror the construction of the hegemony itself, affecting its core principles. Allow me to illustrate this idea by considering the *social question* on the one hand, the *centrality of the school system* in the constitutional fabric of laïcité on the other hand, and their articulation.

One striking aspect of debates and investigations prompted by the anniversary of the creation of laïcité in 1905 on the background of its current uncertainties, has been a renewed insistence on the correlation between the religious question and the social question in France, and the importance this correlation had in giving the leading roles to socialist or liberal-socialist leaders (such as Jean Jaurès and Aristide Briand) who pushed in the direction of an "open" laïcité that would not become equivalent with militant anticlericalism, and even less with an official atheism, but involved a recognition of religious pluralism in the society under the condition of its relative political neutralization.[29] The difficult question, however, which marks the difference between laïcité and other examples of "secularization" in the Western world, concerns the extent to which the educational system was located, not on the side of the "social," but on the side of the "political" (i.e., more than ever thought of in terms of *pouvoir spirituel* as Auguste Comte would say*)*, leading to a quasi monopoly of public education (and especially of *primary* education), to a unified school system where nevertheless it could be argued that *it is the school that "controls" the State as much as the State controls the school.*[30]

One should never forget that the completion and systematization of laïcité comes after the Century of Revolutions in Europe, and especially in France, where there was practically one insurrection for each generation, which each time raised the spectre of communism, and provoked bloody counterrevolutionary repressions. This was once again the case with the Paris Commune (1871), but shortly after that the *Républicains* launched a program of social policies that anticipated the social state, if not the welfare state, and simultaneously they laid the bases of laïcité as a firm ideological foundation for the so-called *pacte républicain*. That these developments also corresponded to the new wave of French colonial imperialism is another aspect of the same conjuncture, undoubtedly decisive for the nationalist construction of hegemony, to which I will return shortly. It was obviously crucial that, on this occasion, a majority of the Socialist movement, under the guidance of Jaurès, rallied the consensus around laïcité, and powerfully contributed to its institution, drawing more or less the same lines of demarcation as in the Dreyfus Affair on the questions of militarism and anti-Semitism. Beyond his philosophical convictions (an interesting combination of Fichte and Marx), it is well known that Jaurès explained that laïcité had to be established in order for "the religious question" to be closed, or *sealed*, and "the social question" to come to the fore, and become the essential object of political debate and activity in France. In short, even if not exactly in Marxist terms, it corresponded to a project of having the *real problems* addressed instead of the *imaginary* ones. Jaurès certainly thought of the necessity of allowing workers with a Christian denomination and workers with atheist convictions to work alongside, adhere to the same unions, and vote for the same Socialist Party—thus depriving the bourgeoisie of her capacity to instrumentalize the religious divisions of the peasantry and the working class. The irony of the situation, but also probably the reason for the success of this strategy, was that the bourgeoisie in the broad sense—including capitalists and the professional class, or *Noblesse d'Etat*, as Pierre Bourdieu calls it—had exactly the same need of a neutralization of the religious issue, in order to invent its own "social" strategies in the class struggle.[31]

Today we frequently hear social activists or sociologists, who are commenting on the volatile conflicts in the new proletarian districts populated by racially discriminated and heavily exploited migrants, explain that laïcité should be a crucial principle—with the necessary historical adaptations, including an effective and full recognition of Islam as a legitimate religion in the French, and more fundamentally, in the *European* space. This would allow it to finally focus on the social problems which call for social and economic solutions, without diverting them and covering them with a religious veil, or fueling the class antagonism with heterogeneous religious passions.[32] There is much truth, I believe, in this discourse—except that, practically, it is a circular one: the removal of the religious veil makes it possible to uncover the social questions whose clarification, in turn, would make it possible to remove or relocate the religious code in its "proper" place . . . This aporia reminds us of the "exceptional" but also highly ambiguous character of the hegemonic compromise that was achieved a century ago, at the time of the foundation of laïcité. It *did*, probably, make it possible for the working class and the Socialist movement to achieve political strength and influence, without which no social state or limitation of the degree of exploitation would have been possible in France—with such further consequences as the politics of the *Front Populaire* (1936–1938) producing an educational reform led by "Radical" Minister Jean Zay (a Freemason), that considerably democratized French society.[33] But it also led to the fact that, at some point, Socialist and Communist parties would rise in defense of laïcité and the state monopoly of education more vigorously than any other objective. This was how they were always able to overcome their political divisions: not on the terrain of the class struggle itself, but inasmuch as they jointly participated in mass demonstrations for laïcité. My generation, I may add, has a vivid memory of that twist: in the 1970s and 1980s, meetings and *journées d'action pour la défense de l'école laïque* tended to replace national strikes for the defense of social rights. In the end, the constitutional instrument used to put aside religious antagonisms would become an end in itself, or the "neutralization of religion" would have replaced "religion" in its role of ideological displacement of the social question. This probably paved the way for the perverse use of laïcité as a code word for nationalist exclusion of the new "Other": the postcolonial proletarian or *immigré*.

Let us now examine the other aspect of the question of hegemony that I mentioned, namely the centrality of the school and the educational program in the construction of laïcité. So much has been already said on this, and still, so much remains to be clarified! I need to be very schematic, though. There is clearly a specific *political* level, which is not purely French, but has equivalents above all in other European countries of dominant Catholic culture (Italy, Spain, Austria, Ireland, Poland . . .), coming from the fact that Catholicism was *both a religion and a centralized Church*, which is not the case—or not to the same extent—for other "religions," including other ("reformed") Christian denominations. As a religion, and a monotheistic one, it is deeply entrenched in the institutions of the patriarchal family and the education which govern the symbolic structures of alliance, genealogy, transmission of experience and knowledge, the distinction of truth and error ("orthodoxy"), individual and social morality ("orthopraxis"), endowing all of them with a sacred (or sacramental) meaning. As a *visible* church, which means a human institution "mixed" with the world but preparing the faithful for her "conversion," it organizes all these processes of meaning and culture in the form of a hierarchic structure of power, which it calls itself *spiritual*—a term that was borrowed from ecclesiastical history by some philosophers who inspired laïcité, particularly Auguste Comte, whose first significant work, written in 1826, was called *Considérations sur le pouvoir spirituel*.[34] Ultimately, it derived from Thomas Hobbes, who in his *Leviathan* from 1651 (the founding text of modern political philosophy), opposed the Catholic doctrine of *potestas indirecta* theorized by Cardinal Robert Bellarmin to justify a distribution of powers between the State and the Church (with the State governing the bodies and the Church governing the souls), not in order to eliminate the idea of the government of the souls, but, on the contrary, to explain that a political sovereignty of the State is possible only if the two powers are exercised in a coherent manner, by a single institution, albeit in two different modalities: "direct" and "indirect," or legal and educational.[35] It is worth recalling here, at least as a symbolic indication, that the Greek term *laos*, whence the French word laïcité is derived, which undoubtedly has a complex history, was originally a theological term (it meant the *people of God*, the *community* of the faithful).[36] Laïcité also has this meaning: in a deep sense it stripped the *laos*, the community, of its intrinsic relationship with the religious institution, and transferred *faith*, or some of its aspects, particularly *the moral aspects* (what the

Germans would call *Gewissen*, now reconciled with *Wissen*, or scientific knowledge), from the religious horizon to the national or political horizon. This meant that laïcité was not only a way to limit the role of religion in the public sphere, it was also a way to have secularism enter the *private, the domestic sphere*, to produce other forms of moralization of the private. It still is, to the extent that it remains alive—and we should notice right away that this lively character of laïcité in the French society largely relies on its implementation in the educational realm. Quite understandably, this was never possible without conflicts and compromises, as we keep witnessing today on issues of sexuality, marriage, procreation, "birth control" and abortion, euthanasia, etc. But in the period of actual hegemony, the conflicts were marginalized and the compromises reinforced the alliance of School and State against other social agencies.

Clearly, none of this was a simple phenomenon of the conjuncture, a matter of politics in the narrow sense, as it is carried on by parties, parliamentary majorities, etc. It concerned the *anthropological fabric of the Nation-State*, and its program of modernizing society.[37] It concerned therefore the possibility, perhaps the necessity, of permanently relativizing the absolute character of cultural memberships and traditions, in order to subjugate them and, to some extent, replace them with a *second-degree membership*, which is the participation in the "community of the citizens," mediated by the State, the Law, the political discourse of the "Republic." So, it amounted, abstractly speaking, to what in other places, following indications from Hobbes, Hegel, and Weber, I have called a double process of *virtual deconstruction* of primary identities, and *virtual reconstruction* of secondary identities, which can be a very violent process in a latent manner at least. In fact, as a process of transformation, a production of the "new human" of the nation, it is always violent, but usually achieved in a "soft" and mostly invisible or imperceptible manner, through the imposition of norms and disciplines, and the intellectual formation (*Bildung*) of subjectivities.[38]

In the French case, this was tendentially achieved through the construction of a central Ideological State Apparatus (to borrow Althusser's formulation), that associated the working of the (mainly public) educational system, and the political and social role of the family ("private" by definition). It is in their interaction that we find the core of the process of civic moralization, and conversely the reason for the permanent expression of laïcité in terms of social ethics and secular or secularized morality, for which the episode of the creation of *morale laïque* by the Third Republic, transforming the school teachers into *secular priests* (or perhaps *preachers*, on the Protestant model), is both typical and only partial.[39] A good testimony of the importance of this combined educational and familial ideological mechanism under the aegis of the State, is the fact that, for a long period, *associations de parents d'élèves* (corporations of student's parents) remained perhaps the single most important political structure of the French civil society, both supporting the political regime and constantly negotiating compromises with the State and the political parties at a *national* level (nothing comparable, therefore, with parents' associations in U.S. society, which are always *local*). A lasting consequence, perhaps a perverse one (but this is not only a sensitive matter, it is also a difficult problem), is the fact that the school system does not easily abandon the objective of *secularizing the family* in order to moralize it, directly or indirectly. Without examining this background, successive episodes of the question of the "Islamic veil" (but also debates about "sexual education" and "birth-control information" for girls) in French schools are impossible to understand—leaving aside (if possible) their instrumentalization by political and religious forces.

Now, as was already the case previously, these considerations call for commentaries and qualifications. Leaving aside—which is obvious—that the reality we are picturing here in terms of hegemony is neither simple nor stable, but a more or less precarious equilibrium, with powerful countertendencies (the Catholic Church, in a sense, never gave up its own "hegemonic" project), I next discuss three complementary aspects.

One of them is a clear consequence of the fact that, laïcité not being a unanimous "civic religion" set up a priori by the General Will, or coinciding with the institution of citizenship as the Rousseauist model would imply, but a social and political compromise expressed in universalistic terms, the "spiritual power" was always shared. In particular, it was split along lines of division of *the public and the private*. Perhaps the most important aspect here concerns the highly contradictory effect of laïcité on the public condition of women in French modern history, and their equivocal inclusionary exclusion, or exclusionary inclusion, in the public sphere. There is little doubt that, particularly after the *Front Populaire* in 1936 and the *Libération* in 1945, educated or rather intellectual women immensely benefited from the working of the public school system which is an essential part of laïcité, as the great feminist historian Michelle Perrot and others have argued.[40] Not only the "daughters of educated men" would become educated themselves, as Virginia Woolf famously wrote (in *Three Guineas*, echoing the protest of Mary Wollstonecraft, but also others). However, there is also little doubt that the French *République laïque* not only was one of the latest Western "democracies" to enfranchise women as active citizens, but it was also one where the resistances to admit women to the legislative and governmental functions (i.e., in Rousseauist terms, the participation in the "indivisible" sovereign) are strongest and most entrenched, as shown by Geneviève Fraisse and others.[41] It seems impossible not to associate this fact—which, for example, explains some of the oddities of the recent debate over *parité*, as perceived from outside France[42]—with the other fact, that part of the historical compromise between Church and State (which some authors ironically called *catholaïcité*), was the reservation of secular morality and patriotism for men, and the long abandonment of women to the more or less complete control of their souls (convictions) and bodies (sexuality) exercised by the Church. Generally speaking, the bourgeois secular Republic tended to use the Church or the Churches (or religious bodies) as a "transmission belt" to control "minorities": women, workers— better a Clerical influence than a Communist one—"natives" in the colonies . . . (whose sum total indeed makes a huge majority of the population).[43]

In the case of the working class, this process of exclusion from full citizenship would certainly have lasted for decades or indefinitely, if it were not for the development of class struggles and the Labour movement, which powerfully challenged it. This takes us back to the program of Jaurès, and the achievements of the Popular Front. But again we are facing a considerable ambiguity. The protracted political struggle within the "constitutional" consensus on laïcité, and the deep identification of the Republic with its educational function, which tried to expand and displace its social limits, produced a profound *national* conviction that the *main form of social equality*, i.e., the one that truly concerns the political community, is *égalité des chances*: equal opportunity provided to individuals by the school system. All bourgeois societies are indeed meritocratic, at least in principle.[44] However, France has transformed meritocracy not only into an instrument of selection for the elites, but into a principle of national unity and cohesion. The access to the *Ecole unique*, and the collective promotion, over several generations, to professional recognition and middle-class standard of living—in short, upward mobility through education— has been the dream of the working class since the beginning of the Third Republic. But this dream has now collapsed, and the French working class is today further away from achieving it than it ever was, the condition of migrants being only one aspect of this general drawback (not even always the worst). This produces at the heart of the public space not only resentment, but despair. And the political consequences of despair are unpredictable . . .

Finally, I would like to say that, obviously, what I have described as the *hegemonic functions of laïcité*: a form of "organic liberalism," a combination of school and family in a single albeit complex "ideological State apparatus" in the service of political consensus, worked only (or only in its typical form) *for the national citizen*. It excluded the colony, or rather it created an interstitial space of huge dimensions, located between the two boundaries which separate the national territory from the empire, and the empire from the external world (today largely reproduced or replicated in a postcolonial manner within the national territory itself).[45] These are certainly no clear-cut boundaries, and the intermediary space is more than any other a space of confrontations between competing logics: this is indeed where the *missionary* dimension of laïcité becomes displayed. It has one foot in emancipatory aspects of modernization, particularly inasmuch as the access to the world culture is involved, and one foot in sheer *racism*, in its typical French guise, which imposes the test of cultural assimilation as an absolute condition for the recognition as "full" or "equal" human being. Fanon never tired of emphasizing this contradiction.[46]

A PARADOXICAL INSTITUTION OF THE UNIVERSAL

This leads me to a last point, which for the sake of brevity I will combine with my conclusions or final hypotheses. The relationship of laïcité with *universalism*, or, as I said in the beginning, the function of laïcité as a paradoxical *institution of the universal*, deserves a whole complex discussion: on a "local" and "singular" point of discursive enunciation, the universal becomes at

the same time *appropriated*, therefore reversed into its opposite, and *expanded*, therefore carried beyond the boundaries
of a specific Nation or Culture. Perhaps we could adopt here
Derrida's oxymoronic composition: the universal becomes *ex-
appropriated*, an idea which indeed also concerns "democracy,"
"scientific knowledge," etc. In short, all the aspects of the universalistic discourses inherited from the Enlightenment. I would
insist again on the violent tension that is at stake here. I see two
tendencies in the history of laïcité, and I don't believe that they
can be easily *isolated* from one another. This is precisely where
we need not only facts, or political analyses, but *interpretation*,
and *deconstruction*. It is not by chance that I quoted Derrida, and
his philosophical oxymoron: ex-appropriation.[47] His expression
also hints at a task, an intellectual action. But if we want to disentangle and separate the inseparable, we might say that laïcité
combines a *theological* and a *sceptical* move.

My guiding thread here is in good part derived from the
Hegelian analysis of the intimate conflict between belief or faith
(*Glauben*) and knowledge, intellectual formation or Enlightenment (*Wissen, Bildung, Aufklärung*) in the *Phenomenology
of Spirit*, which concludes with his famous description of the
revolutionary Terror.[48] This is an indication of how violent the
conflict involved here could become, but the lesson is also that
each antithetic term bears an intrinsic, internal relation to the
other. They are not existing or thinkable *apart* from one another.
So, there is *an element of faith* in the laïcité that has remained
permanent (it was not only acknowledged but proudly vindicated by such Republican philosophers as Ferdinand Buisson,
author of *La foi laïque*). But there is also a deep element of
scepticism that continues the critical "materialist" side of the
radical Enlightenment (in Jonathan Israel's terms).[49]

The element of faith is clearly associated with the missionary dimension, the messianic belief in the virtues of linear
progress that also, indeed, allowed it for the French nation to

present itself as the beacon of civilization for the rest of the world, and proves so difficult to abandon retrospectively—just as it will prove difficult for the United States to abandon the idea that they were showing the world the way to democracy, or that democracy is a specific "American value," when the time comes for that . . . I see no better possibility, in order to highlight the theological element in this belief, than to call it an additional monotheism, or one monotheism *more*. This is a monotheism without a personal God, to be sure, but not without *persons*, as illustrated in the *Religion de l'Humanité* proposed by the Saint-Simonians, Auguste Comte, and "utopian" socialists such as Pierre Leroux (1841). The *Déclaration des droits de l'homme et du citoyen*, which is often allegorically represented as new *Tables of the Law* with a direct allusion to the Revelation of Moses, enunciates the ideal core of this additional monotheism, which indeed would not have been possible without the age-old confrontation between the secular representation of human rights and the theological doctrine of revelation. If you leave aside this discursive or ideological structure, you have difficulty understanding the forms that the rejection of Islam has taken in the French case. Because Islam also is an *additional monotheism* in the French cultural space, which comes "from outside," whereas laïcité comes "from inside," and which has multisecular history whereas laïcité is only slightly more than a century old now. But two candidates competing for a single space is difficult to handle. No wonder Islam is systematically pictured as anti-laïcité, or as the religion which "by nature," is incompatible with laïcité, or whose introduction within the "concordat," the "historical compromise," or the "social contract" that is laïcité would simply destroy it (or spiritually corrupt it, by forcing it to give up its principles). And as a consequence, a sort of new war of religion is lurking, which does not simply oppose traditional religions among themselves, but *two discourses of belief*, across the barrier of revelation. This is what I had in mind when I said that, in a sense, laïcité was less than secular, if we admit that there is something like a "normal" form of secularization—which is problematic.

But in a different sense laïcité is perhaps more than secularization, particularly since secularization or modernization tends to adopt the form of a *general equivalence* of ideas, a process of *communication* where all discourses and the corresponding beliefs or subjectivities become relativized and, by the same token, legitimized. In laïcité there is a cultural element which has to do with the fact that *belief* and *knowledge* are *both inseparable and contradictory*. This would not be a problem if they belonged to separate realms: but this is not the case, even in *scientific* matters, perhaps above all in scientific matters, at least in the case of anthropological disciplines which touch the living, thinking, acting, and feeling subject—from biology to psychology to economics. *Scientism* is the ideology which insists that the domains of belief and knowledge can become radically separated institutionally and epistemologically: but precisely, in a striking illustration of the Hegelian dialectic of the reversal of truth into its opposite, *scientism* itself is a typical and perhaps an extreme form of modern belief or faith. This is what made it possible for Nietzsche, in a famous passage of *The Gay Science* (1882) to exclaim: "we are still pious" (*Inwiefern auch wir noch fromm sind*) (§ 344). So, a permanent critical activity of the understanding—a Cartesian and Spinozistic term that I prefer to "reason"—is needed, which tends to separate, or dislocate, the inseparable: not to keep one side and reject the other, but to make it possible to work with both in a free manner, or in a manner that is somewhat freer. This aspect of scepticism is *also* included in the historical experience of laïcité, and particularly in the experience of critical anthropological thinking within the Academia, whose last ambitious formulation perhaps was structuralism. I tend to associate this side of laïcité with a certain radical legacy of the Enlightenment, and I would agree with Catherine Kintzler that such names as Marquis de Condorcet are very inspirative here, perhaps combined with others: for example, it is a good exercise to read again Rousseau's *Second Discourse* in order to correct the mythology of progress that Condorcet shared with many of his contemporaries, and that was so influential in spreading Western "secular" messianicism.[50]

In lieu of a conclusion, I simply return to my title, presenting it as a genuine *question* which remains open: What future for laïcité? We don't know, but we can suspect that this future must involve a complete philosophical and political reformulation. It would exist only if something like a *laïcité of the future* emerges—perhaps a French "translation" of a much broader and more reciprocal, more widely equalitarian program. But in turn the laïcité of the future, if it is to emerge, would depend on hypothetic transformations of the conditions and functions of the *religions* as such in the world and in each region. *New religions* or creeds with a "religious" dimension: ecology here looks like a good candidate. Or *reformed* versions of the old religions, particularly the old intolerant forms of monotheism. This would also mean that the rules after which the line of demarcation between the religious and the political is drawn, or the legitimate and the illegitimate forms of combining religious values with political objectives, should be redefined. This seems to be inevitable and forms one key objective for a transnational political culture, but also clearly one of the most volatile and hazardous objects of today's and tomorrow's politics.

PART III
STATEMENTS

13.

THREE WORDS FOR THE DEAD AND THE LIVING
(AFTER *CHARLIE HEBDO*)

An old Japanese friend of mine, Haruhisa Kato—formerly a professor at Todai University—wrote to me with this: "I've seen the images of all of France in mourning. I've been deeply moved by all this. Over the years I really loved Wolinski's collections. I have always been a subscriber to the *Canard enchaîné*, and I enjoyed Cabu's "Beauf" cartoons every week. I still have his collection *Cabu et Paris* by my desk, including a number of fine drawings he did of Japanese girls, tourists having fun on the Champs-Élysées." But further on, he offered this reservation: "The January 1 *Le Monde* editorial starts with the words 'A better world? This firstly supposes an intensified struggle against the Islamic State and its blind barbarism.' I was very struck by this statement, a rather contradictory one I thought, that we need a war for the sake of peace!"

Others have written to me from all over the world—Turkey, Argentina, the United States . . . all of them expressing compassion and solidarity, but also concern. Concern for our security, for our democracy, for our civilization—I was about to say, for our souls. I want to reply to these people, at the same time as responding to *Libération*'s invitation to comment. Intellectuals ought to express themselves, not on account of some privileged insight or particular lucidity, but also without reticence or ulterior calculations. It is a duty incumbent upon them: at the hour of danger, they have to spread the word. Today, in this urgent situation, I just want to talk about three words.

The First Is "Community"

Yes, we need community: for mourning, for solidarity, for protecting one another, for reflection. This community is not exclusive, and more particularly it does not exclude those people—whether French citizens or immigrants—whom an increasingly virulent propaganda reminiscent of the darkest hours of our history paints in the colors of invasion and terrorism in order to make them the scapegoats of our fears, our delusions, or our impoverishment. But nor does it exclude those who believe what the *Front National* says, or those who are seduced by Houellebecq's prose.[1] So, the community has to talk to itself. And that doesn't stop at the borders, since it's clear enough that the sharing of the sentiments, responsibilities and initiatives sparked by the current "world civil war" has to be something that's done in common, at an international level, and if possible (Edgar Morin is quite right on this point) within the framework of a "cosmopolitics."[2]

That is why community is not the same thing as "national unity." This latter concept has in practice only ever served disreputable goals: imposing a silence over troubling questions or having people believe that a state of exception is unavoidable. Even the Resistance [during World War II] did not invoke this term (and with good reason). And now we have seen how in calling for a national day of mourning—as is his prerogative—the president of the republic took advantage of it in order to slip in a justification for our military interventions, which he's apparently certain haven't done anything to push the world any further down its current slippery slope. After which we had all the debates (and they're a trap) about which parties are and aren't "national," on whether or not they should bear this name. Is the intention to compete with Ms. Le Pen?

The Second Is "Imprudence"

Were the *Charlie Hebdo* cartoonists imprudent? Yes, but the word has two meanings, which can more or less easily be separated (and of course this is somewhat subjective). Firstly, disregard for danger, a taste for risk, some would call it heroism. But also, indifference toward the disastrous consequences, in the end, of a well-intentioned provocation: in this case, the humiliation of millions of people who are already stigmatized, delivering them to manipulation at the hands of organized fanatics. I think that Charb and his comrades were imprudent in both senses of the word. Today, now that this imprudence has cost them their lives—at the same time exhibiting the mortal threat to freedom of expression—I just want to think about this first aspect of imprudence. But tomorrow and the day after that (and this isn't just a matter for a single day) I really want us to reflect on the most intelligent way of dealing with this second aspect of imprudence and how it relates to the first. And that doesn't necessarily imply any sort of cowardice.

And the Third Is "Jihad"

I'm deliberately finishing with the word that people are so afraid of, since it's high time that we examined all its implications. I have only the beginnings of an idea of this subject, but I'm pretty keen on it: *our fate is in the hands of Muslims*—however imprecise this term is. Why? Because of course it's right to warn against amalgams and to counter the Islamophobia that claims that the Koran and the hadiths call for murder. But that's insufficient.

The only way to answer the exploitation of Islam by jihadist networks—whose main victims both worldwide and in Europe itself are Muslims, lest we forget—is a theological critique, and ultimately a reform of the religion's "common sense," thus making believers see jihadism as a fraud. If not, we will all be caught in the deathly stranglehold of terrorism—with its power of attraction for all the people in our crisis-ridden society who are humiliated and offended—and "securitarian" policies that bludgeon our freedoms, policies being implemented by ever more militarized states. Thus, Muslims have a certain responsibility, or rather a task, incumbent upon them. But that's also our responsibility, and not only because the "we" I'm talking about—in the here and now—by definition includes a lot of Muslims. It's also because the already small chances of such a critique and such a reform will be reduced to nil if we continue to accept the isolating discourse of which Muslims—and their religion and culture—are generally the target.

POSTSCRIPT (2017)

Among the many reactions produced by this article—at times favorable, at times hostile, or simply raising objections—I want to single out those from friends and colleagues who disputed the formula that "our fate is in the hands of Muslims," and the idea that "Muslims have a certain responsibility, or rather a task incumbent upon them." They were feeling or fearing that my words coincide with the dominant discourse in the West that identifies the "roots" of terrorism in Islam, and urges members of the "Muslim community" to acknowledge collective responsibility and undertake a reform of their religion to adapt it to "civilized" standards.[3] I want to reply along three lines:

1. I fully acknowledge the ambiguity of my formulations, which is not only a result of the emotions produced by dramatic events, but which is intrinsic to the situation. Therefore, it cannot be simply eliminated (much less avoided by keeping silent), but it must be worked through, by means of discussions, further reflections, and a collective invention of better formulations. Ambiguities arise from the "enunciative" paradoxes involved in statements being issued at a certain *place* and made in the name of a certain *"we"*. Although, as a consequence of globalization, phrases are heard and can produce effects everywhere, it is not equivalent to speak or write in Paris, or Bagdad, or Timbuktu, or Djeddah, or New York. . . . And to think of oneself as an "independent voice" is not enough to make this independence (from dominant discourses, biased representations, vested interests, etc.) effective. This quite naturally leads to the question of "who is *we*?" Although granted a limited space by the format in which I am writing, I have been very careful to indicate that, in today's world, there is no such thing as an "us vs. them" divide, with "Westerners" (or "Europeans") on one side, and "Muslims" on the other side. To achieve such a divide is one of the goals of terrorism and counterterrorism (including preemptive counterterrorism), and of course its possibility is rooted in the postcolonial distribution of the world. "Muslims," whether they define themselves in terms of a tradition or a religion, do not form a homogeneous *social* or *political* community. They are massively present on each side of the geopolitical borders. The virtual "community" I referred to was a civic community, made of "co-citizens," who overcome divisions, but do not suppress them. A *double inscription* therefore is always at work in the use of "we" in the text, indicating a location where multiple identities and belongings are present, and can clash. It need not be understood in the same manner from every place: exclusionary resonances are part of the problem, common references and ideals would be part of the solution.

2. By writing that "Muslims have a certain responsibility, or . . . task incumbent upon them," I mean to transmit the initiative to subjects who identify as "Muslims" (whichever nationality and allegiance they may have), instead of leaving them in a position to receive instructions and injunctions, more or less explicitly backed with threats. A *responsibility* in the full, active sense is defined and exercised by those very subjects whose actions can make a difference for the public. The word "responsibility" is not automatically synonymous with liability. It is a political and moral shifter, which can serve to either restrict the freedom and deny equal status of some groups, or to enhance their autonomy and historical agency, in particular when it comes to achieving a task of common (or even universal) interest that no others can perform in their stead. I was therefore insisting on the fact that the initiative of Muslims (as many as possible, as diverse as possible, as unanimous as possible) would play the decisive role in counteracting the *religious* conditions of contemporary *jihadism* (which also permanently targets them and destroys their civilization), while also empowering them, because nobody else has a right and capacity to talk *in the name* of Islam (which is not to say that nobody has a right to discuss Islam). What I did not say, however, or not strongly enough, was that, for Muslims to find themselves in a position to speak (and think) freely about their religion and its political uses in the present, *another condition is required*, which is "our" responsibility toward them ("we," the non-Muslim citizens of the world, especially in the Western countries): to ceaselessly and successfully combat Islamophobia and discrimination against Muslims, and more generally renounce military, cultural, and administrative policies that aim at their subjection. This shows that, although there is no symmetry, there exists nevertheless a reciprocity or determination between different "responsibilities."

3. A crucial point remains to be discussed: are there actually *religious* conditions of terrorism? I think this can't be denied. But the "evidence" provided by the *name* which serves as justification, and which has become a global specter, is not enough. As I argued elsewhere (in *Saeculum*), there is no violence (whether legitimate or not) whose causes are purely religious (or purely ideological). Religious determinations make sense only as parts of a complex with many others, which are economic, political, and geopolitical. To "derive" *jihadism* from "Islam" as if religion—or *this religion*—generates violence by virtue of its essence, is sheer absurdity. Religion is but *one* of the ideologies that can become murderous when circumstances permit and if agents appropriate them. It is also not possible to ascribe a religious determination today *only* to movements and groups that invoke an Islamic justification or even a divine mission (such as Al-Qaeda and ISIS), because, with different forms and perhaps weight, this determination is also present on the side of "secular" states (some of which, in fact, are not so secular, since they claim sovereign or transcendent legitimacy, they call themselves "Nations under God"). Most of the time, the "causes" that push individuals of very different origins and culture to undertake criminal actions in the name of Allah or for the defense of the Prophet, include various combinations of psychological instability, social and racial stigmatization, anti-imperialist or anti-modernist imaginary, and political detestation of the established order in the West for which Islam has become the public enemy. Still, I find it very difficult to understand that all these determinations crystallize into a single "sacrificial" outburst of destruction and self-destruction without the symbolic name *jihad*, at the same time fascinating and redeeming, acting as a catalyst. Hence the necessity of a "theological critique" of this concept, i.e., an *immanent elucidation* of its meaning and its powers, combined with accurate history of its uses. Practically, the public opinion in Western societies (academic "Islamology"

notwithstanding) is in a state of mental confusion about these. And, by definition, there is more possibility to resolve the enigma on the side of cultivated people with an Islamic culture, residing in the Orient or the West, including many who are themselves Muslim. It is for them, with their intellectual resources and their moral commitment, to define the kind of exegesis, reformation, or historical critique that can disintricate the contradictory elements of piety and conquest, government of the self and government of others, universalism and communalism, that belong to the meaning of *jihad* in Islam. They will succeed in achieving this convincingly if they feel that they are called by "us" all to provide a vital and exchangeable intelligibility, not to acknowledge a collective guilt. I am convinced myself that the "war of subjectivities" which, according to Fethi Benslama, is an integral component of the global "state of war" into which most of us can become precipitated, is not affecting only Muslim subjects (or those with a Muslim heritage).[4] Nevertheless, since they find themselves on both sides of the battle, as perpetrators and victims, modernists and fundamentalists, speakers and objects of discourse, they must play a central role in laying bare its religious determinations. A crisis of civilization that affects all nations and peoples is not confronted through eliminating or silencing its protagonists. It is collectively resolved only if they raise a legitimate voice.

14

ON "FREEDOM OF EXPRESSION" AND THE
QUESTION OF "BLASPHEMY"

1. FREE SPEECH FROM SUBJECTIVE "PROPERTY" TO "EQUAL LIBERTY"

1.1. Freedom of expression must be considered in an extended sense that includes not only diverse means of expression but the complete situations of communication subjected to conflictual relations of power in a "globalized" world. These are two different extensions, but they become correlative in a public space where not only ideas, discourses, and messages, but also images, spectacles, and reports of collective events are circulating across borders through a number of old and new media.[1]

1.2. "Liberal" definitions and regulations of freedom of expression are conceived in terms of a "subjective right" of the person whose model is *private property*: hence, regulations are conceived as "limitations" imposed before or after *the event* to avoid detrimental effects on others' rights. As John Stuart Mill famously stated (*On Liberty*, 1859): "an opinion only carries intrinsic value to the owner of that opinion, thus silencing the expression of that opinion is an injustice to a basic human right."[2]

1.3. A more adequate model must rely on the representation of speech and expression as a dialogical process including a reciprocity of effects and an *anticipated response* to "speech acts" which is preserved or destroyed: hence it will be conceived as a *public good*, combining "equal liberties," that a democratic constitution ought to collectively maximize. What forms the public good is not only the *result* of free speech, but its *exercise*. This arises both from the "ontological" evidence that opinions (in the generic sense) do not *precede* their expression in the public, but *result* from dialogue, interaction, "differends" (in Lyotard's sense), "excitation" (in Butler's sense), and from the imperative to incorporate the society's powers into its political constitution in a constructive manner, where each individual is empowered when the response of others is accepted as a condition of her own autonomy. Monopolistic, oligarchic or one-sided "appropriation" of the exercise of free speech and the power of expression therefore is not only a contingent limitation of the freedom of expression, but a destruction of its content.[3]

2. TERROR EFFECTS IN THE SPACE OF IMPERFECT COMMUNICATION

2.1. The "regulating idea" of perfect communication or "ideal speech situation" (Habermas) where freedom of speech would be "normative" (i.e., either natural or imposed) must be inverted.[4] The real conditions of "unconditional" democratic exercise of free speech concern the radical transformation of the always already existing situation of "imperfect communication" that is saturated with violence and where terror effects are virtually possible, or become actual.

2.2. It is true, but insufficient, to explain that the social "classes" that own wealth, economic, cultural, and geopolitical power *also* control (i.e., *monopolize*) to a greater or lesser extent the possibilities of legitimate "expression," hence tend to *privatize* the "public good" of free speech.

2.2.1. Why? Because one has to account for the exclusionary effect inherent in the "codes" of dominant discourses, invalidating "subaltern" discourses and preventing their voicing in the public space. This is the structural *discursive* violence: the "subaltern cannot speak" (Spivak) and who cannot speak is/remains a "subaltern" in the constituency.

2.2.2. Structural discursive violence randomly generates different reactions: resistance, claims of the repressed voices (protests, laments), or counterviolence (discursive and nondiscursive), therefore performative displacement or mimetism. A violent reaction to violence is also a *limit form* of expression which may represent the only possibility for oppressed groups (e.g., colonized peoples, the "wretched of the earth" defined by Fanon) or "minorities" to be heard and impose recognition of their rights. Whether it is or becomes self-destructive is perhaps the most difficult political issue, which depends both on a correlation of forces and on ethical orientations of the group.

2.3. It is true that structural discursive violence relegates more or less completely many citizens (perhaps the majority) outside of "citizenship" in the active sense, but this is insufficient: it also deprives the society of the possibility to *know* its own constitution, thus extending a *veil of ignorance* over the constituency.[5]

2.3.1. This is true for the "dominants" as well, who tend to justify this ignorance in terms of "universalistic" discourses. A *negative* characteristic of universalism is therefore its tendency to suppress its own historical conditions, establishing self-referentiality instead of self-reflection or self-criticism. When conceived not as a political construction of the citizens themselves, in their intrinsic plurality, but as an *absolute*, universalism denies its own limits and resistances, therefore it *doesn't know itself.*

2.3.2. "Acts of terrorism" and "counterterrorism" are essentially aiming at *suppressing* every possibility of a "feedback" or "response" that is not mimetic to a first interpellation: therefore, they involve censorship and self-censorship. But the "threat" would not be effective if the "veil of ignorance" did not blind everyone with respect to the identity and the position of her "others," hence herself.

2.4. The political objective of establishing *the conditions of the unconditional freedom* is not simply to create a constitutional framework for the freedom of expression, but to listen to the suppressed or distorted voices, make room for their conflictual, even provoking utterance, and lift the veil of ignorance: in other words, cross and displace every boundary that limited the reciprocity of interpellations. To invent or implement the conditions of the unconditional is politics as such.

3. "BLASPHEMY," "INSULT," AND THE METASTASES OF THE SACRED

3.1. The *Charlie Hebdo* affair, with its multiple contexts, retroactively appears as a multiplier of terror effects, which powerfully contributed to framing perceptions and discourses, before they were "captured" by war.[6]

3.2. On one side, there is need to discuss the claim by authors and publishers of the cartoons that they were uttering a sign of "equality" toward the Muslim citizens.[7] The subtext of this claim is the enactment of a typical discursive violence also illustrated by injunctions to Muslim citizens to publicly "disavow" terrorism if they wanted to be assimilated to the majority and considered "compatriots". They were reduced to silence through the double bind of accepting a negative (criminal) image of their identity or distancing themselves from their own "religion."

3.3. On the other hand, there is need to discuss the claim by Muslim voices that the outrage at the cartoons had nothing to do with *blasphemy* but was linked to a feeling of collective *insult* or *injury* wounding the "community."[8] This seems to be true and untrue.

3.3.1. There is massive use of the category "blasphemy" in Islamic countries (such as Pakistan, Saudi Arabia, and more recently Indonesia) subjected to the influence of fundamentalist interpretations of the shari'a and using tribunals against atheists, or men and women belonging to religious minorities deemed unrespectful of the Koran. On their side, "secularist" discourses use *blasphemy* as a projective category to imaginarily penetrate the theologico-political space of the "Muslim world" without engaging with it, while remaining protected in the "Western secular" space and claiming its state protection; they tend to erect themselves as proud "blasphemers."

3.3.2. Behind the question of "blasphemy" there really lies the question of the importance of *sacred* values, institutions, and words that exist in every society to various degrees, either in religious or secular forms (the latter, essentially *national*), or a combination of both. The same speakers who denounce the repressive effects of the sacred in non-Western societies are blind or biased when it comes to the repressive effects of the sacred in Western democratic societies.

3.3.3. The mimetic response of Islamic fundamentalism (and a fortiori, terrorism) to Western secular (republican) Islamophobia also played on the "confusion" of religious symbolism (the sacred) that is inherited as a shared tradition, with an "organic" unity or solidarity of the believers, by trying to revive an archaic concept of the *ummah*: "insulting the honor" of the Prophet, forcing Muslim women to take off their veils, which are part of their personal identity, are presented as physical injuries inflicted on a collective "body."

3.4. Muslims and non-Muslims alike are thus caught in the production of an "Islamic identity" that relies on projections based on fear, hatred, and above all, ignorance: to "deconstruct" these mechanisms is the task of "intellectuals" of different sides, trying to make free speech *possible, hence* real. Admittedly, their most pressing obligations regard the criticism of ideologies that are dominant in the community/constituency with which they have closer material and moral ties, or to which they "belong."

4. BORDERS INSIDE AND OUTSIDE THE COMMON PLACE

4.1. To decide that certain peoples, bearing a certain "civilization," are essentially incapable of cultivating freedom of speech or expression because of their history and their collective psychology, is a typical form of orientalism, most of the time inherited from colonialism, and participating in the construction of contemporary racism.

4.1.1. A corollary of this prejudice is the self-legitimizing idea that freedom of expression is *per se* a Western democratic "value" which is inherent in the institutions of the liberal state (authoritarian or totalitarian regimes forming a regrettable exception). This can be pushed quite easily to the idea that freedom of expression is threatened from *outside* more than *inside* the liberal state. Hence it should be imposed outside by whichever means to remain protected inside.

4.1.2. A symmetric corollary is *inverted orientalism*: the idea that freedom of expression is a Western democratic "value" which is inherent in the imperialist domination and Eurocentric hegemony. This can be pushed quite easily to the idea that freedom of expression is a weapon to disintegrate non-European societies and cultures, therefore it should be resisted and fought against in order to protect vital collective traditions.

4.1.3. Taken together, orientalist and inverted orientalist discourses define the great *imaginary border* ("faultline," in Huntingtonian jargon) that dramatizes the political confrontations of the global world, making each side of the border, as it is projected on the maps, an object of hatred and fear.

4.2. Whereas the modern Eurocentric "Nomos" of the Earth, in terms of communications as well as political institutions, was based on a primacy of national and imperial borders, the "Nomos" of Globalization coincides with the expansion of electronic communication, seemingly borderless, which relativizes territorial borders and becomes intertwined with the circulation of commodities and labor power in a single market. News and values are themselves distributed like commodities, and the same financial power that displaces humans also controls their access to knowledge. This is the *universal space* where freedom of expression must now define its regime.[9]

4.2.1. Universality, however, is not homogeneity. The "liquidity" (Baumann) of the global communications across boundaries and the "ubiquity" of its network (reaching individuals anywhere on the planet and gathering them into virtual communities), is perfectly compatible with different kinds of "internal borders," which produce new *partitions* of the planetary public space, or reproduce old ones to sustain monopolistic and oligarchic regimes of power. There is a *(dis)location of power*. Among these differences is, tendentially, the distinction of conservative societies (e.g., authoritarian, patriarchic and paternalistic, theocratic—or a combination of these), where it is mainly a deviant opinion or conduct that is censored and punished (as sacrilegious, immoral, unruly), and liberal societies (combining freedom of circulation and freedom of opinion), where it is mainly otherness, alienness, "minority" status that is discriminated against and silenced, sometimes eliminated. Dominations locally and globally obey different patterns, resistances as well, even if they "resonate" or become dissonant. [10]

4.2.2. Visible censorship of media and interdiction of blasphemy, or invisible monitoring and gathering of personal and collective data, are two different forms of "police" restricting expression, which follow different anthropological models and use different techniques. Although they don't add up in a logical manner, they can overlap. It is their concrete combination in a specific moment and place (Erdogan's Turkey, Obama's America) that defines the degree of freedom and equality available for individuals and groups in a given society. It is hardly possible to *hierarchize* societies, countries and civilizations after such criteria, especially in the long term, but it is certainly the case that one may have to choose between them in the present, sometimes as a matter of life and death. Think of Salman Rushdie and Edgar Snowden.

4.3. To maximize freedom of expression in a common globalized world (or simply to create such a world), it is necessary to transgress or suppress certain boundaries, and to radically "democratize" others, i.e., make them more permeable and more symmetrical (which means less discriminatory), and an object of discussion and negotiation among those who "share" them. What is true for the mobility of persons ("migrations") must be true for the mobility of ideas and discourses as well ("translations").

4.3.1. An "international law of nations" in the global age must take the *intensification* and the *democratization* of communication as simultaneous, if not identical, concerns. It must define communication and expression as public goods, a common resource of humankind as such, which needs to be secured and developed. That includes education (e.g., as defined by UNESCO), but also regulation of monopolies and a protection of so-called deviants and dissidents by the international community. As international organizations monitor the distribution of inequalities of income and access to vital resources, they should also monitor the unequal distribution of access to cultural resources, "symbolic capital" (Bourdieu), and means of expression.

5. SECULARISM IS FEARLESS SPEECH

5.1. Freedom of expression as a public good in the global age has national and transnational, juridical and moral (subjective) conditions. As a central institution of *civic* universalism (or a universality based on the agency, rights, and duties of "citizens"), it is conceptually distinct from either religious universalities or the universality of the market. It can be conflicting with their respective logics, but also try to subsume them under norms of autonomy and equality which are meaningful for different subjectivities.

5.2. Why do conflicts inevitably arise in the public sphere? Not only because "opinions" are different, not mutually "translatable," or because class interests and other interests are incompatible, but because subjects are *personally implicated* in their own discourses (which "interpellate" them, or require from them attachment and fidelity, impose guilt and recognition, dignity and shame, etc.). As a consequence, subjects not only perceive and "judge" each other's opinions, but their respective *identities* (histories, cultures, values, ways of life: "Gods" in Max Weber's extended sense).

5.2.1. Religious (or antireligious) discourses and traditions are clearly a very strong apparatus of interpellation in that sense. But the media regime that corresponds to the fully developed market society paradoxically generates equally strong tendencies for individuals to identify their personality with the messages they transmit or the emotions they share. A culture acquired or inherited from the ancestors is a "human capital." We observe today permanent combinations of both mechanisms.

5.2.2. Terror and fear are jointly intensifying the "police of thought," or the political constraints that limit or suppress free speech. Terror is interiorized as fear, and fear is exteriorized as terror, or counterterror, or "state of exception." Fear is terrorized and terrorizing: it is fear of others, aliens, enemies, and fear of oneself or one's fellow citizens.

5.2.3. The opposite of fear and terror, which is *fearless speech*, governs both relations to others and relations to oneself. It includes "speaking truth to power" in the public (be they powers of sovereign authorities or powers of silent social norms), and critically distancing oneself from one's identity as an exclusion of others, inside or outside the "community." In other words, it involves a discussion of all traditions (including the modern or modernist traditions), and an awareness of the fact that the ethical value of any tradition is enhanced by universal recognition, but need not be considered an absolute.[11]

5.3. There is an intrinsic articulation of the idea of freedom of expression as a public good, and a generalized concept of the secular, itself "secularized," which is precisely provided by the practice of fearless speech. Fearless speech accepts the risk of conflict, publicizing the "differend," while opening the possibility of knowledge, and seeking the maximum knowledge of the other (even the enemy). It is therefore a strategy of civility based on the intelligence of identities, relations, and antagonisms, rather than just recognition or respect. This appears to be incompatible with any known imposition of the sacred. It therefore obliges us to disintricate the religious and the sacred. Is that possible? If it becomes real, it will have been possible.

15.
IDENTITARIAN LAÏCITÉ

PRELIMINARY

In the summer of 2016, emotion and outrage were enormous in the wake of a murderous attack perpetrated during the festivities of 14 juillet (the French national holiday) at Nice. A lone driver, of Tunisian origin, who claimed allegiance to the Islamic State in Syria and Iraq (also known as *Daesh*), launched his truck into the crowd, killed 86 people (men, women, and children of different denominations and nationalities), and injured more than 300 others. The mass killing—by a method that has been repeated since then—came shortly after several other murders and assaults committed by Islamic terrorists or attributed to them, particularly the shooting of the *Charlie Hebdo* cartoonists on January 7, 2015, and the massacre at and around the music hall Le Bataclan in Paris on November 13, 2015. The attacks demonstrated again how real was the threat against civilians and ordinary institutions incarnated by Islamist organizations based in the Middle East (where the French army, lest we forget, also participates in military interventions). These organizations' emissaries are either dispatched from Syria and other training places, or are recruited through the Internet from among young French Muslims (men, occasionally women) with a more or less troubled social and psychological background, or, increasingly—as in the killings at San Bernardino and Orlando in the United States during the same period [1]—they are individuals who decided to pledge "allegiance to the Islamic State"; inventing for themselves a sacred mission in the moment of their acting out.

These repeated episodes led France to declare a legal "state of emergency" which, since then, has been continuously prorogated. These incidents also encouraged racist manifestations, including aggression directed at members of the Muslim communities in French cities, especially targeting women wearing "Islamic veils" already forbidden or hardly tolerated in various public places.[2] To make things worse, insistent campaigns of intellectuals, media, and politicians pictured the "multiplication" of Muslim women donning hijabs or other traditional veils as part of a strategic plan to create in France a "secessionist" community that would be controlled by Islamist activists and "Salafist imams," which would therefore pose a threat to national unity and security. It is in this (heavy) context that, right after the Nice assaults, some mayors of towns and cities on the seaside (mainly on the Mediterranean) issued municipal decrees to ban the wearing of "burkinis" (and more generally traditional Muslim attire) on their beaches: it was a ridiculous but also violent symbolic initiative, which immediately induced some brutal scenes of expulsion or coercion that were reported worldwide, and some clashes between the local police, vigilante-type mobs, and young men of Arab origin (e.g., in Corsica).[3] The initiative was acclaimed by Islamophobic groups, "secular feminists," and "republican" politicians. Manuel Valls, the prime minister [at the time], himself supported the ban. But it was criticized by others, including two important (women) ministers in the government (Najat Vallaud-Belkacem and Marisol

Touraine). For his part, French President Francois Hollande remained cautiously silent.

On August 22, 2016, a district judge—ruling against the protest of the *Collectif contre l'islamophobie en France* (Committee against Islamophobia in France, active since 2003)—validated the bans, declaring that such "conspicuous garments" are signs of "religious fanaticism" and part of a "debasement of women" incompatible with the values of a "democratic society." But on August 26, at the request of the same CCIF plus the *Ligue des Droits de l'Homme* (the historic league created at the time of the Dreyfus Affair to combat anti-Semitism), the *Conseil d'Etat* (the highest French court in administrative matters) reversed the ruling, stating that such interdictions issued under the pressure of circumstances "contain a grave damage, manifestly illegal, against such fundamental liberties as the right to circulate, the freedom of conscience, and personal freedom in general."[4] This decision put an end to the wave of initiatives from (mostly right-wing or far-right) local authorities who sought to increase the general tension and customize the stigmatization of Muslims in the name of the defense of laïcité and "secular values" in French society—a society already torn apart by religious and racial divides, and frightened by the terrorist attacks.

However important this ruling has been (and remains) politically, it was also clear that it would only represent one episode in a protracted conflict. Prime Minister Valls immediately declared on his Facebook page that the decision did not "close the fundamental debate" over the wearing of burkinis, because the swimsuit expressed the "political project" to "create a counter-society based on the servitude of women, incompatible with the values of France and the Republic," an attack before which it would be unthinkable to recoil.[5] Other politicians announced that they would introduce a law further extending the ban on "Muslim attire" in public spaces.

On August 30, I published an article on this episode in the journal *Libération*, which I expanded subsequently for a collective volume on "political uses and misuses of laïcité."[6] I present here an English adaptation of this article, as a complement to my previous essay, "What Future for Laïcité?" (from 2005), to signal the transformations that are taking place in this moment.

Laïcité as National Identity Politics

Thanks to the ruling of the *Conseil d'Etat*, we will avoid seeing in France a morality police, charged not with forcing women to wear the veil (as in some other countries), but with forcing them to remove it. The exercise of freedom—so the ruling declares—must have priority over the exigencies of public order, which by definition restrict it, as far as possible. In a democracy, the rights of women are a matter of their decision, and not of a theologico-political grid of interpretation plastered over their behavior to "force them to be free."[7] Laïcité as an institution means an obligation of neutrality of the state toward citizens and not an ideological obligation of citizens toward the state.

I consider (and I am not alone) these juridical demonstrations as fundamental. As they deliver a blow to the attempt to exploit the sentiments—anguish, anger, suspicion—aroused by the series of attacks perpetrated in the name of Islam, in order to combine a fundamentalist *laïcisme* with a strategy of the exacerbation of nationalism, they are going to arouse a counteroffensive. Indeed, this started the day after the ruling of the *Conseil*, with stunning declarations from the prime minister. Other declarations show that, independent of whether the guerilla campaign by certain mayors currently being waged against the judicial order is successful or not, more perilous in the long run will be proposals to legislate by taking new steps in prohibiting public signs of belonging to a certain religion. But the moral and political stakes therein will be very high, because it becomes clear that such legislation would not only require a constitutional revision, it signifies that we are drifting from the state of law toward the state of exception.

Just as important are the implications with regard to the conception and the institution of laïcité. But here a difficulty begins to arise, which requires some philosophical elucidation. There must be a genealogical labor on what laïcité has been in France, and what it is becoming in the present moment.[8] And, on this basis, it is necessary to discuss what must be conserved, prolonged, or restored, but also reformed, so that the signification of the principle does not find itself turned into its opposite.

Historically, the idea of laïcité in France is divided between two conceptions, both issuing from the centuries-long confrontation between Catholicism and Republicanism. Régis Debray has baptized them "republican" and "democratic," but this alternative is not satisfying in my eyes because there are democratic elements on each side, and because both belong to the republican tradition.[9] Both conceptions, in fact, express aspects of the Enlightenment's legacy. I would say that the first—ultimately derived from the Hobbesian doctrine of the government as a "representative" of the multitude, who acts in the citizens' name and in their best interest—is rather statist and authoritarian, while the second, in part derived from the conceptions of Locke on individual self-ownership and "toleration," is more liberal and even includes a libertarian tendency. The first makes laïcité an essential piece of the "normative" primacy of public order over private activities and opinions, whereas the second posits the autonomy of civil society, to which belong the liberties of conscience and of expression, as the "natural" order of things of which the state must be the servant and the protector. The law of separation of 1905 did not so much mark the triumph of the second over the first as a *correction* of anticlerical projects for "laicizing society," by means of guarantees for individual and collective liberties.

Evidently this allows it to be invoked every time the laïcité of the state is threatened in its existence, or in its democratic character, which can happen in many different manners and is probably the case today.[10]

Unlike some excellent interpreters (in particular Jean Baubérot, whose lucidity and erudition I admire and with whom I share many conclusions), I do not think that the "identitarian laïcité" (the program of which we see today developing on the right and the left of the political spectrum) represents a simple accentuation of the Hobbesian heritage or its revenge on the liberal interpretation, even if I can see which dogmatic arguments have favored the orchestration of a juridical, moral, and pedagogical conception of public authority, and its sliding toward the idea of an "order of values" which are baptized as republican and *laïque*, but are in reality nationalist and Islamophobic. I believe that something like a *mutation* has occurred. I find it important to try to understand its ideological content and what made it possible in the conjuncture.

Indeed, the symbolic equation which subtends identitarian laïcité must be reconstructed in its whole extension: what it posits is that *the identity of the Republic* (and the "community of citizens" instituted by the Republican state) resides in laïcité, and, correlatively, that laïcité must serve the *assimilation* of populations of foreign origin (which, put more clearly, means colonial and postcolonial), lest they are liable, by their culture and religious beliefs, to constitute a "foreign body" at the heart of the nation. Making *assimilation* explicitly the other name of "national" and "republican" *identity*, former president Nicolas Sarkozy in particular has enunciated the common element of the discourses which are now circulating from left to right and far right, thus redistributing political and ideological cleavages in a decisive manner. Of course, it can be no innocent coincidence that the notion of assimilation officially formed the ideal objective of French colonization and its "civilizing" mission.[11]

This element of repressed unconscious continuously insists, loudly returning to the fore in favorable circumstances like those we have nowadays.[12] Being obsessed by the necessity of building a dam against "communitarianism," this politics in fact comes to construct (by means of "values," but also of norms and cultural prohibitions) a state communitarianism. And as always, this communitarianism involves a control on the lives of women, completely symmetrical with the control imposed on them by "traditional" structures of patriarchic power blessed by religious laws, whether "oriental" or not, but also, until recently in Europe, by the Napoleonic civil code, which deemed women to be "minors" and relegated them to the condition of "passive citizens." The analogy is undeniable with the process that the statesman Georges Clemenceau described in 1901 as follows: "in order to suppress the religious congregation, we make France a big congregation."[13]

But more serious still, above all in the current conjuncture: the symmetrical opposite or the inverse synonym of *assimilation* is *acculturation*. Now this notion (which is taken from the vocabulary of anthropology and transformed into a category for the interpretation of political and ideological history) is the very spearhead of the ideological offensive of Islamic fundamentalism which denounces the grip of (more or less completely identified) "Christian" and "secular" civilization on Muslim communities in Europe (and on "modernizing" Arab-Muslim societies). From this it draws on occasion a legitimation of *"spiritual" jihad against the West*, as one can read on various Internet sites.[14] The construction of laïcité as collective, national identity, subtended by the idea that the republic implies assimilation (and not only integration into social life and the fulfillment of civic obligations), is thus drawn into a scenario of *mimetic rivalry* with the totalitarian discourse against which, at the same time, French politics pretends to guard itself. As Lacan would say: we receive our message from the Other in inverted form . . . The least we can say is that such a construction will serve neither for understanding the nature of the perils, nor, since *"we are at war,"* for forging solidarity among all citizens.[15]

Obviously, the rise of this intellectual "monster" that is identitarian laïcité is not a phenomenon that can be isolated from multiple tendencies to the exacerbation of nationalisms and to the "clash of civilizations" which, in connection with extreme violence, occur in the world today. Nevertheless, the "French" form is specific. It troubles us profoundly because it tends to reverse the political function of a principle which had played an essential role in our political history: ultimately, a certain *laïcisme* takes the place formerly occupied by a certain *clericalism*. A battle cry with sinister resonances, *"La France aux français,"* or "France belongs to the (pure) French people," now seems to be heard in the form: *"La France aux Laïques"* (France only belongs to the secularists, in other words: anybody who is not and does not exhibit the standard emblems of being a secularist cannot be a French citizen with full rights).[16] It is vital that we react collectively to this. But it is necessary to understand exactly what is happening, to redraw the "fronts" and the "borderlines," and not to replay the old battles in the same way. Today's battles, certainly, keep concerning the "spirit of the laws" (Montesquieu) in the French Republic. However, they are inscribed in a much wider cosmopolitical context, whose tendencies permanently influence our own actions, whether we like it or not. In this context, I hope we can keep (or regain) a capacity of "enlightened" emancipation from darkness and prejudices.

NOTES

PREFACE

1. On "monotheism," I largely agree with Jan Assmann's idea that monotheisms are "counterreligions" (*Gegenreligionen*), which come *second* and *against* what they define as "superstition." In this sense, modern secularisms are like "counter-counterreligions." For the convoluted history of the word, see chapter 10.

2. In *Saeculum*, I quoted from Derrida's description of the perilous place of encounter called "Jerusalem," the object of rival appropriations, which could also become a model of civility, provided certain (very unlikely) conditions are met.

3. Remember the title of Talal Asad's very important (and very critical) essay from 2006: "Trying to Understand French Secularism," in *Political Theologies: Public Religions in a Post-Secular World*, ed. Hent de Vries and Lawrence Eugene Sullivan (New York: Fordham University Press, 2006), 494–526.

4. Followed by an invitation from my friends, editors of the journal *Radical Philosophy*, to contribute to their anniversary issue in 2016, where the piece was published first in English.

1. Translated by Emiliano Battista. This paper was originally presented at the conference "Misère de la critique/Das Elend der Kritik," at the École Normale Supérieure, Paris, on February 5, 2016. The conference was organized as part of the research project ANR-DFG CActuS (The Actuality of Critique, Social Theory, and Critical Sociology in France and Germany), directed by Gérard Raulet (Université Paris-Sorbonne) and Axel Honneth (Goethe-Universität Frankfurt). For the present publication, I have introduced the necessary bibliographical references for the texts I cite or evoke, but I have not changed the character of the talk, or its oral presentation. I would like to extend my gratitude to the editors of *Radical Philosophy* for inviting me to publish in the anniversary issue (*Radical Philosophy*, no. 200, 2016).

2. Georges Politzer, *Critique of the Foundations of Psychology: The Psychology of Psychoanalysis* (1928), trans. Maurice Apprey (Pittsburgh: Duquesne University Press, 1994).

3. In a collection of essays from 1979 titled *Futures Past: On the Semantics of Historical Time*, Koselleck devotes a fundamental essay to the modern concept of "revolution" ("Historical Criteria of the Modern Concept of Revolution"), an idea that he sees as emblematic of what he calls "futures past."

4. It was the Saint-Simonians who articulated this distinction, particularly in the fundamental work from 1829, *Exposition de la doctrine saint-simonienne. Première année*, by A. Bazard and O. Rodrigues, a critical edition of which, by Maurice Halbwachs and Marcel Rivière, appeared in Paris in 1924. Antonio Gramsci makes it a central category of his analyses of hegemony in the *Prison Notebooks*. But it is in effect common to the entire "sociological tradition." See Robert Nisbet, *The Sociological Tradition* (New York: Basic Books, 1966).

5. Among other recent interventions by these authors, see Immanuel Wallerstein, "Structural Crisis, or Why Capitalists May No Longer

Find Capitalism Rewarding," in Immanuel Wallerstein et al., *Does Capitalism Have a Future?* (Oxford and New York: Oxford University Press, 2013); Jean-Luc Nancy and Jean Manuel Garrido, "Phraser la mutation: entretien avec Jean-Luc Nancy," at https://blogs.mediapart.fr/juan-manuel-garrido-wainer/blog/131015/phraser-la-mutation-entretien-avec-jean-luc-nancy

6. See, for example, Wendy Brown, *Undoing the Demos: Neoliberalism's Stealth Revolution* (Cambridge, MA: MIT Press, 2015).

7. I retain the terminology of the emergence of a "pure capitalism," with globalization and the integral financialization of the economy. But I also think it may be preferable, or at least useful, to employ the expression "absolute capitalism" (as do, notably, Franco Berardi and Jacques Rancière), because it indicates more clearly the *self-referential* character of a system in which there is no longer any real exception to the "production of commodities by means of commodities" (Piero Sraffa), and also because it can be pitted against "historical capitalism," the capitalism that not only operated the *great transformation* between the beginnings of primitive accumulation and the dismantling of the "social state," colonization and decolonization, but also provided the framework for the classic configuration of class struggle and the conflict among nations.

8. Immanuel Wallerstein admirably designates this task in the title of his book, *Unthinking Social Science: The Limits of Nineteenth-Century Paradigms* (Cambridge: Polity Press, 1991, 2001).

9. For example, one might compare two devastating "death zones": Syria and the Middle East more generally since the attacks of 9/11 and the American interventions; and West Africa (Guinea, Liberia, Sierra Leone), contaminated by the Ebola virus and essentially abandoned to its own devices by the World Health Organization.

10. See Saskia Sassen, *Expulsions: Brutality and Complexity in the Global Economy*, (Cambridge, MA and London: Harvard University Press, 2014).

11. See Étienne Balibar, *We, the People of Europe? Reflections on Transnational Citizenship*, trans. James Swenson (Princeton: Princeton University Press, 2003).

12. Jacques Derrida, "Faith and Knowledge: Two Sources of 'Religion' at the Limits of Reason Alone" (1996), in *Acts of Religion*, ed. Gil Anidjar (London: Routledge, 2002), 63.

13. See the special dossier on "Governance" in *Parolechiave* no. 56/2, 2016, Carocci editore, Roma.

14. On the history and fluctuations of the notion of the "theologico-political," see the introduction to Jan Assmann's *Herrschaft und Heil. Politische Theologie in Altägypten, Israel und Europa* (Munich: Carl Hansel Verlag, 2000).

15. On the crisis of the "party form" that undergirds and overflows the crisis of the parliamentary system, see Marco Revelli, *Finale di partito* (Turin: Eunaudi, 2013).

16. Jacques Rancière, "Comment sortir de la haine? Grand entretien avec Jacques Rancière," *Le Nouvel Observateur*, February 7, 2016.

17. On the question of inconvertible violence, see my book *Violence and Civility: On the Limits of Political Philosophy*, trans. G. M. Goshgarian (New York and Chichester, West Sussex: Columbia University Press, 2015).

18. See, for example, Jean Birnbaum, *Un silence religioux. La gauche face au djihadisme* (Paris: Seuil, 2016).

19. Karl Marx, "A Contribution to the Critique of Hegel's *Philosophy of Right*: Introduction," in *Marx: Early Political Writings*, ed. and trans. Joseph O'Malley, with Richard A. Davis (Cambridge: Cambridge University Press, 1994), 57–58.

20. From this perspective, there is a radical incompatibility between the Marxist tradition and the "sociological tradition" that found its fullest articulation in Durkheim, for whom religion is always, in the last analysis, the source of what Althusser calls "the society effect"—a function that in turn defines it. See Bruno Karsenti, *La société en personnes. Etudes durkheimiennes* (Paris: Economica, 2006).

21. In this, my position runs against an amalgam that was practiced by the school of reading and interpreting Marx from which I came, and that I helped erect under Althusser's direction: the amalgam of "humanist" philosophical positions and the anthropological question in general. For more on this, see my essay "Anthropologie philosophique ou ontologie de la relation? Que faire de la Sixième Thèse sur Feuerbach?" ["Philosophical Anthropology or Relational Ontology? What to do with the Sixth Thesis on Feuerbach?"], in *La philosophie de Marx*, new and enlarged edition (Paris: La Decouverte, 2014).

22. This implication is something Ernst Bloch places particular emphasis on in his great commentary on the "Theses on Feuerbach" from 1953, later incorporated into volume 1 of *The Principle of Hope*, trans. Neville Plaice et al. (Cambridge, MA: MIT Press, 1986), chap. 19, "Changing the World, or Marx's Eleven Theses on Feuerbach."

23. This formulation is to be found in the preface to *A Contribution to the Critique of Political Economy* (1859), a text that codified the principles of "historical materialism" for a century and a half. I have on occasion said that it states precisely that which, in Marx, has become untenable for us. Deep down, though, this had already been suggested, albeit in different ways, by Benjamin in his "Theses on the Concept of History," and by Althusser's posthumously published reflections on "aleatory materialism." That Marx himself did not stick to the *evolutionism* that informs this formulation is a well-known fact to those readers of his work who stress its permanent refounding and fundamental incompleteness.

24. I think I may have been one of the first, if not the very first, to note that the famous formulation that concludes—or, rather, leaves unfinished—the first volume of *Capital* ("the expropriation of the expropriators" [*Die Expropriateurs werden expropriirt*]), beyond its obviously "French" revolutionary associations, contains a messianic reference as well, drawn from the Biblical formula, "they will oppress their oppressors" (Isa. 14:1—4 and

27:7–9). On the "messianic moment" in Marx in 1844, see my book *Citizen Subject: Foundations for Philosophical Anthropology*, trans. Steven Miller (New York: Fordham University Press, 2017). The expression "secular religion," or "political religion," refers, in particular, to the work of Eric Voegelin.

25. See my study, "Foucault's Point of Heresy: 'Quasi-Transcendentals' and the Transdisciplinary Function of the Episteme," in *Theory, Culture & Society* vol. 32, no. 5–6 (September–November 2015). I also apply this category at length in *Citizen Subject*.

26. Giorgio Agamben, *The Use of Bodies*, trans. Adam Kotsko (Stanford, CA: Stanford University Press, 2014).

27. This was suggested to me by the intensity of the controversies about the compatibility or incompatibility of Islam with the "values," meaning the "norms," of public and private behavior that are more or less sacralized in the secular West of Christian origin. See Étienne Balibar, *Saeculum. Religion, culture, idéologie* (Paris: Galilée, 2012) [Part one of this volume].

28. This point is not self-evident, or something we can take for granted. In the introduction to *Parting Ways: Jewishness and the Critique of Zionism* (New York: Columbia University Press, 2012), Judith Butler takes me to task for postulating the untranslatability of certain discourses, and for identifying this limit with "the religious," something that would make the latter, ipso facto, an obstacle to the common political action of those who profess it (or are labeled as such). I recognize that we have to explore this further. What I mean by "untranslatability," in a Derridean spirit, is not an essential uncommunicability, but the historical impossibility generating the infinite effort directed at transforming or displacing the limit. It is true, however, that the *heterogeneity* of the two instances (culture and religion) in their intertwining (or permanent overdetermination) is the motivation for the position I am outlining.

29. I am transposing here, to the question of anthropological differences and their religious coding, what Kant says about the "character of the species" in his *Anthropology from a Pragmatic Point of View*,

where he suggests that one would have to place oneself in the perspective of an extraterrestrial to define the *specific difference*, the difference that defines the species. But, in practice, this aporia spills over into an endless conflict of interpretations. See Peter Szendy, *Kant in the Land of Extraterrestrials: Cosmopolitical Philosofictions*, trans. Will Bishop (New York: Fordham University Press, 2013).

30. The idea of the "critique of political economy" as the "political economy of labor" that stands opposite and against the "political economy of capital" was revindicated by Marx himself, particularly when he wanted to explain why, after the "decomposition" of the classical school (crowned by Ricardo's work), there could no longer be another bourgeois economic theory other than a "vulgar" or "apologetic" one. There is an absolute opposition on this point between the Operaismo tradition in Italy—which, since Mario Tronti's *Workers and Capital* (1966), has continued to radicalize the identification of labor with the "substance" of value and capital—and the position defended by the German school of *Wertkritik* (see notably, Robert Kurz, *Geld ohne Wert. Grundrisse ʒu einer Transformation der Kritik der Politischen Ökonomie* [Berlin: Horlemann Verlag, 2012]), or, in a different way, the position defended by Moishe Postone in *Time, Labor, and Social Denomination: A Reinterpretation of Marx's Critical Theory* (1993). Postone argues that the reduction of capital to labor (a typically "bourgeois" category) is a compromise that the "exoteric Marx" was prepared to make with the labor movements of his time, and their preoccupation with wage-oriented demands. From the philosophical standpoint, the fundamental reference for me on this issue remains Jean-Marie Vincent, *Critique du travail. Le Faire et l'agir* (Paris: Presses universitaires de France, 1987).

31. See Alys Eve Weinbaum, *Wayward Reproductions: Genealogies of Race and Nation in Transatlantic Modern Thought* (Durham and London: Duke University Press, 2004). See also my article "Exploitation," in *Political Concepts: A Critical Lexicon*, at http://www.politicalconcepts.org/balibar-exploitation/

32. See Robert Castel, *From Manual Workers to Wage Labourers: Transformation of the Social Question* (1995) trans. and ed. Richard Boyd (New Brunswick and London: Transaction Publishers, 2003).

33. For more on the "real subsumption" of health under the operations of financial capital, see Kaushik Sunder Rajan, *Biocapital: The Constitution of Postgenomic Life* (Durham and London: Duke University Press, 2006). On the elaboration of the category of "human capital" by Gary Becker and its interpretation by Foucault, see the critical presentation by Wendy Brown in *Undoing the Demos*.

34. Over the past few years, Antonio Negri, Michael Hardt, Moulier-Boutang, and others have devoted their energies to discussing the recession of manual labor for the profit of intellectual labor and the emergence of "cognitive capitalism." I don't deny that their analyses are interesting, but I do wonder whether—in the spirit of Marx's "progressivism," or even, "futurism"—they have not mistaken one aspect of the "division of labor" in the current economy for the very realization of the future of social development.

35. I refer the reader once again to Saskia Sassen's *Expulsions: Brutality and Complexity in the Global Economy*, as well as to the work of more "orthodox" economists, like Pierre-Noël Giraud, *L'homme inutile* (Paris: Odile Jacob, 2015).

36. See, for example, Danièle Linhart, *La Comédie humaine du travail. De la déshumanisation taylorienne à la sur-humanisation managériale* (Paris: Érès, 2015).

1. CIRCUMSTANCES AND OBJECTIVES

1. I borrow this play on words from Jean-Luc Nancy, *Dis-Enclosure: The Deconstruction of Christianity*, trans. Bettina Bergo, et al. Perspectives in Continental Philosophy (New York: Fordham University Press, 2008), 5: "Philosophy (and science with it) has somehow managed to intimidate itself with its proclaimed

exclusions of a religion from which it never ceased, underhand-edly, to draw nourishment, though without really questioning itself about this 'secularization' and . . . about this consequent 'laicization' or social generalization of secularity. All this can be said otherwise with another term, that of *world*. When the world becomes simultaneously worldwide [*mondial*] and resolutely worldly [*mondain*] . . . how and where is inscribed the necessary assertion that *the sense of the world must be found outside of the world?* [Wittgenstein]."

2. Anis Makdisi Memorial Lecture, delivered on November 12, 2009 at the American University of Beirut (Faculty of Arts and Sciences). I thank Professor Maher Jarrar, Dean Patrick McGreevy, Provost Ahmad Dallal, and Ms. Jean Said Makdisi for their invitation and hospitality. The text of my lecture was published by the university and subsequently reprinted as Etienne Balibar, "Cosmopolitanism and Secularism: Controversial Lega-cies and Prospective Interrogations," *Gray Room*, vol. 1, no. 44 (Summer 2011), 6–25. An early French version of this lecture may be found in *Raison publique*, no. 14 (June 2011). I thank the editors of both reviews for graciously providing a forum for my work.

3. See Balibar, "Quelle universalité des Lumières?" in *Le Bottin des Lumières*, ed. Nadine Descendre (Ville de Nancy: Communauté urbaine du Grand Nancy, 2005), 306–11.

2. SECULARISM AND COSMOPOLITANISM: AN APORIA?

1. *Sécularisme* is the term that, after reflection, I have translated to the English "secularism," although the French word has a partisan connotation that its English cognate does not. The term *laïcité*, left untranslated here, is best reserved for an essentially French his-torical *variant* of secularism, as will appear. Thus the distinction between secularism and laïcité, mandated by the problematic of a confrontation of the "West" with its other, is not quite coextensive with the standard sociological distinction between *sécularisation*

and *laïcité*. The latter distinction is mandated, rather, by intra-European comparisons between regions dominated by the Protestant tradition (where processes of political "modernization" are said to run from civil society to the state) and regions dominated by the Catholic tradition (where such processes are said to run in the other direction). See Jean Baubérot, *Laïcité 1905–2005: Entre passion et raison* (Paris: Le Seuil, 2004), and Emile Poulat, *Notre laïcité publique* (Paris: Berg International, 2003), especially 300ff. See also Marc de Launay, "Sécularisation/Profanation," in *Vocabulaire européen des philosophies*, ed. Barbara Cassin (Paris: Seuil/Le Robert, 2004), 1118ff.

2. If it is not too much to point out, with a grain of salt, the existence of an etymological guiding thread, let us note that, in the Greco-Latin tradition handed down by the church, *saeculum*, treated as an equivalent for the Greek word *eon*, is the "world" or even "the time of the world," whereas *kosmos* (translated into Latin as *mundus*, but also as *universum*) is identified with the "creation" that God entrusted to man. St. Paul opposes "the wisdom of this world" (*sophia tou kosmou*) to "the wisdom/knowledge of God" (*sophia/gnôsis theou*) in 1 Cor. 1:6–24. German language, making use of the two senses of the adjective *weltlich*, preserves, better than French or English, the symmetry between *Weltweisheit* (popular or ordinary philosophy) and *Weltbürgertum* (world citizenship), which Kant discusses in *The Critique of Pure Reason*. The Marxian watchword of a "secularization-realization of philosophy" (*Verweltlichung* or *Verwirklichung*) thus appears as a way of bringing philosophy back to its profane origins, inseparable from its cosmopolitical function, and, simultaneously, as an internal critique of its capture by theological discourse. In a very interesting essay, Jan N. Bremmer sketches a history of the transfer of the words "century" (*siècle*), "secular," and "secularization" from Latin to French, German, and English (Bremmer, "Secularization: Notes Toward a Genealogy," in *Religion: Beyond a Concept*, ed. Hent de Vries [New York: Fordham University Press, 2008], 432–37).

Laïcité has an altogether different etymology: it comes from the Old Greek word *laos*, which designates the community of citizen-warriors. The Septuagint appropriated *laos* to translate the distinction between the "chosen people" (*'am*) and the "nations" (*goyim*); the church later used the word to distinguish the mass of ordinary believers from the "clergy" (*kleros*). Finally, *laos* was turned against the church by the post-revolutionary discourse of the French Republic. See Etienne Balibar, Simone Bonnafous, and Pierre Fiala, eds., "Laïc, laïque, laïcité," in *Mots: Les langages du politique*, no. 27 (June 1991).

3. Joan Wallach Scott, *Only Paradoxes to Offer: French Feminists and the Rights of Man* (Cambridge, MA: Harvard University Press, 1996).

4. See Balibar, "The Antinomy of Citizenship," in *Equaliberty: Political Essays*, trans. James Ingram (Durham, NC: Duke University Press, 2014), 1–32.

3. DOUBLE BINDS: POLITICS OF THE VEIL

1. Still useful on this point is the investigation conducted by Françoise Gaspard and Farhad Khosrokhavar, *Le Foulard et la République* (Paris: La Découverte, 1995).

2. See chapter 2, note 1.

3. Henri Pena-Ruiz, *Qu'est-ce que la laïcité?* (Paris: Gallimard, 2003), 11–12.

4. See Jean Baubérot, *Laïcité 1905–2005: Entre passion et raison* (Paris: Seuil, 2004), 185. Baubérot mentions the term *catho-laïcité*, attributing it to Jean-Paul Willaime (1993). It was in fact used earlier in Edgar Morin, "Le trou noir de la laïcité," in *Le Débat*, no. 58 (January 1990), 35–38. See also Pierre Fiala, ed., "Les termes de la laïcité: Différenciation morphologique et conflits sémantiques," in *Mots: Les langages du politique*, no. 27 (June 1991).

5. "France is an indivisible, secular, democratic and social Republic. It ensures the equality before the law of all citizens, without

distinction of origin, race or religion. It respects all beliefs."
(Constitution of the Fifth Republic, Article 2, which has become
Article 1 with the dissolution of the "community" uniting France
and its former overseas territories). The meaning-effect of the
set of the republic's four attributes (brought together for the first
time in 1946)—its indivisible, secular, democratic, and social
character, all attributes that, doubtless not accidentally, evoke the
attributes of the church according to what is known as the Nicene
Creed: *unam, sanctam, catholicam,* and *apostolicam Ecclesiam*—is
at the center of discussions of the addenda that specify, limit or,
in the opinion of some, contradict the intention indicated by the
title of this article, "On Sovereignty." "It respects all beliefs,"
which echoes Article 1 of the Law of 1905 on the separation of
church and state, is one such addendum. There is no need to
dwell on its importance from the standpoint of a "liberal" conception of laïcité, or, again, its considerable moral and political ambiguity (since, strictly speaking, the subjective wording
of this article does not make it possible to exclude either sects
or racist, denialist ideologies, except to "keep the peace"). The
same holds for the very controversial 2003 addendum that says
that France, while remaining "indivisible," "shall be organized
on a decentralized basis." As for the formula "without distinction of origin, race, or religion," it, too, has been taken from the
1946 Constitution, whose preamble declares that "each human
being, without distinction of race, religion, or creed, possesses
sacred and inalienable rights." At a conference held in the French
senate, Professor Jean-Jacques Israel pointed out that, when
this article was being drawn up, the formula that was ultimately
settled on replaced another that spoke of "sex, religion, and
beliefs," although it is impossible to say how and why the substitution occurred (Israel, "La non-discrimination *raciale* dans les
textes constitutionnels français: présence ou absence," in *Mots*,
no. 33 (December 1992): "Sans distinction de . . . race," 343–50.

6. I have taken a stand on this question on several occasions. See Etienne Balibar, "Le symbole ou la vérité," in *Libération*, November 3, 1989; "Dissonances within Laïcité: The New 'Headscarf Affair,'" in Balibar, *Equaliberty: Political Essays*, trans. James Ingram [Durham, NC: Duke University Press, 2014], 209–32); "Secularism has Become Another Religion," interview, *Tehelka*, March 25, 2009. On the controversy surrounding the Law of March 15, 2004, see Françoise Lorcerie, ed., *La Politisation du voile en France, en Europe et dans le Monde arabe* (Paris: Harmattan, 2005). The fact that no open resistance to this political constraint materialized, contrary to what some had predicted, may be explained in the international conjuncture: the girls wearing the veil, or their friends and family, did not wish to be co-opted by the fundamentalists that vociferously supported their "cause" from outside and called for symbolic or even violent reprisals at a time when Islamophobic currents in French public opinion and French politics were trying to make these girls out to be representatives of the "Movement Against France" (*l'Anti-France*).

7. Gayatri Chakravorty Spivak coined this phrase to capture the spirit in which the colonial administration and Western "Indianologists" reconstructed the rite (*sati*) in which Hindu widows immolated themselves on their deceased husbands' graves; the Westerners' intention was to turn the rite into a symbol of the barbarous native customs that colonization had made it its mission to root out. See Spivak, *A Critique of Postcolonial Reason: Toward a History of the Vanishing Present* (Cambridge, MA: Harvard University Press, 1999), 232ff.

8. Joan Wallach Scott, *The Politics of the Veil* (Princeton, NJ: Princeton University Press, 2007).

9. The same comparison was drawn, to different ends, by the Guadeloupean philosopher Jacky Dahomay, who later resigned from the Haut Conseil à l'Intégration at the same time Edouard Glissant did (December 2008).

10. Scott, *The Politics of the Veil*, 171–72. I cite at length because no French publisher has been willing to issue a translation of Scott's book, notwithstanding her reputation as an eminent scholar.

11. Ibid., 170–71. In many respects, Scott's thesis *reverses* the one argued in Fatima Mernissi, *Beyond the Veil: Male-Female Dynamics in Modern Muslim Society*, 2nd ed. (Bloomington: Indiana University Press, 1987 [1975]). Mernissi contrasts the representations of an "active" feminine sexuality in Islam to the West's representations of it as "passive," linking the veiling of women to a *territorialization* of the masculine and the feminine, whose potential excesses must be checked by assigning them separate domains. On the circumstances in which the veil has been fetishized by both colonialism, which makes it a symbol of indigenous women's oppression, and the anticolonialist movements for which it symbolizes resistance to the West, see Leila Ahmed, *Women and Gender in Islam* (New Haven, CT: Yale University Press, 1992), 144–68; and Monique Gadant, "Femmes alibi," in *Les Temps modernes*, no. 580 (January–February 1995): "Algérie: La Guerre des frères," 221–32. Note that in Koranic Arabic, *hijab* designates both the veil and seclusion (first imposed on women by the Prophet). Here we should keep in mind the distinction between the different types of veils and their uses, often ignored by a Western public opinion that interprets them as *equivalent signifiers*, referring to a single theological *signified*. As has been shown by studies such as Nilüfer Göle, *Musulmanes et modernes: Voile et civilisation en Turquie*, trans. J. Riegel (Paris: La Découverte, 2003), that which, in certain contexts, betokens strict segregation and an extreme form of archaism corresponds, in others, to modernization and relative emancipation: "It is plainly a question of the new visibility of women in public life, even if it is hidden beneath the veil, and, as well, a question of their attempt to escape from the traditional life that awaits them if they accept their fate" (ibid., 148).

4. Cosmopolitics and Conflicts Between Universalities

1. Etienne Balibar, "Sujets ou citoyens: Pour l'égalité," in *Les Frontières de la démocratie* (Paris: La Découverte, 1992), 42–71.

2. Georges Canguilhem, "What is a Scientific Ideology?" [1969], in *Ideology and Rationality in the History of the Life Sciences*, trans. Arthur Goldhammer (Cambridge, MA: MIT Press, 1988).

3. I borrow the idea of "competing universalities" from Judith Butler, who of course takes her inspiration from Hegel. See her contribution to Butler, Ernesto Laclau, and Slavoj Žižek, *Contingency, Hegemony, Universality: Contemporary Dialogues on the Left* (London: Verso, 2000).

4. Etienne Tassin has very clearly brought out the importance of this distinction in Tassin, *Un monde commun: Pour une cosmopolitique des conflits* (Paris: Seuil, 2003). See also Bruce Robbins and Pheng Cheah, eds., *Cosmopolitics: Thinking and Feeling Beyond the Nation* (Minneapolis: University of Minnesota Press, 1998).

5. Obviously, something altogether different is involved when the heads of the British, French, and German governments suddenly declare, in unison, that "multiculturalism has failed." Practically speaking, this means that they have endorsed the widespread and growing representation of the immigrant as a "foreign body" that one must either assimilate by doing away with what makes for his singularity, or eliminate, should assimilation prove impossible. (Note added in 2011.)

6. Charles Taylor, *Multiculturalism and "The Politics of Recognition"* (Princeton, NJ: Princeton University Press, 1992); Will Kymlicka, *Multicultural Citizenship: A Liberal Theory of Modern Rights* (New York: Oxford University Press, 1996); Homi K. Bhabha, *The Location of Culture*, 2nd ed. (London: Routledge, 2004 [1994]); Stuart Hall, *Identités et cultures* (anthology), trans.

P. Chanial and M. Preziosi (Paris: Amsterdam, 2008). For a comparative overview, see Francesco Fistetti, *Théories du multiculturalisme: Un parcours entre philosophie et sciences sociales* (Paris: La Découverte, 2009). For a philosophical discussion of the question, see Emanuela Fornari, *Linee di confine: Filosofia e Postcolonialismo* (Turino: Bollati Boringhieri, 2011). W. E. B. DuBois's category "double consciousness" plays a central role in Franz Fanon (*Black Skin, White Masks*, 2nd ed., trans. Richard Philcox [New York: Grove Press, 2008]).

7. Danièle Hervieu-Léger, *Religion as a Chain of Memory*, trans. Simon Lee (New Brunswick, NJ: Rutgers University Press, 2000), dates the "return of the religious" to the 1970s. Régis Debray, *God, an Itinerary*, trans. Jeffrey Mehlman (London: Verso, 2004) identifies it as the communitarian reaction or resistance on the part of an "esprit de corps" to the progress of a utilitarian, homogenizing globalization. The terminology of a "return of the sacred" is utilized by, notably, the Indian philosopher Ashis Nandy; see "The Return of the Sacred: The Language of Religion and the Fear of Democracy in a Post-Secular World," in *Regimes of Despair* (New York: Oxford University Press, 2013).

8. As everyone knows, this is the perspective lurking behind the notion of the "clash of civilizations" given wide currency by Samuel Huntington. See Marc Crépon's critique in *La Guerre des civilisations: La culture de la peur, II* (Paris: Galilée, 2010), and my own reconsideration, "Eclaircissements (VIII). Le 'Choc des civilisations' et Carl Schmitt: Une Coïncidence?" in Etienne Balibar, *L'Europe, l'Amérique, la Guerre* (Paris: La Découverte, 2003).

9. A famous poem written by Louis Aragon during the German Occupation (1943), *la Rose et le Réséda* (the rose and the mignonette), declared that "celui qui croyait au ciel" and "celui qui n'y croyait pas," the believer and the atheist could fight the same patriotic resistance.

1. See Lila Abu-Lughod's emblematic essay, "Do Muslim Women Really Need Saving? Anthropological Reflections on Cultural Relativism and its Others," *American Anthropologist*, vol. 104, no. 3 (September 2002), 783–90.

2. Jacques Derrida, "Faith and Knowledge," in Gil Anidjar, ed., *Acts of Religion* (London: Routledge, 2001), 72–73. On the non-equivalence between "religion" and *dîn*, see Mohammed Ali Amir-Moezzi, "Religion," in *Dictionnaire du Coran*, ed. Mohammed Ali Amir-Moezzi (Paris: Robert Laffont, 2007), 741ff. On the non-equivalence between "religion" and *dharma*, see Lakshmi Kapani, "Spécificités de la religion hindoue," in *Le Fait religieux*, ed. Jean Delumeau (Paris: Fayard, 1993), 374ff. On the Chinese state's search for something equivalent to "religion" (and "super-stition"), see Vincent Goossaert, "L'invention des 'religions' en Chine moderne," in *La Pensée en Chine aujourd'hui*, ed. Anne Cheng (Paris: Gallimard, 2007), 185ff.

3. Jacques Derrida, "Above All, No Journalists!" trans. Samuel Weber, in *Religion and Media*, ed. Hent de Vries and Samuel Weber (Stanford, CA: Stanford University Press, 2011), 56–93.

4. Régis Debray, *Les Communions humaines: Pour en finir avec "la religion"* (Paris: Fayard, 2005), 59–60.

5. Ibid., 115–16. A series of exchanges took place between Derrida and Debray; Hent de Vries evokes it in the preface to his anthology *Religion: Beyond a Concept* (New York: Fordham University Press, 2008), 92–94. These exchanges bore, notably, on the distinction between "cult" and "culture," and derived another between "religious teaching" and "teaching religion" from it.

6. Talal Asad, *Genealogies of Religion: Discipline and Reasons of Power in Christianity and Islam* (Baltimore: Johns Hopkins University Press, 1993); Asad, *Formations of the Secular: Christianity, Islam, Modernity* (Stanford, CA: Stanford University Press, 2003). Asad radically criticizes French-style laïcité in "Trying to

Understand French Secularism," in *Political Theologies: Public Religions in a Post-Secular World*, ed. Hent de Vries and Lawrence Eugene Sullivan, (New York: Fordham University Press, 2006), 494–526, an essay that ought to be translated into French. Asad, one of the leading lights of the American "new anthropology," is the son of Mohammed Asad (Leopold Weiss), an Austrian-Polish Jew who converted to Islam in 1926 and went on to became one of the founders of Pakistan.

7. See Asad, *Formations of the Secular*, 191ff.

8. Besides the 1978 *Orientalism*, see Edward W. Said, *Covering Islam: How the Media and the Experts Determine How We See the Rest of the World* (New York: Vintage, 1997 [1981]).

9. I have in mind the now famous "Würzburg speech" delivered by Benoît XVI (Joseph Ratzinger) on September 12, 2006, "Faith, Reason, and the University: Memories and Reflections," http://w2.vatican.va/content/benedict-xvi/en/speeches/2006 /september/documents/hf_ben-xvi_spe_20060912_university -regensburg.html. This idea is all the more absurd in that philosophical and scientific rationalism, invented by the Greeks, returned to the Christian West by way of medieval Arab thought. See Philippe Büttgen et al., *Les Grecs, les Arabes et nous: Enquête sur l'Islamophobie savante* (Paris: Fayard, 2009).

10. Asad, *Formations of the Secular*, 78. Let us be fair to Asad: in the framework of a problematic that might be described as "critical culturalism," the accent in his work lies less on *totality* or *identity* than on the regimes of reference to tradition—as both "discursive regime" and "form of life" in Wittgenstein's sense—and on the models of "self-governance" (Foucault) that such a problematic provides. That is why analysis of the conflict between the various types of "reform" by means of which tradition reflects on itself (whether to regenerate itself or modify itself) holds a central place in Asad.

11. It is hard to avoid a sense that the critiques aimed at the category of religion (and, consequently, at a "secularism" supposed to

be its inverted image), when they are leveled by specialists in Judaism or Islam, reflect not only a distance taken from Eurocentrism, but also the pursuit of a quarrel internal to the monotheistic tradition and its successive revelations. This is manifest in Gil Anidjar, *Semites: Race, Religion, Literature* (Stanford, CA: Stanford University Press, 2008), which takes its inspiration from both Asad and Derrida. The very term "monotheism" is part of the problem (see Etienne Balibar: "Note sur l'origine et les usages du terme *monothéisme*," *Critique*, no. 704–705 (January-February 2006), chapter 10 of this volume; Thomas Römer, "Les monothéismes en question," in *Enquête sur le Dieu unique* (Paris: Bayard/Le Monde de la Bible, 2010), 11–15. On the constitution in Europe, from the sixteenth to the eighteenth century, of a historical and philological discipline correlative with the universalization of the category "religion," see Guy G. Stroumsa, *A New Science: The Discovery of Religion in the Age of Reason* (Cambridge, MA: Harvard University Press, 2010).

6. Culture, Religion, or Ideology

1. On the construction of the concept of ideology and the alternatives it contains within it, see Nestor Capdevila, *Le Concept d'idéologie* (Paris: Presses universitaires de France, 2004). Capdevila treats the concept of ideology as "essentially controversial" and, consequently, open-ended, even beyond the various uses to which Marxism puts it. I am reversing the tendency to describe processes of "ideologization" as effects of a degradation of the religious and attempting to lay the groundwork for a project comparable to the one that authors of Marxist inspiration have, following Carl Mannheim, carried out with the dichotomy ideology/utopia. See Michael Löwy, *Redemption and Utopia: Jewish Libertarian Thought in Central Europe, A Study in Elective Affinity*, trans. Hope Heaney (Stanford, CA: Stanford University Press, 1992).

2. Not only does a description of this sort not require us to restrict "the religious phenomenon" to the field of belief; it may also allow us to account adequately for the bodily inscription of religious practice (observable in asceticism as well as in rites or taboos), which institutionalizes the short circuit between law and the gesture. See Mohammed Hocine Benkheira, *Islam et interdits alimentaires: Juguler l'animalité* (Paris: Presses universitaires françaises, 2000). Benkheira centers his analysis of "Islam as a religious system" on an Islamic politics of the body, the essential aspect of which, legally codified in the *fikh* ("Muslims live in the world as jurists"), is not belief, but individual and collective ritual, a translation into practice of the distinction between the licit and the illicit. Compare this with Jean Robelin's reflections in Robelin, *Maïmonide et le langage religieux* (Paris: Presses universitaires de France, 1991), especially 153ff.: "La religion, institution de la culture."

3. Judg. 12:5–6. See Jacques Derrida, *Shibboleth*, trans. Joshua Wilner and Thomas Dutoit, in *Sovereignties in Question: The Poetics of Paul Celan*, ed. Thomas Dutoit and Outi Pasanen (New York: Fordham University Press, 2005) [Perspectives in Continental Philosophy], 1–64.

4. Clifford Geertz, "Religion as a Cultural System," in Geertz, *The Interpretation of Cultures* (New York: Basic Books, 1973), 87–125. See Talal Asad's commentary in Asad, "The Construction of Religion as an Anthropological Category," in *Genealogies of Religion: Discipline and Reasons of Power in Christianity and Islam* (Baltimore: Johns Hopkins, 1993), 27–54. See also Bruno Karsenti: "In the long term, then, indications are that a kind of inversion has come about. It seems that there has been a shift from a universal religion exercising its domination and penetrating every culture in the imperial context of the "first modernity" to a universal culture in which religion concentrates, and expresses better than any other type of phenomenon . . . the irreducible particularity subsisting in the life of concrete societies.

Religion, the hard core of whatever is specific to a culture, would appear to belong, for reasons of principle, to the realm of the non-universalizable. What universality do we mean, however, when we invoke culture in order to include religion in it? After all, culture, too, can be reduced to a localized conceptual creation, the invention of a type of society at a determinate moment of its history. In a word, it too . . . can be considered relative. Is this to say that the claim to universality, while changing motives, has not really changed bearers—that the religion of the imperial West has merely yielded to a new type of ethnocentrism, centered on forms of progress of the human spirit as unified by the concept of culture, itself an appanage of the West's, but a West that is now 'enlightened'? The part of illusion this vision contains is well known." (Karsenti, "Structuralism and Religion," in *Faire des sciences sociales*, ed. Isabelle Thireau et al. [Paris: EHESS, 2012]). On the connection between "anthropological" and "humanistic" concepts of culture, see Terence Turner, "Human Rights, Human Difference: Anthropology's Contribution to an Emancipatory Cultural Politics," *Journal of Anthropological Research*, vol. 53, no. 3 (1997): 273–91. (I thank Olivier Remaud for calling this important text to my attention.) See also the unjustly neglected analyses in Edmond Ortigues, *Religions du livre, religions de la coutume* (Paris: Sycomore, 1981). For Karsenti, who is endeavoring to rehabilitate these analyses, the distinction between the two types of "religion" has to be interpreted as the index of a gradual differentiation within the underlying phenomenon of "symbolic transmission."

5. Max Weber, "Intermediate Reflections: Religious Rejections of the World and their Directions," trans. and ed. Hans Gerth and C. Wright Mills, in *From Max Weber*, ed. Gerth and Mills (New York: Oxford University Press, 1946 [1915]), 323–59. I here use both the standard English translation of the Weberian category of *Veralltäglichung*, "routinization," as well as "reduction to the level of daily life." The former is closer to the literal meaning of

the German word, while the latter better brings out the change in normative modality associated with Weber's comparison of the three types of "legitimation of domination." See my lecture to Pierre Macherey's study group: https://f-origin.hypotheses .org/wp-content/blogs.dir/165/files/2017/09/03-11-2004 _Balibar.pdf as well as Frédéric Keck's comments: https:// f-origin.hypotheses.org/wp-content/blogs.dir/165/files /2017/09/03-11-2004_kecknotebalibar.pdf.

6. Louis Althusser, "Is it Simple to be a Marxist in Philosophy?" trans. Grahame Lock, in *Essays in Self-Criticism* (London: New Left, 1976), 187.

7. RELIGIOUS REVOLUTIONS AND
ANTHROPOLOGICAL DIFFERENCES

1. See Etienne Balibar, "The Ill-Being of the Subject," in *Citizen Subject, Foundations for Philosophical Anthropology*, trans. Steven Miller (New York: Fordham University Press, 2016), 173–302. I would have been unable to undertake this reversal of perspectives without Jacques Derrida's critique of the theme of "ontological difference" in Heidegger: Derrida, "Geschlecht I: Ontological Difference, Sexual Difference," in Derrida, *Psyche: Inventions of the Other*, vol. 2, ed. Peggy Kamuf and Elizabeth Rottenburg (Stanford, CA: Stanford University Press, 2008), 7–26. Other texts were also of decisive importance here, especially Claude Levi-Strauss, "Cosmopolitanism and Schizophrenia," in Levi-Strauss, *The View From Afar*, trans. Joachim Neugroschel and Phoebe Hoss (Chicago: University of Chicago Press, 1992), 177–85, and Michel Foucault, *Abnormal: Lectures at the Collège de France, 1974–1975*, ed. Arnold I. Davidson, trans. Graham Burchell (New York: Picador, 2004). For a different argument (inspired by Bataille, Lacan, and Deligny) that is nevertheless comparable as far as its critical effects on the idea of a human condition are concerned, see Bertrand Ogilvie, "Anthropologie du

propre à rien," in Ogilvie, *Le passant ordinaire*, no. 38 (January-March 2002) and *Ogilvie, La Seconde Nature du politique: Essai d'anthropologie négative* (Paris: L'Harmattan, 2012).

2. This is shown, in particular, by Gershom Scholem's work on Jewish messianism: *Major Trends in Jewish Mysticism* (New York: Schocken, 1995), and *Sabbatai Sevi, The Mystical Messiah* (Princeton: Princeton University Press, 1976).

3. This does not mean that the culture that distributes social roles constitutes an incontestable determinism: every culture, even if it is based on an organization of spheres of activity and a status hierarchy, contains possibilities of reversal and play. That point is one of the themes of a book that has modified the relations between feminism and anthropology: Marilyn Strathern, *The Gender of the Gift: Problems with Women and Problems with Society in Melanesia* (Berkeley: University of California Press, 1990). It is also the point at which these two discourses encounter the problematic of "power" in Foucault's sense: see Foucault, "Sex, Power, and the Politics of Identity: An Interview," in *Ethics. Subjectivity and Truth: Selections from the Essential Works of Foucault, 1954–1984*, vol. 1, ed. Paul Rabinow and N. Rose (New York: New Press, 1998), 163–174.

4. I borrow this phrase from Leszek Kolakowski, "La revanche du sacré dans la culture profane," *Revue du MAUSS*, no. 22: "Qu'est-ce que le religieux?" 2003 (1973): 57. Bataille's terminology—"excess," "expenditure," the "accursed share"—points in the same general direction, while accentuating the register of the ambiguous (already present in the Roman notion of the "sacred," on which Girogio Agamben bases his problematization of *homo sacer*).

5. See Michael Löwy, *The War of the Gods: Religion and Politics in Latin America* (London: Verso, 1996). Because of Bartolomé de Las Casas's early denunciation of the conquest and the oppression of American Indians, liberation theology has adopted him as one of its own. His work and action do indeed constitute a privileged

object of reflection about the possibilities of subversion, even radical subversion, inherent in the Christian theology of the incarnation. Yet Las Casas is precisely *not* a "revolutionary." See Nestor Capdevila, *Las Casas: Une politique de l'humanité* (Paris: Le Cerf, 1998).

6. On the generalization of the masculine-feminine distinction in the "Medina surats" of the Koran, see Denis Gril, "Femme," in M. A. Amir-Moezzi, *Dictionnaire du Coran*, 338ff. Fethi Benslama undertakes an undoubtedly debatable, yet very suggestive psychoanalytical interpretation of the relationship between the scheme of genealogical transmission and the ambiguousness of the role of the feminine in Islam, particularly as revealed by the figure of Hagar, the wife "cast out" by Abraham, from whom the Arabs and the Prophet himself are supposed to have descended (Fethi Benslama, trans. Robert Bononno, *Psychoanalysis and the Challenge of Islam* [Minneapolis: University of Minnesota Press, 2009]). There is no avoiding the comparison, although it is by no means easy to make, with other figures of originary repression in the Western monotheisms, particularly the *virginity* of the Mother of the Savior, which would seem to introduce a "matriarchal" element into Christianity, but at the price of accentuating the prohibition of the "fleshly." See Marina Warner, *Alone of All her Sex: The Myth and Cult of the Virgin Mary* (New York: Vintage, 1983).

7. See Reza Azlan's commentary on Armina Wadud, *Qur'an and Women: Reading the Sacred Text from a Women's Perspective* (Oxford: Oxford University Press, 1999), in Azlan, *No God but God: The Origins, Evolution, and Future of Islam* (New York: Random House, 2005), 73ff. See also Margot Badran, "Islamic Feminism: What's in a Name?" *Al-Ahram* (January 2002): 17–23; Badran, "Exploring Islamic Feminism," Center for Muslim-Christian Understanding, Georgetown University, November 30, 2000. My understanding of the relationship between *shari'a*

and *fikh* is based on *Dictionnaire du Coran*, ed. M. A. Amir-Moezzi (Paris: Bouquins), 818ff.

8. Saba Mahmood, *Politics of Piety: The Islamic Revival and the Feminist Subject* (Princeton, NJ: Princeton University Press, 2005). What makes Mahmood's study fascinating is her depiction of the way women appropriate a function of *interpreting* the law that is traditionally an exclusively male prerogative; this leads them not to "reverse" the socially institutionalized relations of dependency prescribed by the Koran, but to come forward, vis-à-vis their husbands, as the spokeswomen of a higher authority (God) in order to demand that the men respect it more conscientiously than they would if left to their own devices. (Women thus make themselves, as it were, their guardians' guardians.) This is also women's way of "exercising governance," as best they can, in a situation in which being single or being repudiated by one's husband is tantamount to social death. We have here a dialectic that Mahmood seeks radically to distinguish from a problematic of "resistance" or "emancipation," but that nonetheless confers a subversive function on religious tradition (within certain political limits).

9. Danièle Hervieu-Léger, ed., *Religion et écologie* (Paris: Le Cerf, 1993); Isabelle Stengers, *Au temps des catastrophes: Résister à la barbarie qui vient* (Paris: Les Empêcheurs de penser en rond, 2009).

8. SECULARISM SECULARIZED: THE VANISHING MEDIATOR

1. Gayatri Chakravorty Spivak, *Death of a Discipline* (New York: Columbia University Press, 2003); Paul Gilroy, *Postcolonial Melancholia* (New York: Columbia University Press, 2004).

2. See the work of André Tosel, especially *Scénarios de la mondialisation culturelle*, vols. 1 and 2 (Paris: Kimé, 2011), and Iain Chambers's interesting "The 'Unseen Order': Religion, Secularism and

Hegemony," in *The Postcolonial Gramsci*, ed. Neelam Srivasta and Baidik Bhattacharya (Oxford: Routledge, 2011).

3. Slavoj Žižek overstates his case, but touches on a fundamental question when he writes: "This ecology of fear has every chance of developing into the predominant form of ideology of global capitalism, a new opium for the masses replacing declining religion: it takes over the old religion's fundamental function, that of having an unquestionable authority which can impose limits." Žižek, "Unbehagen in der Natur," in *In Defense of Lost Causes* (London: Verso, 2008), 439.

4. I here borrow Bruce Robbins's formulation in "Said and Secularism," in *Edward Said and Jacques Derrida: Reconstellating Humanism and the Global Hybrid*, ed. Mina Karavanta and Nina Morgan (Cambridge: Cambridge Scholars, 2008), 140–57.

5. On this point, see especially Giacomo Marramao, *Dopo il Leviatano: Individuo e comunità* (Turin: Bollati Boringhieri, 2000); Marramao, *Potere e secolarizzazione: Le categorie del tempo* (Turin: Bollati Boringhieri, 2005).

6. Etienne Balibar, "Strangers and Enemies: Further Reflections on the Aporias of Transnational Citizenship," Globalization Working Papers, 06/4, McMaster University, March 16, 2006: http://www.globalautonomy.ca/global1/article.jsp?index=RA _Balibar_Strangers.xml. See also Balibar, *Violence and Civility* (New York: Columbia University Press, 2014).

7. Ghislaine Glasson-Deschaumes and Rada Ivekovic, eds., "Sur l'expérience de l'exil et son pouvoir critique," *Transeuropéennes*, no. 22 (Spring–Summer 2002): Traduire, entre les cultures. See also Edward Said, *Convergences: Inventories of the Present, Reflections on Exile and Other Essays* (Cambridge, MA: Harvard University Press, 2002).

8. One finds a somewhat different idea in Jan Assmann, "Translating Gods: Religion as a Factor of Cultural (Un)Translatability," in *Religion: Beyond a Concept*, ed. Hent de Vries (New York: Fordham University Press, 2008), 139–49. Assmann opposes,

from this standpoint, the "monotheisms" to the "polytheisms," bringing them into relation with two types of empires. This distinction itself may be regarded as an ideal type. However, there is an underlying tension between two types of problematics: those that (as in Assmann, or, in a different way, in Ortigues) insist on the *ambiguity* of the notion of religion, and the one I am sketching here, in which the religious as such represents the untranslatable, while cultures are susceptible, if not of mutual translation, then at least of mutual interpretation and comprehension.

9. I am using the word *differend* in the sense Jean-François Lyotard gives it in *Differend: Phrases in Dispute*, trans. Georges Van Den Abbeele (Minneapolis: University of Minnesota Press, 1989): a juxtaposition of sentences from different regimes that thwarts the continuity and reciprocity of dialogue, thus constantly requiring us to invent another "sentence."

10. Fredric Jameson, "The Vanishing Mediator, or Max Weber as Storyteller" (1973), in *The Ideologies of Theory: Essays 1971–1986*, vol. 2: *Syntax of History* (London: Routledge, 1988), 3–34.

11. On the confrontations between moral discourses, with specific reference to the conflicts generated by decolonization, see Hans Schelkshorn, *Diskurs und Befreiung*: *Studien zur philosophischen Ethik von Karl-Otto Apel und Enrique Dussel* (Amsterdam: Rodopi, 1997). For a more profound consideration of the intercultural as an alternative to neoliberal globalization, see Raul Fornet-Betancourt, *La philosophie interculturelle: Penser autrement le monde*, preface by Fred Poché (Paris: Atelier/Editions ouvrières, 2011).

12. Frédéric Brahami, *Le Travail du scepticisme: Montaigne, Bayle, Hume* (Paris: Presses universitaires de France, 2001).

13. Warren Montag, "Lucretius Hebraizant: Spinoza's Reading of Ecclesiastes," in *European Journal of Philosophy*, vol. 20, no. 1 (March 2012), 109–29. See also Yirmiyahu Yovel, *Spinoza and Other Heretics*, 2 vols. (Princeton, NJ: Princeton University Press, 1992).

9. Envoi

1. See Nilüfer Göle's very good remarks on this in her article, "La laïcité républicaine et l'Islam public," in *Pouvoirs. Revue française d'études constitutionnelles et politiques*, no. 115 (November 2005): 73–86. She relates this confrontation (in the case of France and Turkey) to a "didactic secularism" (Ernest Gellner): "Comparing the two Republics also highlights the fundamental importance of the law. . . . The law is the vector which changes practices, as shown by the Turkish civil code breaking with the religious law, the *shar'ia*. . . . The law does not arise from negotiating with the society, but it appears as a didactic instrument to change mores, social and cultural habits. . . ." (79).

2. A discussion continues about whether globalization, which reverses the hierarchy between commodity universalism and civic universalism in the public space, produces a development or a degeneracy of the juridical norm that is applicable to persons and their "intercourse." On this point, see Giacomo Marramao, *Dopo il Leviatano* (Turin: Bollati Boringhieri, 2000), and Mireille Delmas-Marty, *Le relatif et l'universel* (*Les forces imaginantes du droit*, I) (Paris: Le Seuil, 2004).

3. In my essay, "The Ill-Being of the Subject," in *Citizen Subject* (New York: Fordham University Press, 2016), I tried to demonstrate that civic-bourgeois universalism—as expressed in the discourse of human rights that directly communicates with a program of the secularization of the world—does not suppress the discriminating function of anthropological differences, even if it reproduces in its own language the eschatological promise of their overcoming.

4. Hegel, in the *Phenomenology of Spirit*, famously called "femininity" an "eternal irony of the community." How not to add that "masculinity," as an eternal vanity, or incurable paranoia of the individual, seems to pertain to every religion or culture, with no monopoly?

5. I am referring to Bruno Karsenti, *Moïse et l'idée de peuple. La vérité historique selon Freud* (Paris: Cerf, 2012); and Geneviève Fraisse, *Muse de la raison. La démocratie exclusive et la différence des sexes* (Paris: Alinéa, 1989).

6. Bertrand Ogilvie, *La seconde nature du politique. Essai d'anthropologie négative* (Paris: L'Harmattan, 2012).

7. See interesting analyzes on this point by Jean Robelin, focusing on "religious coding of bodies," in "Corps et sacré" in *Noesis*, no. 12 (2007): 207–24.

8. Etienne Balibar, *Equaliberty. Political Essays*, trans. James Ingram (Durham, NC: Duke University Press, 2014).

10. NOTE ON THE ORIGIN AND USES OF THE WORD "MONOTHEISM"

The present text was originally published in the review *Critique* (see the special issue titled "God," [January-February 2006], nos. 704–705, pp. 19–45). It had been meant to represent only a note to the article on "monotheism" that I was committed to contribute for the issue, until I discovered the need to reconstruct a missing history that I initially thought I could sum up by just citing a few obvious references. More recently, similar considerations have been offered by Thomas Römer, in *L'invention de Dieu*, chapter 12, "Du Dieu *un* au Dieu *unique*" and notes (Paris: Le Seuil, 2014). After the publication of my article in French, I received several contributions, indicating sources that I had neglected or ignored, particularly from my colleague at University Paris-Sorbonne and the Ecole Normale Supérieure, Jean-François Courtine, who gave me several very interesting German references in Kant, Goethe, Novalis. . . . The Kantian references, in addition to confirming the overwhelming prevalence of the debate on the (perilous) affinities of "monotheism," "pantheism," and "atheism" at the origins of German Idealism, also suggest that I may have overlooked the importance of his debate with Moses Mendelssohn, with whom I lack familiarity. On Hegel, see note 32.

1. For example, Jean-Luc Nancy's recent undertaking, *Disenclosure: The Deconstruction of Christianity*, trans. Bettina Bergo (New York: Fordham University Press, 2008), two chapters of which are titled, respectively, "Atheism and Monotheism" and "The Deconstruction of Monotheism." Nancy asks, among other things, in what sense the "self-interpretive" nature of Christianity privileges it when it comes to deconstructing monotheism in general without prejudice to the pluralism constituting it.

2. *Le Coran*, trans. Denise Masson (Paris: Folio-Gallimard, 1967), cxi; *Le Coran*, ed. and trad. Jacques Berque (Paris: Sinbad, 1990). The *shirk*, opposed to the *tawhîd*, is thus occasionally translated as "associationism" rather than "polytheism." See Ibn 'Arabi, *La Profession de foi*, trans. R. Deladrière (Paris: Sinbad, 1995), 83. [Translator's Note: I have here cited from *The Koran* (the *Quran*), trans. E. H. Palmer (Oxford University Press, 1951), 20, 80, and 17, respectively. One passage cited here is not to be found in Palmer's translation at or near where it is supposed to be].

3. See Reza Aslan, *No god but God: The Origins, Evolution, and Future of Islam* (New York: Random House, 2005), 214–16.

4. Deutero-Isaiah is a striking exception (Isa. 41–43). See Françoise Smyth-Florentin, "Du monothéisme biblique: Émergence et alentours," in *Archives de Sciences Sociales des Religions*, vol. 59, no. 1 (January-March 1985): 5–16.

5. Emmanuel Levinas, *Beyond the Verse: Talmudic Readings and Lectures*, trans. Gary Mole (Bloomington and Indianapolis: Indiana University Press, 1994).

6. Roger Arnaldez, "Philon d'Alexandrie," in *Dictionnaire des philosophes* (Paris: Presses universitaires de France, 1984).

7. Jean Trouillard, "Procession néoplatonicienne et création judéo-chrétienne," in *Néoplatonisme: Mélanges offertejs à Jean Trouillard*, *Les Cahiers de Fontenay*, no. 19 (March 1981): 8.

8. H. D. Saffrey and L. G. Westerink, Introduction to Proclus, *Théologie platonicienne*, Book III (Paris: Les Belles Lettres, Budé, 1978), lxxi. Proclus takes the concept of *theologia* from Aristotle, distinguishing it from *theomuthia*. See Victor Goldschmidt, *Questions platoniciennes* (Paris: Vrin, 1970), 144ff., and Luc Brisson, *Introduction à la philosophie du mythe*, vol. 1: *Sauver les mythes* (Paris: Vrin, 1996), 121–45.

9. Endre von Ivanka, "Le problème des 'noms de Dieu' et de l'ineffabilité divine selon le pseudo-Denys l'Aréopagite," in *L'analyse du langage théologique: Le nom de Dieu. Actes du colloque organisé par le Centre international d'études philosophiques de Rome, Rome, 5–11 janvier 1969*, ed. Enrico Castelli (Paris: Aubier-Montaigne, 1969), 201–206.

10. See, for example, Adolf von Harnack, *Mission et expansion du christianisme aux trois premiers siècles*, trans. Joseph Hoffman, preface by Michel Tardieu (Paris: Les éditions du Cerf, 2004), 48ff.; *The Expansion of Christianity in the First Three Centuries*, ed. and trans. James Moffatt (Charleston, SC: BiblioBazaar, 2009 [New York: Putnam, 1905]).

11. "Well then, about eating this consecrated food: of course, as you say, 'a false god has no existence in the real world (*ouden eidôlon en kosmôi*). There is no god but one' (*ouden theos heteros ei mè heis*). For indeed, if there be so-called gods, whether in heaven or on earth—as indeed there are many 'gods' and many 'lords'—yet for us there is one God, the Father, from whom all being comes, towards whom we move (*heis theos ho patèr ex'hou ta panta kai hèmeis eis auton*); and there is one Lord, Jesus Christ, through whom all things came to be, and we through him (*heis kurios Ièsous Khristos di'hou ta panta kai hèmeis di'autou*)" (1 Cor. 8:4–6, New English Bible).

12. Philippe Borgeaud, *Aux origines de l'histoire des religions* (Paris: Seuil, 2004), 51.

13. Erik Peterson, *Der Monotheismus als politisches Problem*, in *Ausgewählte Schriften*, vol. 1: *Theologische Traktate* (Würzburg: Echter Verlag, 1994), 23–81.

14. "All men love and fear this unique God, who decreed, in the very period in which he wished to reveal Himself to us, the unity of this empire, with the result that the same laws that are subjected to the unique God impose themselves everywhere." (*Subiecto* would appear to be a misreading of *subiectae*.)

15. Peterson, *Der Monotheismus*, 55–56.

16. Peterson was contested on this point by Carl Schmitt in part 2 of his *Political Theology*, which was belatedly in 1969 a response to what he saw as a complete refutation of his own viewpoint (see Carl Schmitt, *Théologie politique* [Paris: Gallimard, 1988], 83–166); *Political Theology: Four Chapters on the Concept of Sovereignty*, trans. George Schwab (Chicago: University of Chicago Press, 2006), and *Political Theology II: The Myth of the Closure of any Political Theology*, trans. Michael Hoelzl and Graham Ward (Cambridge-Malden: Polity, 2008). Jan Assmann discusses this confrontation in the introduction to *Herrschaft und Heil: Politische Theologie in Altägypten, Israel und Europa* (Munich: Carl Hanser, 2000), which focuses on the evolution and significance of the concept of "political theology."

17. Roger Arnaldez (*À la croisée des trois monothéismes: Une communauté de pensée au Moyen-âge* [Paris: Albin Michel, 1993]) suggests another angle that should be explored so as not to create a false impression of exhaustiveness. It concerns the exchange of the arguments that Jews, Christians, and Muslims directed against the *dualism* of the Mazdeans and, later, the Manicheans, an exchange that did not lead to mutual recognition under a common name. Admittedly, this debate bore on human freedom rather than divine monarchy. But are they separable?

18. Francis Schmidt, "Naissance des polythéismes, 1624–1757," in *Archives de Sciences Sociales des Religions*, vol. 59, no. 1 (January–March 1985). See also "La discussion sur l'origine de l'idolâtrie aux XVIIe et XVIIIe siècles," in *Rencontres de l'École du Louvre: L'idolâtrie* (La Documentation française, 1990).

19. Ralph Cudworth, D. D., *The True Intellectual System of the Universe: The First Part; wherein, All the Reason and Philosophy of Atheism is Confuted; and Its Impossibility Demonstrated* (London: Fromann Verlag, 1964, and Thoemmes Press, 1995). Chapter 4 (pp. 192–632) discusses the question of polytheism, the question as to whether the idea of a unitary God underlies paganism, the relations between Platonism and the theology of the Trinity, and so on.

20. David Hume, *The Natural History of Religion*, ed. A. Wayne Colver (Oxford: The Clarendon Press, 1976), 61.

21. As Philippe Borgeaud reminds us (*Aux origines de l'histoire*, 65ff), students of the Bible are happy to ascribe the emergence of the prophetic tradition and, consequently, the birth of "true monotheism" (as distinct from the *henotheism* of the ancient Hebrews) to this encounter between the two religions during the Babylonian exile.

22. Edward Gibbon, *The History of the Decline and Fall of the Roman Empire*, ed. David Womersley, 3 vols. (Harmondsworth, Great Britain: Penguin, 1994).

23. Edgar Quinet, *Le Christianisme et la Révolution française* (Paris: Fayard, 1984), 118.

24. *Das älteste Systemprogramm des deutschen Idealismus*, in *L'absolu littéraire: Théorie de la littérature du romantisme allemand*, trans. Philippe Lacoue-Labarthe and Jean-Luc Nancy (Paris: Seuil, 1978), 53–54; *The Literary Absolute: The Theory of Literature in German Romanticism*, trans. Philip Barnard (New York: SUNY, 1988). See the whole dossier of the controversy in *Mythologie der Vernunft: Hegels ältestes Systemprogramm des deutschen Idealismus*, eds. Christoph Jamme and Helmut Schneider (Frankfurt: Suhrkamp, 1984).

25. One of the rare commentaries on this formula is to be found in Françoise Dastur, "La poésie comme origine: Hölderlin et Heidegger," in *À la naissance des choses: Art, poésie et philosophie*

(Paris: Encre marine, 2005), 144–45. Dastur sets the text in relation with Hölderlin's essay "On Religion" and discerns a critique of Kant's theory of the sublime in it. These symmetries reflect the spirit of the times, but nowhere do they reach the same conceptual intensity. Witness the sentence that Fichte cites in his 1799 *Réponse juridique à l'accusation d'athéisme*: "Religion can consist in polytheism just as well as in monotheism, in anthropomorphism just as well as in spiritualism" (*Querelle de l'athéisme suivie de divers textes sur la religion*, ed. Jean-Charles Goddard [Paris: Vrin, 1993], 100).

26. See the book published by Citizen Dupuis in Year Three of the Revolution (1795): *Origine de tous les cultes, ou Religion universelle*, which proposes to integrate a Christianity purged of its superstitions into a religion of "God the Universe," of which the ancient mythologies of the heavenly bodies are supposed to have had a premonition.

27. *The Critique of Pure Reason* appeared in 1788 and *Religion Within the Limits of Reason Alone* in 1793. Robespierre instituted the Cult of the Supreme Being in 1794.

28. I have consulted *Symbolik und Mythologie der Alten Völker, besonders der Griechen*, von Dr. Friedrich Creuzer, Professor der Althen Literatur zu Heidelberg, Erster Theil . . . Zweite völlig umbearbeitete Ausgabe, Leipzig und Darmstadt, 1819, and *Religions de l'Antiquité, considérées principalement dans leurs formes symboliques et mythologiques*, ouvrage traduit de l'allemand du Dr. Creuzer, refondu en partie, complété et développé par J. D. Guigniaut . . . Tome Premier, Première partie, Paris, MDCCCXXV. For an attempt to put Creuzer's work in perspective, see Christoph Jamme, *Introduction à la philosophie du mythe*, vol. 2: *Époque moderne et contemporaine*, trad. A. Pernet (Paris: Vrin, 1995); *Einführung in die Philosophie des Mythos*, vol. 2: *Neuzeit und Gegenwart* (Darmstadt: Wissenschaftliche Buchgesellschaft, 1991).

29. Georg-Friedrich Creuzer and Gottfried Hermann, *Briefe über Homer und Hesiodus, vorzüglich über die Theogonie* (Heidelberg: August Ostwald, 1818).

30. Ernest Renan, "Des religions de l'antiquité et de leurs derniers historiens" (1853), in *Études d'histoire religieuse* (1857) (Paris: Gallimard, 1992), 35–78; *Studies of Religious History*, trans. O. B. Frothingham (New York: Carleton, 1864), [trans. note: probably p. 62 to around p. 100. The book is available on line, see www .archive.org]

31. It may be asked, with regard to what follows, whether we do not have hints of a *fourth approach* (it might be called *projective*) to the constitution of the notion of "monotheism" in post-revolutionary Europe, which was also the Europe of the emancipation of the Jews and the beginnings of European colonization of the Islamic world. This approach would discern monotheism above all *in the "Eastern" other*, equivocally associating Islam with Judaism via the reference to a "Semitism" that is either idealized or made to serve as a negative foil. This very clearly holds for Renan after 1850, but the phenomenon would have to be documented for the preceding period, particularly in the English-speaking countries.

32. Following the publication of this essay in French, my colleague Jean-François Courtine signaled to me a single exception, all the more remarkable, to this exclusion: in his *Encyclopedia of the Philosophical Sciences* from 1830 (par. 573), Hegel names "monotheism" to characterize the Hindu religion of Brahma. This reference is repeated in his account of *Bafhavad Gîta* (in the *Philosophy of Religion*), both times with a reference to the essay by Thomas Colebrooke: "On the Vedas, or the Sacred Writings of the Hindus," in *Asiatic Researches*, vol. 8 (1808) by the Asiatic Society of Calcutta.

33. F. W. J. Schelling, *Les divinités de Samothrace*, trans. Samuel Janké-lévitch, in *Les âges du monde* (Paris: Aubier-Montaigne, 1949), 212; *The Deities of Samothrace*, ed. and trans. Robert J. Brown

(Missoula, MT: Scholars Press, 1977). In contrast, the question of monotheism plays no role in Schelling's 1809 treatise *On the Essence of Human Freedom*, which bases its treatment of the division of the idea of God on the alternative between Good and Evil (he occasionally calls the latter "the inverted God" [*der umgekehrte Gott*]).

34. *La philosophie de la mythologie de Schelling d'après Charles Secrétan (Munich 1835–36) et Henri-Frédéric Amiel (Berlin 1845–46)*, ed. L. Pareyson and M. Pagano (Milan: Mursia Editore, 1991).

35. F. W. J. Schelling, *Der Monotheismus, Erste Vorlesung*, S.W., XII, 13. See A. Pernet's translation, *Le Monothéisme*, with an introduction by Xavier Tilliette (Paris: Vrin, 1992), 27–28.

36. In *The Education of Mankind* (1780), Lessing posits (in paragraph 1) that "revelation is to mankind what education is to the individual."

37. Xavier Tilliette has observed that Schelling, while taking up the Paulinian theme of *kenosis*, goes on to make a strange substitution here: "Paganism is the Revelation's veritable Old Testament. . . . Paradoxically, the Biblical Revelation appears to be superfluous. . . . It is easier to understand the embarrassment into which Judaism plunged Schelling when one knows that, for him, Christ is not the Jewish Messiah, but the 'Light of the pagans,' *Lumen gentium*" (*L'Absolu et la philosophie: Essais sur Schelling* [Paris: Presses universitaires de France, 1987]), 247.

38. According to the equivalence posited in 1709 by the inventor of this notion. See John Toland, *Pantheisticon*, eds. O. Nicastro and M. Iofrida (Pisa: Edizioni ETS, 1996), 20–21; *Pantheisticon: A Modern English Translation*, trans. Jason Cooper (Lulu Press, 2014).

39. On Schelling's combination of the themes of the humanization of God (or "anthropomorphism"), Being as Potentiality, and the God who is always still to come, see Jean-François Courtine, *Extase de la Raison: Essais sur Schelling* (Paris: Galilée, 1990), 203–59.

40. F. W. J. Schelling, *Historical-Critical Introduction to the Philosophy of Mythology*, trans. Mason Richey (New York: SUNY, 2008).

41. One is struck by the fact that Schleiermacher uses "polytheism" only once and never uses "monotheism" in *Reden über die Religion* (1799), in which he introduces concepts that were to enjoy phenomenal success (such as "virtuosity" and "holy melancholy"). Schleiermacher's transition from Judaism to Christianity is organized around the idea of prophecy, while his definition of religious sentiment as an intuition of the infinite nature of the universe is marked by unmistakably pantheistic accents. This fact seems to me to substantiate the hypothesis that Creuzer and Schelling influenced Schleiermacher's adoption of a "new" terminology.

42. *Schleiermacher Kritische Ausgabe*, vol. 7, part 1 (Berlin: Walter de Gruyter, 1980), 49.

43. Jan Assmann, *Das verschleierte Bild zu Sais: Schillers Ballade und ihre griechischen und ägyptischen Hintergründe* (Stuttgart: Teubner, 1999); Pierre Hadot, *The Veil of Isis: An Essay on the History of the Idea of Nature*, trans. Michael Chase (Cambridge, MA: Belknap Press, 2008).

44. *Schleiermacher Kritische Ausgabe*, vol. 13, part 2, 514–32. The line that runs from here to the question that Peterson asked himself in 1935, in a completely different conjuncture, to be sure, would seem to be a straight one.

45. *De la religion considéré dans sa source, ses formes, et ses développements* (1824–1825), after Mary Pickering, *Auguste Comte: An Intellectual Biography*, vol. 1 (London: Cambridge University Press, 1993), 273. In a posthumous book, *Du polythéisme romain considéré dans ses rapports avec la philosophie grecque et la religion chrétienne* (1833), Constant systematically opposes polytheism and theism (he says of theism that the religion of the Hebrews "gave the world the signal").

46. See Alfonso M. Iacono, *Le fétichisme: Histoire d'un concept* (Paris: Presses universitaires de France, 1992). De Brosses's text has recently been translated into English; see *The Returns of Fetishism*,

ed. Rosalind C. Morris and Daniel H. Leonard (Chicago: University of Chicago Press, 2017).

47. *Doctrine saint-simonienne: Exposition* (Paris: Librairie nouvelle, 1854), 313–28. This is one of the rare editions containing the *two years* of the Course taught by Bazard and Olinde Rodriguès.

48. Profoundly influenced by Freemasonry, the Saint-Simonians also saw Lessing as an intellectual ancestor, and translated his *The Education of Mankind* into French in 1832.

49. Georges Canguilhem demonstrates this in "Histoire des religions et histoire des sciences dans la théorie du fétichisme chez Auguste Comte," in *Études d'histoire et de philosophie des sciences* (Paris: Vrin, 1968).

50. Auguste Comte, *Cours de philosophie positive*, fifty-fourth lecture, new edition (Paris: Hermann, 1975), vol. 2, 332.

51. Ibid., 330.

52. Comte, *Cours de philosophie positive*, 53e leçon; Comte, *Système de politique positive ou Traité de sociologie instituant la Religion de l'Humanité* (Paris: 1929 [1853]), vol. 3, 240. Comte discusses Buddhism as a "subversive" religion in the same text.

53. Comte, *Système*, 471. We should, however, note Comte's vacillation over Islam from one text to the other, as well as the ambiguity of his formulations on Islam.

54. Comte, *Système*, vol. 1, 244

55. See Marc Augé, *Génie du paganisme* (Paris: Gallimard, 1982).

56. The work of Stanislas Breton, from *Unicité et monothéisme* (1981) through *Philosophie et mystique* (1996) to *L'avenir du christianisme* (1999) provides a striking illustration of this point. Henri Corbin, too, sets out from the Neoplatonist heritage when he distinguishes, after Ibn 'Arabi, what he calls the esoteric or ontological *tawhîd* from the exoteric or theological *tawhîd* (*Le paradoxe du monothéisme* [Paris: Éditions de l'Herne, 1981]).

57. Jan Assmann, *Moses der Ägypter: Entzifferung einer Gedächtnisspur* (Frankfurt: Fischer, 1998); *Moses the Egyptian: The Memory of Egypt in Western Monotheism* (Cambridge, MA: Harvard University

Press, 1997); *Assmann, Die Mosaische Unterscheidung, oder der Preis des Monotheismus* (Munich: Carl Hanser Verlag, 2003); *The Price of Monotheism*, trans. Robert Savage (Stanford, CA: Stanford University Press, 2009).

11. "GOD WILL NOT REMAIN SILENT": ZIONISM, MESSIANISM, AND NATIONALISM

1. First published (in French) in *Agenda de la Pensée Contemporaine*, no. 9 (Hiver, 2007). English translation in *Human Architecture, Journal of the Sociology of Self-Knowledge*, vol. 7, no. 2 (Spring 2009), 123–34. Review essay of the following three books: Jacqueline Rose, *The Question of Zion* (Princeton, NJ: Princeton University Press, 2005); Idith Zertal, *La nation et la mort. La Shoah dans le discours et la politique d'Israël*, translated from the English by Marc Saint-Upéry (Paris: La Découverte, 2004), *Israel's Holocaust and the Politics of Nationhood* (Cambridge, 2005); Amnon Raz-Krakotzkin, *Exil et souveraineté. Judaïsme, sionisme et pensée bi-nationale*, trans. Catherine Neuve-Eglise (Paris: La Fabrique, 2007), preface by Carlo Ginzburg.

2. Regarding my own hypotheses on this matter, see the article I wrote with Jean-Marc Lévy-Leblond: "Guerre en Orient ou paix en Méditerranée?" in *Le Monde*, August 19, 2006; the non-abridged version is available at http://www.lemonde.fr/web /article/0,1-0@2-3232,36–804577,0.html. English translation: "A Mediterranean Way for Peace in the Middle-East," in *Radical Philosophy*, November 2006.

3. The translation of this work was refused by an important French publisher. Jacqueline Rose, professor at the University of London, is also the author of *The Haunting of Sylvia Plath*, (Virago, 1991); the collective work *Why War: Psychoanalysis, Politics and the Return to Melanie Klein* (Oxford: Blackwell, 1993); *On Not Being Able to Sleep: Essays on Psychoanalysis in the Modern World* (London: Chatto, 2003); and an introduction to the new

English translation of Freud's essays on "mass psychology" (London: Penguin Classics, 2004).

4. See in particular Gershom Scholem, *Le messianisme juif. Essais sur la spiritualité du judaïsme* (Paris: Calmann Lévy, 1974), in which one finds the essay on "redemption through sin"; and *Sabbataï Tsevi, le messie mystique 1626–1676* (Lagrave, France: Verdier, 1990). The most complete presentation in French of the intellectual career of Scholem is that of David Biale, *Gershom Scholem. Cabale et contre-histoire* (Paris: Editions de l'éclat, 2001).

5. See Scholem, *Le messianisme juif*, 27.

6. Ibid., 40.

7. Ibid., 42.

8. Ibid., 139ff., and *Sabbataï Tsevi*.

9. On the subject of the "neutralization of messianism" in Scholem, see Biale, *Gershom Scholem*, 132ff.

10. Most of the political interventions by Scholem between 1916 and 1974 are translated in the collection *Le prix d'Israël* (Paris: Editions de l'Eclat, 2003). The letter to Rosenzweig, unknown for a long time, also plays a central role in the much more critical analyses of Raz-Krakotzkin, who stresses that it is through a "typically messianic interpretation of the situation" that Scholem "warns against the messianic danger hidden by secularization (laicisation)" (Raz-Krakotzkin, *Exil et souveraineté*, 133). Raz-Krakotzkin's "ambivalent" relationship, according to Carlo Ginzburg, with the work and personality of Scholem, is influenced by the critiques by the new generation of Kabbalah specialists of his "national" conception of older messianism (see Moshe Idel, *Messianisme et mystique*, [Paris: Cerf, 1994]).

11. See in particular the exchange with Shalom Lappin in the online journal Dissent, https://www.dissentmagazine.org/democratiya _article/a-question-of-zion-a-reply-to-shalom-lappin.

12. Rose refers here to the key article by Edward Said (to whose memory her book is dedicated), "Zionism from the point of view of its victims" (1979).

13. This formula was used by the socialist leader Shmuel Yavne'eli in 1918, quoted by Rose (*Question of Zion*, 150). The theme of "national shame" is also analyzed by Zertal. It is incorporated by Raz-Krakotzkin into a much more general framework of the abjection of the "exiled" Jew, a notoriously insistent element in the formation of the Israeli national character.

14. Before 1933, Scholem too identified with this current. He wrote: "I am, in this respect, a religious Ahad-Haamist." See *Le prix d'Israël*, 163. See also Biale, *Gershom Scholem*, 40ff. and 171–75.

15. Rose, *Question of Zion*, 96ff.

16. Idith Zertal, *Israel's Holocaust and the Politics of Nationhood* (Cambridge: Cambridge University Press, 2005). Author of many studies of the history of the state of Israel and emigration to Palestine, Zertal was professor at the Hebrew University of Jerusalem and the Interdisciplinary Center of Herzliya. She currently teaches in Basel. Her most recent work, written with Akiva Eldar, is *The War Over Israel's Settlements in the Occupied Territories, 1967–2007* (New York: Nation Books, 2007).

17. On the institution of the "exclusive link" between the memory of the Shoah and the site of Jerusalem by the Yad Vashem law, and its relation to other policies regarding "places of memory," see Zertal, *La nation et la mort*, 120. On the reticence of certain Shoah survivors, see 130ff.

18. This point is particularly important regarding the Nasser regime's propaganda in the days preceding the Israeli attack of June 1967, presented as a case of legitimate preventive defense. See Zertal, *La nation et la mort*, 166.

19. Ibid., 144ff., in particular concerning the contacts established by the Grand Mufti Hadj Amin Al-Husseini.

20. Sociologists of Luhmannian inspiration would employ here the category of "*Selbstthematisierung*" or "self-characterization." See Ulrich Bielefeld, *Nation und Gesellschaft. Selbstthematisier-ungen in Frankreich und Deutschland* (Hamburg: Hamburger Edition, 2003).

21. On "the long processus of banalization of the Shoah," see Zertal, *Nation et mort*, 88, 156, etc.

22. In the extended version of the mythical narrative, which ties modern episodes to antiquity (the destruction of the Second Temple, the revolt of Bar Kochba and the battle of Massada), this chain makes it possible to legitimate the idea of a national and territorial identity that goes back a millennium, in which the diaspora represents little more than a "nonhistory" or a tragic parenthesis prior to reconquest. Raz-Krakotzkin discusses the fiction of the revolt of Bar Kokhba and its opposition to the rabbinic tradition in *Exil et souveraineté*, 100ff.

23. Zertal, *La nation et la mort*, 36ff. Following others, Zertal stresses the fact that the most prominent surviving leader of the revolt of the Warsaw ghetto, Marek Edelman, always opposed this trans-figuration of the insurrection into an episode of "Zionist" hero-ism, and more generally the idea that the creation of the state of Israel represented not only an historical consequence, but the very "meaning," revealed a posteriori, of the Shoah (see 47ff.).

24. This occurred in particular as a result of a 1950 law "against war criminals and the authors of crimes against humanity" present in Israel itself: see Zertal, *La nation et la mort*, 83ff. In practice, the law targeted Jews, themselves Shoah survivors (such as former kapos and room supervisors in the concentration camps) but ended up exonerating notables who had negotiated with the Nazis in the name of the Judenräte of central Europe. The law resulted in the scandal of the Kastner trial (1952), for which Ben Gurion conceived the Eichmann trial as a symbolic reparation (112ff.).

25. According to Zertal, who follows Arendt on this point, but also other historians (including the British historian Hugh Trevor-Roper, who was quite sympathetic to Israeli objectives), the trial was conceived strictly in this perspective.

26. Zertal, *La nation et la mort*, 268–69 ("L'ange de la mort d'Auschwitz"). Let us recall that Edward Said, who swam against the current in his own camp, called for the Palestinians and Arabs

to take this psychology into account and, beyond this, to make of the Jewish genocide and the rights it entailed (which did not include in his view the right to dispossess others) one of the conditions for the solution of the Israeli-Palestinian conflict. See *The Question of Palestine* (London: Vintage, 1981); *The Politics of Dispossession* (London: Vintage, 1994).

27. Her controversy with Scholem attests to this. This controversy turned on "love for Israel" vs. "love for the Jewish people" (Ahavat Israel), to which she counterposes not the "love of humanity" but that of individuals and friends. See Hannah Arendt, *The Jew as Pariah: Jewish Identity and Politics in the Modern Age* (New York: Grove, 1978), 240–251, as well as Scholem, *Fidélité et utopie. Essais sur le judaïsme contemporain* (Paris: Calmann Lévy, 1978), 213–28. On Arendt's conception of the "Jewish question" before and after the Eichmann trial, see Martine Leibovici, *Hannah Arendt, une Juive. Expérience, politique et histoire*, preface by Pierre Vidal-Naquet (Paris: Desclée de Brouwer, 1998).

28. The author is senior lecturer in history of Judaism at the University of Beersheva. Several of his previous publications are about Catholic censorship and the transformations of Jewish thought it brought about in classical Europe.

29. The close exchanges between Scholem and Benjamin on theology and the philosophy of history, (up to the "Theses" of 1940, submitted to Arendt and published by her) are the subject of a book by Eric Jacobson: *Metaphysics of the Profane: The Political Theology of Walter Benjamin and Gershom Scholem* (New York: Columbia University Press, 2003). See also Michael Löwy, *Avertissement d'incendie. Une lecture des thèses "Sur le concept d'histoire"* (Paris: Editions de l'Eclat, 2001).

30. Raz-Krakotzkin, *Exil et souveraineté*, 209.

31. This is tantamount to criticizing the notion, inscribed in the Israeli constitution, of a state which is "democratic" because it is "Jewish" (and for Jews exclusively). This idea of the "land

of exile" is tied to a "secular" elaboration of the religious tradition for which the land of Israel does not constitute the place or the instrument of salvation but rather that place where the Jews attempt to continue to "live in exile," as long as all of humanity is not yet liberated from slavery or oppression. It converges with the critique of statism in Benjamin and the opposition pointed out by Arendt between the position of the "parvenu" and that of the "pariah." See Raz-Krakotzkin, *Exil et souveraineté*, 199–201.

32. This is so because it actually reaches the point of preferring self-destruction to the sharing of the land: see the passage on the "Samson option" and the taboo on naming the Israeli nuclear weapon, Raz-Krakotzkin, *Exil et souveraineté*, 152ff.

33. Raz-Krakotzkin, *Exil et souveraineté*, 45ff., 197ff.

34. Ibid., 196–203 (with reference to Baruch Kurzweill and Yeshayahou Leibowitz). The nationalist religious parties are indeed in the forefront of the colonization of the occupied territories.

35. Raz-Krakotzkin speaks of "forced de-Arabization," 83. He draws in particular on the work of Gil Anidjar, philosopher and historian, who studied with Derrida and is author of *"Our Place in Al-Andalous": Kabbalah, Philosophy, Literature in Arab Jewish Letters*, (Stanford, CA: Stanford University Press, 2002); *The Jew, the Arab: A History of the Enemy* (Stanford, CA: Stanford University Press, 2003); and most recently, *Semites: Race, Religion, Literature*, (Stanford, CA: Stanford University Press, 2008). Israeli suppression of the Judeo-Arab element at the heart of its own historic identity is the obverse side of the fantasized discourse of "Christian" Europe, which placed the Jew and the Arab, at least since the Renaissance, in the position of absolute enemies, both internal and external, forming a single enemy at a deeper level.

36. See in particular chapters 1 ("La négation de l'exil dans la conscience sioniste") and 2 ("Le retour à l'histoire"). Scholem discusses in particular the relations between Jewish messianism and Christian millenarism in *Sabbataï Tsevi*, 105ff.

37. See in particular chapter 7: "Arendt, Benjamin, Scholem et le binationalisme."

38. This responsibility is carefully distinguished from culpability: see 206ff.

39. One will find, I believe, an idea of this sort implicit in certain recent writings by Jean-Claude Milner: see his *Les penchants criminels de l'Europe démocratique*, (Lagrave, France: Verdier, 2003), in particular § 55, 97ff.: "In truth, there is only one real obstacle [to the expansion of European "peace," synonym of "unlimited society"] . . . and that is the existence of a state named Israel. For Israel presents itself as a limited whole, in the form of a nation-state, claiming secure and recognized borders. Such language is reputed to be intrinsically warlike . . .".

40. Raz-Krakotzkin, *Exil et souveraineté*, 111, 199. This formula is all the more striking to me since during the period of perestroika, when the French communist philosopher Lucien Sève (a long time personal friend and theoretical opponent of Althusser on "theoretical humanism"), with whom I was commenting the events, asked me in a falsely naïve way (and with real anxiety) what I thought of the U.S.S.R., I replied exactly that: "It's a state like any other . . ."

12. WHAT FUTURE FOR *LAÏCITÉ*?

1. This chapter was originally a paper presented at the international conference "Laïcité/Secularization," in the Maison Française of Columbia University, New York, November 12, 2005. It has been updated and revised for inclusion in this book.

2. I will return to the etymology of "laïque" (adjective) and "laïcité" (noun), which are important to recall. See "Laïc, laïque, laïcité," a special issue of the journal *Mots*, no. 27 (June 1991), eds. Simone Bonnafous, Etienne Balibar, and Pierre Fiala. In modern English, "laïcité" is usually translated (at the risk of confusion) as "secularism" except when an author wants to draw attention

to the specific character of the French doctrine and institution. In German, the neologism *Laiʒität* has been coined to this effect. Latin languages copy the French: *laicità* in Italian, *laicidad* in Spanish (which is inscribed in the 1917 Mexican Constitution). More interesting is the fact that Turkish has transcribed the French (*laiklik*) to mark the antireligious character of the secular state (and army) created by Atatürk, producing a violent opposition that is triumphant today. In 2005, the French senate adopted a *Déclaration universelle de la laïcité*, which—surprisingly—has been endorsed by representatives of twenty-nine countries (including the United States and the United Kingdom).

3. I have attempted to discuss this dialectical problem—now the subject of a grand *querelle* in philosophy—in my book *Des Universels. Essais et conferences* (Paris: Editions Galilée, 2016).

4. The Treatises of Westphalia (1648) that instituted the *Ius Publicum Europaeum*, or the international order and the balance of power between independent nation-states (most of them kingdoms or empires at the time), also involved a "sovereign" right of states to control the public exercise of religion in their territories (*Ius circa sacra*), and led to the division of populations among state religions (or the religion of each sovereign): *cujus regio ejus religio*.

5. Historians conventionally identify the establishment of laïcité in France with the "law of separation of church and state," passed in 1905 by the Third Republic, which put an end to a century of fluctuations between clerical and anticlerical policies. In 1946, after the end of World War II and the collapse of the Vichy Regime that had again heavily favored interventions of the Catholic Church in public affairs, laïcité was incorporated in the Constitution of the Fourth Republic as a defining principle, together with national indivisibility, democracy, and social welfare. "Separation" of course contained an echo of the idea of the "wall of separation" claimed by the American colony of Rhode Island in the seventeenth century, but it referred to a distance rather than a "wall."

6. Although addressing a similar issue and drawing on the important research of Jean-Paul Willaime, I differ on the conclusions:
whereas I suggest that laïcité is a consequence of the failure of the
"Rousseauist" project, Willaime claims that it forms its deferred
realization: see Willaime, "La religion civile à la française,"
in *Autres Temps. Les cahiers du christianisme social*, no. 6 (1985);
"La religion civile à la française et ses métamorphoses," in *Social
Compass* 40(4), 1993.

7. In his *Prison Notebooks*, Gramsci pays extensive attention to the
differences between the Italian situation, in which the "modernization" of the state was prevented by the position of the Catholic
Church as a "sovereign enclave" within the nation, and the French
situation, where the state becomes the instrument of the "passive
revolution" operated by the bourgeoisie through the transformation of Jacobinism into a republican common sense, in spite
of the resistances of the "Catholic party," supporting successive
monarchic and bonapartist restorations (see André Tosel, *Etudier
Gramsci*, [Paris: Editions Kimé, 2016]); for readers of Italian:
Fabio Frosini, *La religione dell'uomo moderno. Politica e verità nei
«Quaderni del carcere» di Antonio Gramsci* (Rome: Carocci, 2010).

8. See Ernst Kantorowicz: *The King's Two Bodies: A Study in Medi-
eval Political Theology*, (Princeton, NJ: Princeton University
Press, 1957); Julia R. Lupton and Graham Hammill eds., *Political
Theology and Early Modernity* (Chicago: Chicago University
Press, 2011).

9. A remarkable recent critical edition and commentary of Marx's
essay was provided by Daniel Bensaid: *Karl Marx, Sur la Question
juive* (Paris: La fabrique, 2006).

10. Jean-Jacques Rousseau, *The Social Contract*, book 1, chapter 6.
See my essay "Apories rousseauistes," in *L'anthropologie et le
politique selon Jean-Jacques Rousseau. Etudes réunies par Michèle
Cohen-Halimi* (Les Cahiers Philosophiques de Strasbourg, Tome
13, 2002). "Civil Religion" is introduced in the penultimate chapter of the (unfinished) work: IV, 8.

11. Michel Foucault, "*Omnes et Singulatim*: Towards a Criticism of 'Political Reason'" (the Tanner Lectures on Human Values, delivered at Stanford University, October 10 and 16, 1979).

12. The much disputed phrase: "on les forcera d'être libres" ("In order then that the social compact may not be an empty formula, it tacitly includes the undertaking, which alone can give force to the rest, that whoever refuses to obey the general will shall be compelled to do so by the whole body. This means nothing less than that he will be forced to be free," *Social Contract*, 1, 7, in G. D. H. Cole's translation). This is clearly a transposition of the church's use of *compelle eos intrare* (Luke 14:23).

13. See Balibar, *Equaliberty. Political Essays*, trans. James Ingram (Durham, NC: Duke University Press, 2010).

14. "Article 6—The law is the expression of the general will. All the citizens have the right of contributing personally or through their representatives to its formation. It must be the same for all, either that it protects, or that it punishes. All the citizens, being equal in its eyes, are equally admissible to all public dignities, places and employments, according to their capacity and without distinction other than that of their virtues and of their talents."

15. See the classic essay by Robert N. Bellah, "Civil Religion in America," *Daedalus*, (Winter 1967), vol. 96, no. 1, 1–21; also, Philippe Portier, "La religion en France et aux Etats-Unis. Retour sur une comparaison tocquevillienne," *Social Compass* (June 2010), 180–93.

16. Ernst H. Kantorowicz, Pro Patria Mori in Medieval Political Thought, *The American Historical Review*, vol. 56, no. 3 (April 1951), 472–92.

17. Jean Baubérot, *Vers un nouveau pacte laïque?* (Paris: Seuil, 1990).

18. John Locke (1632–1704) published *A Letter Concerning Toleration* in 1689 (first in Latin, then English), the same year that the British Parliament (which had been preceded by the colony of Maryland) published the Act of Toleration. On ambivalent effects of the idea of "tolerance," see Wendy Brown, *Regulating Aversion: Tolerance*

in the Age of Identity and Empire (Princeton, NJ: Princeton University Press, 2008).

19. See Baubérot, *Vers un nouveau pacte laïque?* and Patrick Weil, *Politiques de la laïcité au XXe siècle* (Paris: Presses universitaires de France, 2007).

20. The Third Republic, installed after the collapse of the Second Empire in 1871, was unable to establish a formal "Constitution" because of its internal conflicts. It only adopted a set of "constitutional laws" regulating the administration and separation of powers (1875).

21. The legal disposition of this "separation" now has unexpected (some would say: perverse) consequences. The state and public corporations are prohibited from subsidizing "churches," in the sense of denominations; but the *churches as buildings* have mostly become properties of the towns where they are located: their maintenance and reparations are therefore paid for with public money. On the other hand, the towns are prohibited from subsidizing the *construction* of mosques for the Muslim communities in France, which face not only racist prejudices, but financial and legal obstacles. When Muslim associations resort to funding from Arab (more generally Islamic) countries, they are immediately suspected of offering a point of entry for an Islamic "fifth column" within national territory.

22. Pierre Rosanvallon, *Le moment Guizot* (Paris: Gallimard, 1985).

23. Emile Poulat, *Notre laïcité publique* (Paris: Berg International, 2003); Jean Baubérot, *Histoire de la laïcité en France* (Paris: Presses universitaires de France, 2013); Jacqueline Lalouette, ed., *L'État et les cultes 1789–1905–2005* (Paris: La Découverte, 2005). A major new contribution, discussing the *longue durée* of the question of "laïcité" in France, has now been published: Philippe Portier, *L'Etat et les religions en France, une sociologie historique de la laïcité* (Rennes, France: Presses universitaires de Rennes, 2016). Antithetic views can be found (in their best formulation) in Claude Nicolet, *Histoire, Nation, République,*

(Paris: Odile Jacob, 2000); and Catherine Kintzler, *Penser la laïcité*, (Paris: Minerve, 2014).

24. The "Vendée," Victor Hugo's last and most extraordinary novel: *Quatre-Vingt Treize* (written after the Paris Commune in 1872, published in 1874) is just about that.

25. See Balibar, *Equaliberty*.

26. The best recent discussion of Gramsci's elaboration of "hegemony" (in French) is: Fabio Frosini, "Hégémonie: une approche génétique," *Actuel Marx*, 2015, vol.1, no. 57 (Paris: Presses universitaires de France).

27. An interesting collection of essays combining Foucault and Gramsci to theorize resistances to power is *Gramsci and Foucault: A Reassessment*, ed. David Krebs, (Abingdon, UK: Routledge, 2016).

28. This is the key element in Weber's definition of legitimate power, which leads to the "paradoxical" definition of democracy as "illegitimate domination" (in *Die Stadt*, a posthumous essay translated into English as *The City* [The Free Press, 1958]), i.e., a political regime in which *obedience and disobedience are equally possible* therefore normalizes conflict (see a great commentary by Catherine Colliot-Thélène in her *Etudes Wébériennes. Rationalités, histoires, droits* [Paris: Presses universitaires de France, 2001]).

29. See works by Poulat (*Notre laïcité publique*, 2003) and Baubérot (*Histoire de la laïcité en France*, 2013), already quoted. On the importance of Jaurès, who represented socialism in this compromise, and famously identified democracy and laïcité in a mass meeting at Castres in 1904, distancing himself from "workerist" *anticléricalisme*, see Antoine Casanova, *Jean Jaurès. Laïcité et République sociale* (Paris: Editions Le cherche midi, 2005).

30. The seminal essay by Comte is "Considérations sur le pouvoir spirituel" from 1825; see Auguste Comte, *Du pouvoir spirituel* (Paris: Livre de Poche Collection Pluriel, 1978), with an introduction by Pierre Arnaud. Essential commentaries are provided

by Pierre Macherey in his magnum opus: *Études de "philosophie française." De Sieyes à Barni* (Paris: Publications de la Sorbonne, 2013).

31. This is in part the object of the great study on the origins of the welfare state (with particular emphasis on the French case): Robert Castel, *Les métamorphoses de la question sociale. Une chronique du salariat* (Paris: Fayard, 1995). English translation: *From Manual Workers to Wage Laborers. Transformations of the Social Question* (New Brunswick, NJ: Transaction Publishers, 2003).

32. Michel Wieviorka, *La Diversité: rapport à la Ministre de l'Enseignement supérieur et de la Recherche* (Paris: Robert Laffont, 2008).

33. Zay was arrested by the Vichy government, and murdered by fascist militias in 1944. On the educational reform of the Popular Front in the spirit of laïcité, see Antoine Prost, *Du changement dans l'École—Les Réformes de l'éducation de 1936 à nos jours* (Paris: Seuil, 2013).

34. See Bruno Karsenti, *Politique de l'esprit: Auguste Comte et la naissance de la science sociale* (Paris: Hermann, 2006).

35. See Thomas Hobbes, *Leviathan or the Matter, Forme, & Power of a Common-wealth Ecclesiasticall and Civill* (1651), chapter 42, "Of Power Ecclesiastical." This distinction of course has a long and complex history until our times (which includes Gramsci's distinction between "dictatorship" and "hegemony," and above all Althusser's distinction between "repressive state apparatus" and "ideological state apparatus").

36. This is a stunning history of semantic "translations": *laos* is an archaic term in classical Greek (mainly used in Homer, where it names the "people" or "assembly" of the warriors, as opposed to their "kings"). It was "resuscitated" by the Septuagint, the group of Hellenistic Jewish scholars who translated the Hebraic Bible into Greek, therefore preparing for its universalist reading: they needed a Greek name for *'ham* (the "elect" people of God) that would be neither *demos* nor *ethnos* (which they reserved for the

"nations," *ethne*, in Latin *nationes* or *gentes*). In Christianity, *laos* is transferred to the church as "assembly" of the faithful, which is the "New Israel." Once Latinized and transformed into adjective, *laicus* (as opposed to *clericus*, from the Greek *klèros*) becomes the name of the ordinary believers, who are not priests (in progressive versions of Catholicism, the hierarchic relation tends to be inverted: the "clerics" are viewed as *servants*, not *masters* of their flock). In modern French, an orthographic distinction is observed: *laic* keeps the religious, ecclesiastic meaning, whereas *laïque* refers to *laïcité*, which of course has no ecclesiastic equivalent (except perhaps . . . to the church itself, as an antonym), and to its institutions (such as *école laïque*) or its own supporters (not to say believers). Founding fathers of laïcité were still aware of the symmetry and made use of it: see for example the classical treatise by Ferdinand Buisson (an active "dreyfusard" and Nobel Peace Prize winner): *La foi laïque*, 1912. Contemporary thinkers prefer to speak of *"laïcité interieure"* to name the conviction of a supporter or "activist" of laïcité (e.g., Claude Nicolet). See my additional entry on "demos, ethnos, laos" for the *Dictionary of Untranslatables*, eds. B. Cassin, E. Apter, J. Lezra, and M. Wood (Princeton, NJ: Princeton University Press, 2014).

37. See Balibar, "Homo nationalis: An Anthropological Sketch of the Nation-Form," in *We, the People of Europe?*, trans. James Swenson (Princeton, NJ: Princeton University Press, 2003).

38. See my contribution to the Conference at Cerisy in 1994 on "Violence et politique: La violence des intellectuels," in *Lignes*, no. 25(1995), Editions Hazan.

39. See the works by Buisson (*La foi laïque*,1912) and Nicolet (*Histoire, Nation, République*, 2000) already mentioned.

40. See Geneviève Fraisse and Michelle Perrot, eds., *Histoire des femmes en Occident*. Volume 4, *le XIXe siècle*, (Paris: Plon, 1991); and Michelle Perrot, "La laïcité, un atout pour les femmes," in *Valeurs mutualistes*, no. 231 (May 2004).

41. Geneviève Fraisse, *Les deux gouvernements: la famille et la cité* (Paris: Gallimard, collection Folio-Essais, 2001).

42. See Joan Wallach Scott, *Parité! Sexual Equality and the Crisis of French Universalism* (Chicago: University of Chicago Press, 2005).

43. About colonies, see in particular *La France en terre d'islam. Empire colonial et religions, XIXe-XXe siècles*, (Paris: Belin, 2016).

44. Immanuel Wallerstein, "The Ideological Tensions of Capitalism: Universalism vs. Racism and Sexism," reprinted in *The Essential Wallerstein* (New York: The New Press, 2000), 344, etc.

45. See Balibar, "Sujets ou Citoyens. Pour l'égalité," in *Les Temps Modernes*, no. 452 (1984).

46. Among recent new work on Fanon, see (in French), Seloua Luste Boulbina, *L'Afrique et ses fantômes. Ecrire l'après* (Paris: Présence africaine, 2015); Matthieu Renault, *Frantz Fanon. De l'anticolonialisme à la critique postcoloniale* (Paris: Editions Amsterdam, 2011).

47. Derrida's uses of this typically "deconstructive" category are scattered among his works beginning with *Eperons. Les styles de Nietzsche* (1978) and *Donner le temps* (1991).

48. See Balibar, *Des Universels*, quoted.

49. Jonathan Israel, *Radical Enlightenment: Philosophy and the Making of Modernity, 1650–1750* (Oxford: Oxford University Press, 2001). However, the expression was invented by his predecessor, Margaret Jacob, *The Radical Enlightenment: Pantheists, Freemasons and Republicans* (London: George Allen and Unwin, 1981).

50. Catherine Kintzler, *Condorcet, l'instruction publique et la naissance du citoyen*, préface de J. C. Milner, third édition, revue et augmentée (Paris: Minerve, 2015). Condorcet did apparently invent the notion of the "civilizing mission" of Europe with respect to "Barbarian" peoples, legitimizing colonization. See Bertrand Binoche, *La Raison sans l'Histoire. Echantillons pour une histoire comparée des philosophies de l'Histoire* (Paris: Presses universitaires de France, 2007).

French original: "Trois mots pour les morts et pour les vivants," *Libération*, January 9, 2015. (This translation is taken from a blog by David Broder, with some corrections. Another one, by Mike Watson, was published on the Verso blog on January 16, 2015). This paper was written and published after the shooting by Islamist terrorists (claiming allegiance to Al-Qaeda in Yemen) in Paris on January 7, 2015, before another group belonging to the same network attacked Jewish customers at a kosher supermarket in Paris, killing four of them, before being killed themselves by special forces who liberated the other hostages, on January 9, 2015. Cabu (Jean Cabut) and (Georges) Wolinski were two of the *Charlie Hebdo* cartoonists killed in the attack (together with ten others, including a police officer, a protection services officer, and a visiting columnist).

1. A reference to the novel *Soumission* (*Submission*), released a few hours before the attack on *Charlie Hebdo*, whose intentions remain ambiguous, but which was widely perceived as a denunciation of the way Muslims are "seizing power" in Europe.

2. The reference is to an article by Edgar Morin, "La France frappée au coeur de sa nature laïque et de sa liberté," in *Le Monde*, January 8, 2015.

3. Among other circumstances, I want to recall a public discussion with Talal Asad and Mohamed Amer-Meziane at Columbia University, New York, on November 14, 2016, titled "Beyond the Secular State? Secularism, Empire, Hegemony."

4. Fethi Benslama: *La guerre des subjectivités en Islam* (Fécamp, France: Editions Lignes, 2014).

14. ON "FREEDOM OF EXPRESSION" AND THE QUESTION OF "BLASPHEMY"

The following theses—or rather hypotheses—originate in a session of the Literary Seminar, directed by Bruce Robbins at

Columbia University, New York), December 3, 2015. I presented and commented on sections 1 to 3. My "respondent" was Souley-mane Bachir Diagne, who presented his own (better informed) version of the question of "blasphemy" and its alleged equivalents in Islamic tradition. Sections 4 and 5 and footnotes have been added subsequently. In expanding the draft, I have greatly benefited from a response by Robbins published in Politics/Letters, no. 4, on April 14, 2016, titled "Power Talking" (http://politics slashletters.org/power-talking-a-commentary-on-balibar/). The first theses themselves are published as *http://politicsslashletters.org/on-freedom-of-expression-and-the-question-of-blasphemy/*.

1. "Freedom of expression" and "free speech" are closely related but not completely equivalent phrases. Fundamental documents, to begin with the First Amendment of the U.S. Constitution, use complex formulas which amount to defining a general right of expression or explain the first in terms of the second: "Congress shall make no law respecting an establishment of religion, or prohibiting the free exercise thereof; or abridging the freedom of speech, or of the press; or the right of the people peaceably to assemble, and to petition the Government for a redress of grievances." The French tradition quite generally uses *liberté d'expression*, and the Universal Declaration of Human Rights has the apparently redundant formula: "right to freedom of opinion and expression," indicating that it is the "free" or independent opinion/expression that must be kept "free" or immune of constraints and interdictions.

2. "Subjective right" means a right attached to the individual person as inalienable property (John Locke's "property in one's person," including "life, liberty, and estates"), even if it is granted by some "objective" legal order, and subject to *limitations of use* which prove necessary to make one's right compatible with the right of others (Kant's definition of the law as "what prevents from preventing liberty"). The classical "declarations of rights" of the American and French revolutions enumerate fundamental

subjective rights and impose their constitutionalization as foundations of republican citizenship. The indisputable importance of subjective rights (including *habeas corpus* and freedom of conscience/speech) arises from their capacity to impose limits on the arbitrary power of authorities over individuals. Their limitation, as I argue here, arises from the fact that they make it impossible to *positively* define a right or empowerment inherent in collective action or interaction (except through the legal fiction transforming collective subjects into "corporate" individuals or persons, very often an instrument of monopolistic power relations).

3. "Public good" is an ancient notion of political philosophy, attached to the representation of the "city" as a community of its own citizens, whose limitations (exclusion of women, children, servants and wage laborers, aliens, colonized people) become progressively (albeit never entirely) transgressed with the modern democratization of citizenship and the collective struggles it involves. It becomes associated with the idea of "public service" or "public obligations" in the constitutions of twentieth-century "social states," especially in the fields of education, health, welfare, albeit with inequalities nationally and internationally, and a more or less reversible achievement. Interestingly, in parallel with a renewed interest for the use, conservation, and destruction of the "commons," contemporary economists and political theorists have started to expand the definition of a "public good" as a thing or service that can only become used collectively (or remains "indivisible" by its very nature), applying it to the issue of *information* at a national and transnational level: see Chantal Peyer and Urs Jäggi, *L'information est un bien public*, report for "Pain pour le prochain" before the UN World Summit on the Information Society (Switzerland, 2003): https://www.kirchen.ch/ecouter-entendre/actualite/IMG/information_bien_public.pdf.

4. Jürgen Habermas introduced the pragmatic concept of the "ideal speech situation" (ISS) in the early 1970s, as a "rhetorical" counterpart to his definition of the public sphere (*öffentlichkeit*) that

makes democratic institutions possible. The fact that he later shifted to a more formalistic theory of "communicative action" does not make it less interesting. The ISS is defined by the following rules: 1. Every subject with the competence to speak and act is allowed to take part in a discourse. 2a. Everyone is allowed to question any assertion whatever. 2b. Everyone is allowed to introduce any assertion whatever into the discourse. 2c. Everyone is allowed to express their attitudes, desires and needs without any hesitation. 3. No speaker may be prevented, by internal or external coercion, from exercising his rights as laid down in (1) and (2).

5. Of course, I am borrowing the expression that was coined by John Rawls, who made it the cornerstone of his resurrection of social contract foundations for political theory, opening a new moment in the history of the discipline and liberalism in general (*A Theory of Justice*, 1971). In Rawls, the veil of ignorance is a theoretical *fiction* which incorporates the ideal neutralization of differences, interests, inequalities, and power situations and must be imagined at the origin to ground the political and economic order on "fair" rules of distribution. This can include the distribution of knowledge itself, of course. In my inverted use, the veil of ignorance is very *real*, and it is continuously produced by the fact that power unevenly distributed (through class distinctions, monopoly of "symbolic capital," construction of internal enemies, etc.) generates misperception of the other and isolation from the social relations as they actually work.

6. The murderous attack on the *Charlie Hebdo* journal in Paris on January 7, 2015, perpetrated by members of Al-Qaeda, killing ten members of its editorial staff, was the origin of the reflections condensed in the current "Theses." See chapter 20, "Three Words for the Dead and for the Living." The terrorists invoked the reproduction by the French satiric journal (as did others in the world, including the "Muslim world") of the Danish cartoons in *Jyllands-Posten* (2005), including one that represented the Prophet Muhammad carrying a bomb. Mass demonstrations expressing

outrage and occasionally seeking revenge were in part (but in part only) prompted by Danish imams who toured Islamic countries with a selection of the most offensive publications. The Western press, the politicians, and intellectuals sometimes expressed reservations (especially from religious denominations), but generally they defended "free speech," blaming the conflict on the intolerance of Muslims.

7. In a later commentary of the chain of events, one of the editors of *Jyllands-Posten* (a conservative journal) explained that they were trying to make it clear that Muslim citizens in the Danish society were "our equals" and therefore should be treated as equals, including satirically (see interview of Flemming Rose in *Libération*, November 27, 2015).

8. This distinction is specifically emphasized by Saba Mahmood in her contribution to the collective volume *Is Critique Secular? Blasphemy, Injury, and Free Speech*, by Talal Asad, Wendy Brown, Judith Butler, and Saba Mahmood (New York: Fordham University Press, 2013). Mahmood Mamdani suggests a different distinction: "Bigotry, however, is not blasphemy. Blasphemy is the practice of questioning a tradition from the inside, bigotry is an assault on that tradition from the outside. If blasphemy is an attempt to speak truth to power, bigotry is the reverse: an attempt by power to instrumentalize truth. A defining feature of the cartoon debate is that bigotry is being mistaken for blasphemy" ("On Blasphemy, Bigotry and the Politics of Culture Talk," in *Waiting for the Barbarians, A Tribute to Edward W. Said*, eds. Müge Gürsoy Sökmen and Başak Ertür [London: Verso, 2008]). Both are trying to disentangle the fact that "blasphemy" in the cartoon controversy was at times vindicated on both sides.

9. "Nomos of the Earth" (involving a double play on words: law/ distribution of the land/the planet) is the title (and central concept) of Carl Schmitt's postwar work (1950) on *Ius Publicum Europaeum* and international law, advocating a distribution of

geopolitical influence into a limited number of "zones of influence" *(Grossraum)* modeled on the U.S. Monroe Doctrine. Deliberately or not, Samuel Huntington's notion of the "clash of civilizations" seems to be aiming at a revival of this scheme in the postcolonial and postsocialist world.

10. "Victims are not obliged to remain victims. In other words, power is not fixed and unified. Butler has of course insisted time and again that those who are empowered in one place may well be weak and victimized in another, and vice versa. The complexly intertwined histories of class, race, gender, and sexuality ought to have made that clear." (Robbins, *Power Talking*, 2016).

11. "Fearless speech" (the title of his Berkeley lectures in 1983) was analyzed by Foucault as a modern version of ancient *parrêsia*, the capacity to criticize opinions and mores in public. It forms the guiding thread of his last courses at the Collège de France. In the namesake volume (*The Reith Lectures: Speaking Truth to Power*, London, 1993), drawing on earlier works by Foucault, Edward Said associated it with a general idea of the intellectual function as "speaking truth to power," which I am trying to expand beyond the professional and cultural limits of its definition.

15. Identitarian Laïcité

1. December 2, 2015 and June 12, 2016, respectively.

2. The first law *(loi Stasi)*, banning veils for girls in high schools, was passed in 2004 after a national debate. A second law, banning burkas and other "full-body covering," was passed in 2010, because burkas concealed the face from identification. According to official sources, reported anti-Semitic actions (including insults, threats, injuries, murders, vandalism of religious buildings, etc.) rose by 80 percent in 2015–2016, while similar Islamophobic actions rose by 280 percent.

3. One of the most widely reproduced videos shows local police officers at Nice forcing a middle-aged woman to undress (although she is not exactly wearing a burkini): https://fr.sputniknews.com/france/201608241027429039-burkini-plage-nice/.

   (The burkini is "modest swimwear" that covers hair and body, which was created and marketed by an Australian designer in 2004 as being in conformity with "Islamic tradition.")

4. See http://www.conseil-etat.fr/Decisions-Avis-Publications/Decisions/Selection-des-decisions-faisant-l-objet-d-une-communication-particuliere/CE-ordonnance-du-26-aout-2016-Ligue-des-droits-de-l-homme-et-autres-association-de-defense-des-droits-de-l-homme-collectif-contre-l-islamophobie-en-France.

5. See https://www.facebook.com/notes/manuel-valls/assumons-le-d%C3%A9bat-sur-le-burkini/1125932284153781).

6. This essay is an adaptation of my article, published in the French journal *Libération*, on August 30, 2106, titled *Laïcité ou identité?* A longer version is included in the collective volume *Usages et mésusages politiques de la laïcité*, ed. Christine Delory-Momberger and Béatrice Mabilon-Bonfils (Editions de l'Aube, La Tour d'Aigues, 2016). In adapting my longer piece, I was helped by two translations of the *Libération* article that have appeared on the web: http://www.versobooks.com/blogs/2823-etienne-balibar-laicite-or-identity, *and* https://darkprecursor.net/2016/08/30/etienne-balibar-laicite-or-identity-english-translation/.

7. This is an (ironic) reference to Rousseau's famous phrase in *The Social Contract*, book 1, chapter 7, "The Sovereign":

   In order then that the social compact may not be an empty formula, it tacitly includes the undertaking, which alone can give force to the rest, that whoever refuses to obey the general will shall be compelled to do so by the whole body. This means nothing less than that he will be forced to be free; for this is the condition which, by giving each citizen to his country, secures him against all personal dependence. In this lies the key to the working of the political machine; this alone legitimises civil undertakings, which, without it, would be absurd, tyrannical, and liable to the most frightful abuses. (Trans. G.D.H. Cole)

8. I borrow the idea of a "genealogy of secularism" from Talal Asad, while disagreeing on several points (not all . . .) of the application he makes to the case of French laïcité in his important essay, "Trying to Understand French Secularism," in *Political Theologies: Public Religions in a Post-Secular World*, ed. Hent de Vries and Lawrence E. Sullivan, (New York: Fordham University Press, 2006).

9. See Régis Debray: "Etes-vous démocrate ou républicain?" The very influential essay was originally published in *Le Nouvel Observateur* on November 30, 1989, and was republished by the same journal on April 28, 2015: http://tempsreel.nouvelobs.com /politique/20150428.OBS8077/etes-vous-democrate-ou -republicain-par-regis-debray.html.

10. The Law of Separation of Church and State was passed in 1905 after decades of confrontation between the Catholic party and the Secularist party, with a "liberal" force (where some Protestant intellectuals and some Socialist leaders like Aristide Briand and Jean Jaurès had a strong influence) imposing a clear divide between the private and public realms. See my essay in this volume "What Future for Laïcité?" (chapter 12) with references to contemporary historians.

11. See Gérard Noiriel's intervention before the Commission of the French National Assembly on March 25, 2011, at http://ldh-toulon .net/le-modele-francais-d-immigration.html; also Emmanuelle Saada, "Entre 'assimilation' et 'décivilisation': l'imitation et le projet colonial républicain," in *Terrain. Revue d'ethnologie de l'Europe*, no. 44 (March 2005) « Imitation et anthropologie ».

12. Let us not forget, however, that in practice "laïcité" as a legal system was not implemented in the colonies, but only in the

metropolis, because it concerned rights and duties of the *citizens*, not the *subjects* of the empire. This is also a contemporary mutation, which creates a double bind: "assimilation" is now requested to apply to those whom one wants to exclude from citizenship, of which they would be unworthy or for which they would remain unfit. See Achi Raberh, "1905: quand l'islam était (déjà) la seconde religion de France," in *Multitudes 59. Été 2015, Décoloniser la laïcité?*

13. Quoted by Jean Baubérot, *La laïcité falsifiée*, rev. ed., (Paris: La Découverte, 2014), 59. Georges Clemenceau (nicknamed "The Tiger" after leading the patriotic effort during World War I) had been a prominent leader of the "secularist" party at the time of the "separation" (Parti Radical), taking sides against the most extreme anticlerical wing. He is also (in)famous in the Labor Movement for his bloody suppression of strikes in the same years as minister of the interior. Clemenceau is frequently invoked as a model by former Prime Minister Manuel Valls (a right-wing Socialist).

14. Here is an interesting example (writing extensively and in excellent French, apparently located in Yemen) which specifically targets the "acculturation of French Muslims": *l'Observatoire des Islamologues de France* at *www.islamologues-de-france.com*.

15. "We are at war" is a quotation from the French president after the November 2015 attacks, repeated after the July 2016 attack.

16. "La France aux Français": this nationalist slogan was introduced during the anti-Semitic campaign at the time of the Dreyfus Affair and became the motto of the newspaper *La Libre Parole*, created by Edouard Drumont, a founder of French modern anti-Semitism (and a deputy of Algiers). It was periodically resurrected, notably by the Vichy regime, which outlawed foreigners and deported Jews to Nazi Germany during the Holocaust. See Pierre Birnbaum, *"La France aux Français": histoire des haines nationalistes* (Paris: Seuil, 2006).

Honneth, Axel, xii, 168*n1*
Hugo, Victor, 216*n24*
*Human Architecture, Journal
 of the Sociology of Self-
 Knowledge*, 205*n1*
humanists, philosophy and,
 171*n21*
human nature, split (*homo
 duplex*), 58
Hume, David, 77, 78, 80, 83
Huntington, Samuel, 182*n8*,
 224*n9*

"ideal speech situation" (ISS),
 150, 222*n4*
identitarian laïcité, 164, 166
identity: Muslims with
 "Islamic," 154; national, 7,
 99, 162–66, 208*n22*
ideology, vii, viii, x; alternatives,
 48; Althusser on, 46;
 Capdevila on, 185*n1*; with
 religion and culture, 34–41;
 universality with, 36
idolatry, ix, 71, 73, 77, 84
"imprudence," *Charlie Hebdo*
 and, 143
Industrial Revolution, xxxv
insult, with blasphemy and
 sacred, 152–54
inverted orientalism, 154–55
Iran, 113
*Is Critique Secular? Blasphemy,
 Injury, and Free Speech*
 (Asad, T., Brown, W.,
 Butler, J., Mahmood, S.),
 224*n8*

Islam, ix, xxi, xxxii, 186*n2*;
 blasphemy and, 153;
 Christianity and, 172*n27*;
 colonization and, 201*n31*;
 Comte on, 204*n53*;
 feminine in, 190*n6*;
 French republicanism and,
 14–16; fundamentalism
 and blasphemy, 153–54;
 fundamentalism and
 women, 27; with identity
 and Muslims, 154; "Jihad"
 and, 143–44, 147–48; laws
 and, 58–59; monotheism
 and, 69–70; mosque
 movement and, 46; sexuality
 and, 15–17, 180*n11*; with
 terrorism stereotypes, x, xi
Islamic feminism, 45, 46
Islamic veil. *See* hijab
Islamophobia, xi, 13, 62, 161, 179*n6*
Israel, 101, 104; colonization
 and, 108–9, 210*n34*;
 Constitution, 209*n31*;
 land and, 209*n31*, 209*n32*;
 Palestine and, 94–95; with
 "secular" state, 113; with war
 criminals law, 208*n24*
Israel, Jean-Jacques, 177*n5*
*Israel's Holocaust and the Politics
 of Nationhood* (Zertal), 100
ISS. *See* "ideal speech situation"
Ius Publicum Europaeum
 (Schmitt), 212*n4*, 224*n9*

Jacob, Margaret, 219*n49*
Jameson, Fredric, viii, 54

Jaurès, Jean, 126–27, 133, 216*n*29

"Jerusalem," 167*n*2

Jews: Arabs and, 210*n*35; Holocaust, 100, 103, 208*n*26, 228*n*16; with messianism, 96, 210*n*36; Palestine, with return to, 97; Septuagint, 217*n*36. *See also* Israel

"Jihad," 143–44, 147–48

Judaism, ix, xxi, 78, 80; Christianity and, 97; Kabbalah, 96, 97, 206*n*10; monotheism and, 70–71; polytheism and, 70–72

Justin, 76

Jyllands-Posten (journal), 224*n*7

Kabbalah, 96, 97, 206*n*10

Kant, Immanuel, 55, 79, 172*n*29, 176*n*2

Kantorowicz, Ernest, 116, 119

Karsenti, Bruno, 186*n*4, 195*n*5

Kato, Haruhisa, 141

kenosis, 202*n*37

Kintzler, Catherine, 138

kleros ("clergy"), 176*n*2

Kolakowski, Leszek, 189*n*4

Koran, 70, 144, 153, 191*n*8

Koselleck, Reinhart, xvi, xx, 168*n*3

kosmos (creation), 176*n*2

Kymlicka, Will, 23

labor, xxxvi; division of, 44, 174*n*34; with value and

capital, 173*n*30; women and, xxxv

Lacan, Jacques, 165–66

laïcité: with bourgeois hegemony and *potestas indirecta*, 124–34; citizenship and, 121–22; community and, 114; in context, 110–16; Debray and, 29–30; defined, 118, 129–30, 162; equality and, 119; etymology of, 10, 176*n*2, 211*n*2, 217*n*36; in historical context, 212*n*5; identitarian, 164, 166; implementation of, 227*n*12; laws and, 57; as national identity politics, 162–66; "pact of," 11; religion and, 122–23, 130; school system and, 11, 126; secularism and, 10, 136–37, 175*n*1; state and, 121; with theologico-political complex, nation as citizens and civic religion, 116–24; universal and, 134–38; universalism and, 111, 134

"Laïcité/Secularization" conference, 211*n*1

Laizität, 211*n*2

Lalouette, Jacqueline, 122, 215*n*23

land: Israel and, 209*n*31, 210*n*32; with Palestine, myth of, 99

language, sacred, 98

laos, 129, 176*n*2, 217*n*36

Las Casas, Bartolomé de, 189*n*5

"Misère de la critique/Das Elend der Kritik" conference (2016), 168n1

mobility, freedom of expression and, 156

modernization, of state, 213n7

Mohammed (prophet), 70

Monde, Le, 141

mondialisation du monde ("globalization of the globe"), 20

monotheism, 74, 167n1, 201n31, 203n41; Christianity and, 73, 87, 89–90; etymology, 69; Islam and, 69–70; Judaism and, 70–71; origins, 76; polutheos and, 71–72; polytheism and, 76–93; relative, 82

Monotheismus als politisches Problem, Der (Peterson), 74

Monroe Doctrine, 224n9

Montaigne, Michel de, 54

More, Henry, 76

Morin, Edgar, 177n4, 220n2

Moses (biblical figure), ix, 71, 76, 136

mosques: laws, 215n21; movement, 46

Mots (journal), 211n2

Moulier-Boutang, Yann, 174n34

multiculturalism, 18; condition for, 51–52; cosmopolitanism and, 23–25; failure of, 181n5

Muslims: Charlie Hebdo and, 152–53, 223n6; with "Islamic identity," 154; "Jihad" and, 143–44, 147–48; with power, 220n1; racism against, 12–13; responsibility of, 146

Nancy, Jean-Luc, 174n1, 196n1

Nandy, Ashis, 182n7

Napoleonic civil code, 165

Nasser, Gamal Abdel, 207n18

nation, 176n2; as community of citizens with laïcité, 116–24; sacralization of, 108; social hypocrisy and, 124; state and, 130; as trans-historical entity, 119

national identity, 7, 99; Bar Kokhba and, 208n22; politics with laïcité, 162–66

nationalism, Zionism and, 97, 100, 103, 105, 109

national unity, "community" and, 142

Natural History of Religion, The (Hume), 77

Nazism, 45, 100, 101, 120, 208n24, 228n16

Negri, Antonio, 174n34

Neoplatonism, 72, 75, 80, 84, 90, 204n56

New Christianity: Dialogues Between a Conservative and an Innovator, The (Saint-Simon), 86

Nicene Creed, 137, 177n5

Nice Riviera, x

Nietzsche, Friedrich, 82

9/11, 169n9

"Nomos" of Globalization, 155

popular philosophy
(*Weltweisheit*), 176*n*2
Portier, Philippe, 215*n*23
Postone, Moishe, 173*n*30
potestas indirecta. See bourgeois
hegemony
Poulat, Emile, 122, 215*n*23
power: instability of, 124–25; *Ius
Publicum Europaeum* and,
212*n*4; legitimate, 216*n*28;
Muslims with, 220*n*1;
sacralization of, xxiii, 44, 51;
"speaking truth to," 225*n*11;
victims and, 225*n*10
Prison Notebooks (Gramsci),
168*n*4, 213*n*7
private space, 57–60, 130
prix d'Israël, Le, 206*n*10
Proclus, 72
Protestants, 84, 106, 175*n*1
public good: defined, 222*n*3;
freedom of expression
as, 157; with free speech,
exercise of, 150
public institutions, culture and
religion with, 19
public space, 57–60
pure capitalism, xix, xxxv, 169*n*7

Al-Qaeda, 223*n*6
Quatre-Vingt Treize (Hugo),
216*n*24
Question of Zion, The (Rose),
96
Quinet, Edgar, 78

racism, 134; anti-Semitism, 99,
107, 108; multiculturalism

and, 181*n*5; against Muslims,
12–13
radicalize, defined, 44
Radical Philosophy (journal),
167*n*4, 168*n*1
Raison publique (journal), 175*n*2
Rancière, Jacques, 31
Raulet, Gérard, xii, 168*n*1
Rawls, John, 223*n*5
Raz-Krakotzkin, Amnon, 103–4,
206*n*10, 207*n*13, 210*n*35;
Israel and, 109; orientalism
and, 105–6; secularized
political theology and, 106–7
reason, Roman Catholicism with
faith and, 32
redemption (*Erlösung*), 39
Reden über die Religion
(Schleiermacher), 203*n*41
religion, 170*n*20, 203*n*41;
anthropological difference
and, 45–47; Asad, T., and,
30–31, 33; civic, 116–24,
132; with code, construction
of, 30–31, 33; Communism
and, 45; "counterreligions,"
92, 167*n*1; criticism of,
184*n*11; culture and, 17–18,
33, 45–46, 172*n*28; culture
and public institutions with,
19; culture with ideology
and, 34–41; Debray and, 26,
28–30; Derrida and, xxxi,
26, 27–28; discrimination,
124; etymology, 27, 29; free
speech and, 157–58; laïcité
and, 122–23, 130; with Law
of Separation of Church

EUROPEAN PERSPECTIVES

A Series in Social Thought and Cultural Criticism

LAWRENCE D. KRITZMAN, EDITOR

Claudine Fabre-Vassas, *The Singular Beast: Jews, Christians, and the Pig*

Tahar Ben Jelloun, *French Hospitality: Racism and North African Immigrants*

Alain Finkielkraut, *In the Name of Humanity: Reflections on the Twentieth Century*

Emmanuel Levinas, *Entre Nous: Essays on Thinking-of-the-Other*

Zygmunt Bauman, *Globalization: The Human Consequences*

Emmanuel Levinas, *Alterity and Transcendence*

Alain Corbin, *The Life of an Unknown: The Rediscovered World of a Clog Maker in Nineteenth-Century France*

Carlo Ginzburg, *Wooden Eyes: Nine Reflections on Distance*

Sylviane Agacinski, *Parity of the Sexes*

Michel Pastoureau, *The Devil's Cloth: A History of Stripes and Striped Fabric*

Alain Cabantous, *Blasphemy: Impious Speech in the West from the Seventeenth to the Nineteenth Century*

Julia Kristeva, *The Sense and Non-Sense of Revolt: The Powers and Limits of Psychoanalysis*

Kelly Oliver, *The Portable Kristeva*

Gilles Deleuze, *Dialogues II*

Catherine Clément and Julia Kristeva, *The Feminine and the Sacred*

Sylviane Agacinski, *Time Passing: Modernity and Nostalgia*

Luce Irigaray, *Between East and West: From Singularity to Community*

Julia Kristeva, *Hannah Arendt*

Julia Kristeva, *Intimate Revolt: The Powers and Limits of Psychoanalysis*, vol. 2

Elisabeth Roudinesco, *Why Psychoanalysis?*

Régis Debray, *Transmitting Culture*

Steve Redhead, ed., *The Paul Virilio Reader*

Claudia Benthien, *Skin: On the Cultural Border Between Self and the World*

Julia Kristeva, *Melanie Klein*

Roland Barthes, *The Neutral: Lecture Course at the Collège de France (1977–1978)*

Hélène Cixous, *Portrait of Jacques Derrida as a Young Jewish Saint*

Theodor W. Adorno, *Critical Models: Interventions and Catchwords*

Julia Kristeva, *Colette*

Gianni Vattimo, *Dialogue with Nietzsche*

Emmanuel Todd, *After the Empire: The Breakdown of the American Order*

Gianni Vattimo, *Nihilism and Emancipation: Ethics, Politics, and Law*

Hélène Cixous, *Dream I Tell You*

Steve Redhead, *The Jean Baudrillard Reader*

Jean Starobinski, *Enchantment: The Seductress in Opera*

Jacques Derrida, *Geneses, Genealogies, Genres, and Genius: The Secrets of the Archive*

Hélène Cixous, *White Ink: Interviews on Sex, Text, and Politics*

Marta Segarra, ed., *The Portable Cixous*

François Dosse, *Gilles Deleuze and Félix Guattari: Intersecting Lives*

Julia Kristeva, *This Incredible Need to Believe*